NEOLIBERAL NONFICTIONS

Cultural Frames, Framing Culture

Robert Newman, *Editor*
Justin Neuman, *Associate Editor*

NEOLIBERAL NONFICTIONS

The Documentary Aesthetic from Joan Didion to Jay-Z

DANIEL WORDEN

University of Virginia Press
CHARLOTTESVILLE AND LONDON

University of Virginia Press

Printed in the United States of America on acid-free paper

First published 2020

9 8 7 6 5 4 3 2 1

LIBRARY OF CONGRESS CATALOGING-IN-PUBLICATION DATA

Names: Worden, Daniel, 1978– author.
Title: Neoliberal nonfictions : the documentary aesthetic from Joan Didion to Jay-Z / Daniel Worden.
Description: Charlottesville : University of Virginia Press, 2020. | Series: Cultural frames, framing culture | Includes bibliographical references and index.
Identifiers: LCCN 2019044485 (print) | LCCN 2019044486 (ebook) | ISBN 9780813944159 (hardcover) | ISBN 9780813944166 (paperback) | ISBN 9780813944173 (epub)
Subjects: LCSH: Documentary mass media and the arts—United States. | Neoliberalism in popular culture—United States.
Classification: LCC NX180.D63 W67 2020 (print) | LCC NX180.D63 (ebook) | DDC 302.23—dc23
LC record available at https://lccn.loc.gov/2019044485
LC ebook record available at https://lccn.loc.gov/2019044486

The choice of the documentary medium is as gravely distinct a choice as the choice of poetry instead of fiction.

—JOHN GRIERSON, "FIRST PRINCIPLES OF DOCUMENTARY"

We have, it seems to me, a very curious sense of reality—or, rather, perhaps, I should say, a striking sense of irreality.

—JAMES BALDWIN, *NOTHING PERSONAL*

CONTENTS

Acknowledgments ix

Introduction: The Documentary Aesthetic 1
1 Money Trees 21
2 Emergence in Retrospect 47
3 Neoliberal Style 68
4 True Crime 86
5 Speculative Ecology 105
Conclusion: The Meaning of Memoir 127

Notes 147
Bibliography 159
Index 171

ACKNOWLEDGMENTS

Work on this book was supported by the School of Individualized Study and the College of Liberal Arts at the Rochester Institute of Technology, a Dorot Foundation Fellowship from the Harry Ransom Center at the University of Texas at Austin, a Faculty Assembly Women's Committee Grant from the University of Colorado at Colorado Springs, and a Research Allocations Committee Grant from the University of New Mexico. Thanks to the Harry Ransom Center, the New York Public Library's Manuscripts and Rare Books Division, and the Schomburg Center for Research in Black Culture's Manuscript, Rare Books, and Archives Division, the collections of which were crucial to my thinking and this book.

I owe many thanks to the people who allowed me to test out some of this material in public. Special thanks to Carleton University's speaker series on the production of literature for a really invigorating experience. Thanks also to fellow panelists, respondents, and audience members at meetings of the American Comparative Literature Association, the American Literature Association, the American Studies Association, the Association for the Study of the Arts of the Present, the Marxist Literary Group, the Modern Language Association, the Norman Mailer Society, and the Petrocultures Research Group. Those experiences were invaluable.

Along with those groups, I also benefited immensely from the National Endowment for the Humanities seminar "Magazine Modernism," organized by Sean Latham at the University of Tulsa; the National Endowment for the Humanities institute "City of Print: New York and the Periodical

Press," organized by Mark Noonan at the New York City College of Technology (CUNY); and a National Humanities Center summer institute in literary studies, organized by Walter Benn Michaels. These experiences, the ideas generated during them, and the friendships that have continued from them have been crucial to my thinking.

I worked on this book at a few different institutions, and I am especially happy that I was able to finish it in the School of Individualized Study and the College of Liberal Arts at the Rochester Institute of Technology. Thanks to James C. Hall for giving me a place to work that fits, and thanks to Therese Mulligan and Sharon Beckford-Foster for their support. Thanks, as well, to everyone at SOIS and RIT's Department of English for making me feel at home, and thanks to my many wonderful colleagues at RIT and in Rochester.

I owe special notes of thanks to the following people, who have provided a community of thinkers and friends that is more than I could have hoped for. You have each made this book better. Thanks to Jesse Alemán, Jennifer Ashton, David M. Ball, Ross Barrett, Bart Beaty, Alexander Beecroft, Brent Ryan Bellamy, Sara Blair, Margot Bouman, Steve Brauer, Christopher Breu, Sarah Brouillette, Nicholas Brown, Max Brzezinski, Joel Burges, Tom Cerasulo, Hillary Chute, Michael W. Clune, Sam Cohen, Danielle Coriale, Todd Cronan, Jeff Diamanti, Jeff Drouin, Sari Edelstein, Cristie Ellis, Joseph Entin, Leigh Gilmore, Jason Gladstone, David Greven, Gary Harrison, Brooks Hefner, Andrew Hoberek, Melissa Homestead, Mitchum Huehls, Caren Irr, Holly Jackson, Eva-Lynn Jagoe, Joseph Jeon, Brian Johnson, Catherine Keyser, Sean Latham, Graeme Macdonald, Ted Martin, Adam McKible, Walter Benn Michaels, Alan Nadel, Mathias Nilges, Mark Noonan, Franny Nudelman, Kirsten Bartholomew Ortega, Charles Palermo, Mikel Parent, Nancy Pedri, Joan Saab, Emilio Sauri, Tim Scheie, Ben Schreier, Jesse Schwartz, Jeff Severs, Chip Sheffield, Lisa Siraganian, Rachel Greenwald Smith, Min Hyoung Song, Janet Stewart, Dan Stout, Imre Szeman, Lisa Uddin, Melina Vizcaino-Alemán, Kathleen Washburn, Jennifer Wenzel, Benjamin Widiss, Maria Windell, Nicolas Witschi, Benjamin Woo, and Alex Young. Many thanks, as well, to Eric Brandt, Helen Chandler, and Morgan Myers at the University of Virginia Press, series editors Justin Neuman and Robert Newman, and this manuscript's thoughtful peer reviewers for making this a better book.

Earlier versions of some parts of this book appeared in journals and edited volumes, and I am grateful for the guidance of the book and journal editors. Chapter 2 is derived in part from "Amnesiac Fugue: Didion's Style and Neoliberal America" and my contribution to "On Joan Didion: An

Introduction" in *A/B: Auto/Biography Studies* 31.3 (2016), © the Autobiography Society, available online at https://www.tandfonline.com. An earlier version of chapter 3 appeared as "Neoliberal Style: Alex Haley, Hunter S. Thompson, and Countercultures" in *American Literature* 87.4 (2015), © Duke University Press. Earlier versions of chapter 5 and the conclusion appeared, respectively, in *Neoliberalism and Contemporary Literary Culture,* edited by Mitchum Huehls and Rachel Greenwald Smith (Johns Hopkins University Press, 2017) and in *Remaking Reality: U.S. Documentary Culture after 1945,* edited by Sara Blair, Joseph B. Entin, and Franny Nudelman (University of North Carolina Press, 2018).

I appreciate the support and assistance of the Paula Cooper Gallery, the Fraenkel Gallery, Sarah Glidden, Jessamyn Lovell, A. Laurie Palmer, Penguin Random House, Ed Piskor, the Saturday Evening Post Society, the Allan Sekula Studio, Taryn Simon Projects, the Jeff Wall Studio, and the Wylie Agency in securing image and text permissions, so that this book can be illustrated with work in the documentary aesthetic.

Lastly, thanks to Catherine Zuromskis and Clementine, who are the whole deal. Thanks, too, to my family: Katharine Croke, John Vennema, and Peter; Diane and Peter Vennema; Cory, Jessalynn, and Quinn Worden; Dan and Brenda Worden; and the Captain, Peter Zuromskis.

This book is dedicated to Michael "Timo" Gilmore and Jonah Worden.

NEOLIBERAL NONFICTIONS

Introduction: The Documentary Aesthetic

Sarah Glidden's book of comics journalism *Rolling Blackouts* begins with an Iraqi refugee speaking to an American. The Iraqi woman is drawn facing the reader, and in seven panels, she speaks haltingly, countering her willingness to be interviewed with her frustration: "Welcome. But. I never liked you. . . . No, no, I talk with you, but . . . I not like your government. I not like . . . EVERYBODY"[1] (fig. 1). The woman's red hijab stands out against the muted colors worn by the figures behind her, and in the seven panels, she gestures, rubs her forehead, and looks downward. Glidden's sequential illustrations convey the woman's kindness and disgust, yet channel her feelings less toward the individual reading the page than toward "EVERYBODY," a more abstract audience of which the reader is merely a part. In the page's final panel, Glidden further broadens perspective to include the American journalist conducting the interview, Sarah Stuteville, with a caption asking, "What is journalism?"[2] (fig. 2). The answer to this question is, in part, provided on the facing page, on which Glidden explains that her book is a work of comics journalism: "These true events and real dialogue have been crafted into a story, but a person's life is not a story. . . . The idea that I was turning someone else's life into a story fit for consumption is not something I took lightly while I was working on this book, and it will probably always make me uncomfortable. But stories are how all of us try to make sense of a chaotic world, and I think it's worth it, discomfort and all."[3] The discomfort that Glidden describes is made clear in the interview, as the interviewee's halting dialogue expresses her own resentment as well as her desire to be understood, to be documented.

Figure 1. Panel from *Rolling Blackouts: Dispatches from Turkey, Syria, and Iraq,* Sarah Glidden, Drawn & Quarterly, 2016. (Courtesy of the artist)

The discomfort, inequality, and compensatory social value of this exploitative relation between artist and subject is the focal point of Glidden's comic. By including a journalist talking to a subject from the vantage point of a cartoonist and by posing the question "What is journalism?," the comic anchors its narrative in the layered relations between reader, artist, journalist, and subject. Journalism is, for Glidden, an interpretive relation, one that takes on less the qualities of objective reporting as it was defined in the early twentieth century than the aesthetic qualities associated with

Figure 2. Panel from *Rolling Blackouts: Dispatches from Turkey, Syria, and Iraq,* Sarah Glidden, Drawn & Quarterly, 2016. (Courtesy of the artist)

more contemporary and subjective approaches to documentary. Indeed, comics journalism differs in key ways from traditional journalism. For one, comics journalists like Glidden conceptualize projects not only as article-length publications but also as book-length, long-form endeavors. Because of the time-consuming process of comics-making, comics journalism typically cannot appear on the tight, even instantaneous deadlines that define mainstream journalism today. Moreover, comics journalists such as Glidden devote many pages of their works to personal testimony, in a way that documents events through emotion and the artist's hand.

The entanglement of subjective experiences with history is a hallmark of documentary, from the oral histories and iconic photojournalism of the Great Depression to more contemporary preoccupations with relationality and confession in memoirs and social media. Glidden's comics journalism documents personal relations that are uncomfortable because of their overdetermination by structural forces: a war that the American cartoonist did not authorize, displacement and violence occasioned by a terrorist attack with which the Iraqi refugee had nothing to do, and the transactional logic of journalism itself. Yet these structural forces resonate within personal moments. This framing—how the personal is inevitably inflected by structures outside of the frame of Glidden's panels—is key to the "documentary aesthetic" I will elaborate in this book. *Rolling Blackouts* is as much about the process of making journalism as it is itself a work of journalism, and this reflexivity is a major characteristic of documentary art of the past fifty years. The documentary aesthetic occurs across contemporary media and places personal moments in relief against structural forces. In so doing, documentary works make visible how our social relations and desires are produced within compromised conditions, and how individual connections and artistic exertions can offer new visions of redemption, making, and belonging.

Glidden's focus on individual testimony is a signature element of documentary art today, not only in comics but in other media as well. For example, in Errol Morris's celebrated documentary films, his Interrotron camera allows subjects being interviewed to speak directly to the camera, occluding the presence of the interviewer behind the lens. In Morris's 2003 documentary film *The Fog of War,* Robert McNamara reflects on his role in World War II, his tenure as secretary of defense from 1961 to 1968, and the legacy of the Cold War and the Vietnam War. Intercut with graphics and archival footage, the focus of the documentary is Morris's interview with McNamara. McNamara gazes and speaks directly at the viewer, and while the director's voice is heard, Errol Morris does not appear on camera. The Interrotron puts a subject in intimate dialogue with the viewer, projecting personal testimony as historical knowledge.

Yet this transparent intimacy is also mediated through the Interroton and Morris's direction. In one instance, McNamara recounts protests against the Vietnam War, specifically Norman Morrison's self-immolation in 1965 and the 1967 March on the Pentagon. Morris asks, "What effect did all of this dissent have on your thinking? I mean, Norman Morrison is '65, this is '67." McNamara responds, "Well, it was a very tense period. A very tense period for my family, which I don't want to discuss." Morris follows up with another question, "How was your thinking changing during this period?" McNamara then closes the scene by saying, "I don't think my thinking was changing. We were in the Cold War. And this was a Cold War activity." Morris's disembodied voice serves as a rejoinder to the directness of his Interrotron perspective on McNamara. While McNamara's gaze, speech, and framing lend him an immediacy and a sense of intimacy with the viewer, Morris's voice broadens the space in which the film takes place, reminding the viewer that McNamara is speaking to someone, and that what seems like honest testimony and reflection might also be calculated performance. McNamara's transparency is thrown into question, and his melancholic rumination on the "fog of war" is briefly placed in stark contrast with his sense that the Cold War justified his decisions. In this moment, McNamara's reflections are made visible as impersonal, as in fact eliding his personal life. The quagmire of the Vietnam War is represented as a dual or twinned event, both personal and structural yet not fully explicable, and therefore differently mystified, by either explanatory frame. Similar to the confessional segments ubiquitous in reality television, Morris's Interrotron footage manifests intimacy and engagement—we lock eyes with McNamara—as a stylistic device that persists even as McNamara's intimacy with us is exposed as a contrivance by his unwillingness to bear his soul for the camera that is positioned to facilitate such a gesture.

Glidden's *Rolling Blackouts* shares key features with Morris's *Fog of War:* witness testimony, explanatory text or voiceover, artistic reimagination of real-life moments, attention to media footage and recording devices as mediators of experience, and subjective accounts of large-scale events. These two works are examples of how documentary has become an aesthetic mode in our age. Detached from traditional journalism and no longer bound to a specific media form, documentary is now a mode of artmaking, with associated tropes and genre conventions. Like realism and romance, documentary connotes a mode of engagement with character, narrative, and society, and a series of stylistic tropes that connect art to the world. What makes the documentary aesthetic unique, though, is its use of media forms ubiquitous to postwar journalism. While the realist novel of the eighteenth and nineteenth centuries employed devices like letters, newspapers, and diaries to ground narrative in an inherently prosodic reality, contemporary documentary works rely on media forms that have emerged in the twentieth century as signature modes of recording reality, such as photography, film, and recorded voice. Works that fall outside standard definitions of documentary can engage in the documentary aesthetic, through their reliance on these devices.

For example, Adam McKay's 2015 film *The Big Short* engages in the documentary aesthetic in an emblematic way. Adapted from Michael Lewis's nonfiction book of the same name, the Hollywood film adaptation is not a documentary in the way that other films about the 2008 financial crisis were, such as Charles Ferguson's 2010 *Inside Job,* which features talking heads and a voice-over narrator typical of contemporary documentary film. Instead, *The Big Short* uses actors to dramatize the events and figures in Lewis's book. Yet many of the basic terms used in the film's dialogue and central to the film's plot—about how some fund managers, bankers, and investors predicted and profited from the collapse of the U.S. housing market—would be confusing for viewers not familiar with financial instruments. This problem is solved by three scenes featuring celebrities who appear not as characters in the film but as themselves. Anthony Bourdain, Selena Gomez, and Margot Robbie speak directly to the camera, and they explain how financial instruments and the derivatives market work. Along with asides to the camera from Deutsche Bank bond salesman Jared Vennett (played by Ryan Gosling), in which he reassures viewers that what takes place in the film actually took place in the real world, these scenes function as structural and systemic explanations, rendering what is otherwise dramatic content into information about how our lives and loans are commodified in abstract ways. *The Big Short*'s stylized asides make explicit the complex financial transactions that travel alongside our everyday lives, and this coextension of life and finance is indicative of the cultural moment from which the documentary aesthetic emerges. Within our neoliberal culture, public life is increasingly imagined as a series of market transactions, mediated by the financial sector to which we are beholden. In *The Big Short,* the documentary tactic of using expert testimony to present major points and concepts reinforces the film's connection to reality.

The two levels of representation in *The Big Short*—character-based restaging of real events and fact-based exposition—function similarly to Glidden's self-reflexive nod to her own discomfort with journalistic representation, or Morris's voice disrupting McNamara's monologue in front of the Interrortron. By framing personal relations in uncomfortable and often confusing proximity to structures of exploitation, these varied works all participate in the documentary aesthetic, a major mode of artmaking in our contemporary moment. Documentary arts have a history that reaches back at least to the origins of film and photography, and even further if one considers autobiographical works such as Augustine's *Confessions* (ca. 400) or even fictional works written in a documentary format such as Daniel Defoe's *A Journal of the Plague Year* (1722). Yet the documentary aesthetic that I describe in this book captures the distinctly post-1960s moment of documentary art, when documentary forms across media converge on personalized and subjective experiences coupled with structural analysis and critique. The use of documentary tools to creatively represent reality has roots in a range of media-specific practices, including print journalism, photojournalism, documentary film, oral history, ethnography, lyric poetry, and the essay. In the post-1960s moment, these practices commingle to document how the radical transformations of late capitalism work both subjectively and systematically.

From confessional poetry and performance art to cinéma vérité and the New Journalism, documentary emerges as an aesthetic across media in the 1960s and 1970s. Many aesthetic, cultural, economic, and political events make this possible, from the emergence of conceptual art, which privileges the artist's ideas over the art object, and the first-person voice championed by many writers associated with the New Journalism of the period, to the critical edge honed by journalists covering the Vietnam War and the legitimization of media like photography, video, and comics in the art museum.[4] Propelled by the increasing availability of portable audio and video equipment, these aesthetic, cultural, and economic currents led to the emergence of a documentary aesthetic across media, including but not limited to comics, film, photography, prose, and even installation art. This documentary aesthetic has thrived over the past sixty years as a rejoinder and accompaniment to the ways in which finance capitalism and its intensifications of exploitation, dispossession, and state-sanctioned violence have made the world seem vertiginous and precarious. Documentary presents subjects and the structures that determine them today, thus making visible the forms of exploitation that have defined life during the economic, political, and social struggles of the late twentieth and early twenty-first centuries. In so doing, documentary art has emerged as a major way through which we understand our world—a mode that both articulates the culture we inhabit and holds out the possibility of charting a path for new relations to each other and to the structures that both define us and rely on us. In conceptual art, photography, film, comics, music, and literature, the documentary aesthetic seeks to explain the world, motivate change, and trigger a sense of obligation to lost histories and collectives-to-come.

After the 2008 financial crisis, the idea that high finance is too complex for most of us to understand became commonplace. Indeed, it often seems too complex for even experts to understand, as was evident even before the 2008 crisis in Warren Buffett's characterization of derivatives as "financial weapons of mass destruction" because of their volatility and capability to scuttle the very financial institutions that created them.[5] Finance capitalism's unknowability is not something early architects of postwar economic policy feared but instead was a foundation to their worldview. As the neoliberal thinker Friedrich A. Hayek argues in his influential 1945 essay "The Use of Knowledge in Society," the free market produces equilibrium because it is not understood: "The whole acts as one market, not because any of its members survey the whole field, but because their limited individual fields of vision sufficiently overlap so that through many intermediaries the relevant information is communicated to all."[6] As Hayek posits, and as would come to be increasingly the case in the late twentieth century, the systemic and structural operations of finance capitalism have real effects on our world, but the systems themselves seem removed from our everyday lives. Profits are generated by finance capitalism in mysterious, opaque ways, disconnected from the production and consumption of particular things, yet Hayek's claim, which has become a truism of neoliberal rationality, is that the free market produces the best possible conditions for all of us, or at least those conditions which we deserve according to our worth. While this acceptance and endorsement of exploitation has, in part, always existed under capitalism, in which credit and financialization are always operative, it has escalated in our recent past, resulting in massive economic inequality, accelerating environmental crises, and penetrative modes of exploitation and dispossession.[7]

The term "neoliberalism" has become a common descriptor of the increasing financialization and privatization of late capitalism, and neoliberalism's historical trajectory aligns with the emergence of the documentary aesthetic across media. As David Steadman Jones has shown, neoliberal ideology emerges in the aftermath of World War II and becomes intellectually influential in the United States by the 1960s.[8] The two major historical moments that signal the full-blown emergence of neoliberal economic and political policy in the United States between World War II and the Reagan administration are 1971, the moment when the U.S. dollar was unhinged from gold entirely under the "Nixon Shock," and 1973, when the oil embargo led to economic crisis. These moments are bound up in the larger turmoil of the 1960s and 1970s, which encompassed not just the period that has been described as the Great Inflation but also the continued presence of a visible counterculture in the United States. From cinema vérité to the New Journalism, from experimental photography projects to installation art that documented the financial workings of the museum as an institution, documentary art across media forms flourished in this context, and just like neoliberal thought, documentary art across media has become a definitive cultural mode since the 1960s.[9] Neoliberal culture did not appear fully formed in the twenty-first century but instead emerged out of the commingling of economic policy, foreign policy, consumer culture, and postwar political consciousness. This long history of neoliberalism, from its emergence within postwar liberalism to its entrenchment in global economics after the economic crises of the 1970s, is captured in the documentary aesthetic, from Joan Didion's writings about the ends of liberalism in the 1960s, discussed in chapter 2, to contemporary autobiography in the forms of hip hop and prose memoir, as discussed in chapter 1 and the conclusion, respectively.

Another way to characterize the late twentieth-century period in which the documentary aesthetic becomes prominent across media is through the category of postmodernism, influentially described by Fredric Jameson as a state of vertigo and displacement.[10] It has become something of a truism in cultural theory that we are unable to position ourselves in history or in the economy in the late twentieth and early twenty-first centuries.[11] Our everyday lives feel precarious, determined by debt, structured by endless and expanding work. Works of art that try to make sense of this contemporary predicament by placing the unsustainable reality of finance capitalism in relation to personal experiences of that reality employ the documentary aesthetic. I use the term "documentary aesthetic" to identify a wide swath of contemporary art—works in comics, film, literature, music, photography, and mixed media—that has become a dominant force in contemporary culture. Rather than embracing the essential drift of signifiers and the spectacle of consumer capitalism, documentary art presents the cultural flows recognized by figures like Jameson as indicative of postmodernism alongside the structures of extraction, dispossession, and exploitation that make those postmodern spectacles possible. The documentary aesthetic aims to juxtapose the often abstract reality of finance capitalism with precarious everyday life, through which finance capitalism appears as a structuring reality but one that is rarely encountered as a system. While not always named as such, finance capitalism is operative today as an overarching logic by which people are transformed into human capital, public resources are privatized to generate profit for corporate interests, and environmental and social crises become occasions for the accumulation of wealth by global elites. As in Glidden's *Rolling Blackouts,* these systemic modes of exploitation and dispossession (displacement in the service of the attempted privatization of Iraqi oilfields, for example) are often experienced relationally and unevenly. Documentary art can make awkwardness, anger, despair, and other emotions meaningful against structural and systemic backgrounds.

Works that employ the documentary aesthetic engage in juxtaposition, offsetting emotion and personal experience with the structures that produce their possibilities. Because of the cultural logic of neoliberalism, which prioritizes individual agency over collective belonging, a genre like the memoir expresses both personal and structural facets of our moment. Along with more traditionally documentary forms such as photography, memoir participates in the documentary aesthetic through its accounts of individuality within an ideology that has remade what individuality means within economic structures. In our contemporary moment, from the cell phone video footage of police brutality that has contributed to the emergence of Black Lives Matter, to the testimony of sexual assault and school shooting survivors that propelled the #MeToo and #NeverAgain movements, the documentary aesthetic mobilizes subjects by making evident the personal costs of exploitative structures.

Defining Documentary

Documentary is often used as a medium-specific term. It most commonly refers to films made in the tradition established in the early twentieth-century by Robert Flaherty and John Grierson. As the preeminent documentary film scholar Bill Nichols has noted, documentary film also emerges in modernist film practices, through works by Russian filmmakers like Dziga Vertov and in the dadaist films of Luis Buñuel, among others.[12] In 1933, Grierson influentially defined documentary film as the "creative treatment of actuality," and documentary filmmakers' attempts to represent actuality required the creation of a new mode of filmmaking.[13] This new mode synthesized existing genres (the newsreel, the romance, the short film capturing real life) into a distinctive genre unto itself. As Walter Benjamin noted in his famous essay "The Author as Producer," the crises of the early twentieth century required a reorientation of aesthetic forms and their valences: "We are in the midst of a mighty recasting of literary forms, a melting down in which many of the opposites in which we have been used to think may lose their force."[14] Documentary film was one of those forms that "melted down" the divisions between fact and fiction, news and narrative, information and craft.

The emergence of documentary film was accompanied in the early twentieth century by other documentary experiments in text and image, such as James Agee and Walker Evans's 1941 *Let Us Now Praise Famous Men.* As Benjamin makes clear in his critique of Albert Renger-Patzsch's 1928 photobook *The World is Beautiful,* photographs without captions produce a dangerous aestheticization of exploitation. Agee and Evans's work attempts to work against that with text, complementing and contextualizing photographs with personal stories of suffering and dispossession. This history of documentary experimentation forms the cultural background of the contemporary documentary aesthetic, and what makes this latter documentary aesthetic distinct is less its utter break with this previous experimental work than its embrace of aesthetics. In *Let Us Now Praise Famous Men*, for example, Agee distances the project from the category of "Art" in the work's preamble: "Above all else: in God's name don't think of it as Art. . . . Official acceptance is the one unmistakable symptom that salvation is beaten again, and is the one surest sign of fatal misunderstanding, and is the kiss of Judas."[15] As Robert Coles notes in his reflection on documentary art and ethics, Agee and many other modernist documentarians who focused on poverty express "an angry nervousness that belies a sense of complicity in some wrongdoing, or an embarrassment connected to one's good luck as it is rubbed into one's awareness by the sight of others utterly down on their luck."[16] Agee's rejection of the category of art resonates with this nervousness, just as, in John Tagg's reading of Walker Evans's photography from the 1930s, Evans struggles to "disallow all frames of meaning, all nets in which his work might be caught," whether the sentimental rhetoric of magazine photojournalism or the rarefied aestheticism of the art museum.[17] Unlike this modernist moment, in which figures like Agee, Evans, Margaret Bourke-White, and many others were establishing the unique conditions of documentary expression as somewhere in between an indexical record and an aesthetic representation, contemporary documentary artists adapt the discourses and styles associated with both fine art and popular journalism as ways to make documentary more varied. If documentary artists of the early and mid-twentieth century struggled to articulate a place for their work within and outside of modernist aesthetics—more grounded than abstraction, yet different from mass culture—then contemporary documentary art surpasses those tensions and blends overtly artistic techniques with reportage, to give both its artistic and journalistic valences more immediacy.

Today, as during modernism, we are in a moment where documentary matters more than ever. Yet the documentary aesthetic that surrounds us today is one of a different historical moment than that developed during modernism. In the intervening decades, modern media such as film, photography, and even comics have become fully legitimized as art forms, in ways that were still matters of contest and debate in the early twentieth century. Image creation has become more democratized, as portable cameras and digital technology promise to make everyone an image-maker, thus lessening the cost of entry into the documentary mode.[18] Fine art has also shifted considerably, and in our contemporary moment, when archival art, relational art, conceptual art, and installation art are no longer critiques of but welcome components of museums and art galleries, documentary art flourishes even in these rarefied sites.[19] The often documentary and personal inflections of blues, folk, and rock music in the early and mid-twentieth century has extended into the modes of authenticity refined in rap, country, and punk in the late twentieth and early twenty-first centuries. And, in literary culture, writers have long troubled the line between creative writing and reportage, resulting recently in the widespread adoption of "creative nonfiction" as a category in MFA programs in creative writing to reflect the popularity and significance of a range of documentary prose, from the memoir and the essay to immersive journalism and magazine feature writing.

Our contemporary documentary aesthetic is more available, varied, and multimedia than documentary practice in the early twentieth-century, and our relation to history itself has also changed. Early documentary films like Flaherty's *Nanook of the North* (1922) used film to make visible ways of life or modes of existence that were inaccessible to urban viewers through everyday experience, due to geographical and cultural distance or to the limits of human perception. Today, documentary art tends to present less a unified vision of either primitive or current life than a kind of tension, often staged as a problem or symbolic contrast that the documentary artwork itself, or the documentary artist herself, cannot resolve. This reflexive turn is due to a relation to history that Hayden White has described as emerging during modernism: "It appeared impossible to tell any single authoritative story about what really happened—which meant that one could tell any number of possible stories about it."[20] That is, documentary presents not an objective history but a perspectival one.[21] What keeps the documentary aesthetic from slipping into a kind of solipsism, though, is its staging of a relation between individual experience and the structures that make that experience available. Rather than providing a definitive account of a subject, contemporary documentary art makes visible a tension, one often left naggingly unresolved. This irresolution—the memoirist who lacks total recall, the film director who leaves subjects to speak for themselves, the photographer who provides no captions or explanatory titles—reminds us that stories are incomplete and partial.

The art and literature of our age is documentary, and it produces a way of thinking of everyday life's relation to economic and social structures. Documentary art has become a site for aesthetic experimentation amid what seem to be intractably compromised conditions. Refined during the first half of the twentieth century by the solidification of the "standard of objectivity" in print journalism and the formalist aesthetic of New

Deal–era photojournalism and documentary film,[22] early modes of documentary became the subjects of critique by the 1960s. This critique was made perhaps most influentially in Susan Sontag's account of photography as a way of exerting force over the world: "To photograph is to appropriate the thing photographed. It means putting oneself into a certain relation to the world that feels like knowledge—and, therefore, like power."[23] Or, as reiterated in her later book *Regarding the Pain of Others:* "Photographs objectify: they turn an event or a person into something that can be possessed."[24] This critique, which hinged upon the increasing availability and visibility of photographs of atrocities, from the Vietnam War to the torture of prisoners at Abu Ghraib, questioned photography's claim to indexicality, foregrounding how images themselves cannot be thought to have a particular political, emotional, or social meaning, or, even worse, are part of the violence that they depict.[25] With this critique in mind, it makes sense, then, that documentary expression would enter an expanded field.[26] The documentation of actuality has become an aesthetic rather than an explicitly objective or mechanical process, and thus documentary artists use tactics from conceptual art, experimental film, performance art, creative writing, and other modes of aesthetic production.

For example, in Godfrey Reggio's *qatsi* trilogy (1982–2002), film footage is edited together with no narration. The only sound in the films is Philip Glass's musical scores, which sometimes involve chorales singing phrases in the Hopi language. Lauded as films that critique modern capitalism, the exploitation of the third world, and the vacuity of digital culture, none of the *qatsi* trilogy films make an explicit argument. Instead, the films make an impression on the viewer, through juxtaposition and the cumulative force of the films' scores and vantage points. Through the perspectival switching and unifying musical scores comes something like a structural understanding of capitalist accumulation, human collectivity, and commodity pleasures. At the same time, the films create a voyeuristic spectacle, especially the second film in the trilogy, *Powaqqatsi,* which focuses on the "third world" broadly, with footage of "the emerging, land-based cultures of Asia, India, Africa, the Middle East and South America."[27] This broad montage of different locations continues a longstanding tendency in documentary to present the other as primitive, staged for consumption by privileged audiences.

The primitivism inherent in the films' use of the Hopi language also gestures to the exploitative mode in which documentary film has often been considered to operate. This complicity with imperialism is less a failure of an individual artist or work, though, than a quality of privileged life in finance capitalism. *Powaqqatsi* presents economic difference as a difference, thus foregrounding the film's own privileged perspective. The valences of this necessary complicity have been articulated in recent years by different critics, in different ways. David Joselit has noted, in the context of institutional critique, that "either art's power is ethically corrupt or its power is nonexistent," and that therefore art should seek to use its power within an inherently compromised landscape.[28] Writing about postmodern critiques of documentary, Julian Stallabrass asks, "Who or what can avoid complicity in the systems they inhabit? To admit complicity is a first step, not a final condemnation."[29] And Walter Benn Michaels has emphasized the ways that ethical approaches to photography mask the ways in which photographs can produce a structural account of capitalism: "For the critique of capitalism, a good picture is better than a good attitude."[30] One notable feature of documentary art today is its projection of the exploitative gaze as a condition of viewing and of living, and thus its ability to make visible the limits that determine lives. Those determining limits also constitute the horizon of possibilities in our contemporary moment, as we work to build a future different from our exploitative present and past. As Tina M. Campt has asked of contemporary photographs of African Americans that are at once exploitative and also resonances of personhood beyond structures of exploitation, "How do we create an alternative future by living . . . the future we want to see, while inhabiting its potential foreclosure at the same time?"[31] This potential future and its potential foreclosure is the operative tension of the documentary aesthetic today, as it makes visible the limits of the present while also positing a mode of being that moves beyond our neoliberal culture.

One contemporary example of how the documentary aesthetic persists within, rather than outside of, exploitative structures is a book titled *The 2015 Baltimore Uprising: A Teen Epistolary.* The 268-page book was published by the Research and Destroy New York City collective, and it collects hundreds of tweets from April 19, 2015, the day Freddie Gray died in a hospital following physical abuse by Baltimore police officers, to May 1, 2015, when Gray's death was ruled a homicide. The collection of tweets documents the affects, communication and organization networks, and activist strategies of the youth who took to the streets of Baltimore. On one hand, the very existence of the book is a testament to how a social media platform like Twitter has become a default mode of communication today, even when those communications are about revolution and riot. These tweets and their authors are fodder for monetization by a social media giant, which uses personal data for financial gain. Yet, at the same time, the book makes clear how Twitter has led to something like a new language and relation to society, a platform to organize and express newfound consciousness of structural exploitation. The book concludes with a tweet that reads "The riots ain't over," an enjoinder to think of the enthusiasm contained within the book—"Fucking shit up is one of the funniest things to do yall know that lol"—as a marker of the continuing crisis of exploitation in our time.[32] This crisis is intensely personal, perhaps even more so because it is partially organized around individual users of things like social media. Yet the tweet book is also structurally impersonal in its focus on the networks of information generated by a mass of users. From within the framework of a social network that mines user data for profit can emerge a critical intervention in structural exploitation.

Our era's documentary aesthetic charts neoliberalism's erosion of public welfare and inflation of individualism, offering a heightened sense of the irreconcilability of the individual with society. The documentary aesthetic names a transmedia process through which artists turn everyday lives and the structures that both exploit them and give them meaning into objects of contemplation. Documentary works present the contradictions of contemporary culture as operating both through the unprecedented ubiquity of finance capital in everyday life and through a surplus of subjective experience determined by, yet detached from, those structures. The documentary aesthetic that this book will present first emerged in the 1960s, through the critique of traditional conceptions of objectivity. These critiques were popularized by cinéma vérité, the New Journalism, and conceptual art critical of the museum as an institution. However, the documentary aesthetic importantly differs from the conceptions of postmodernism that critics have often used to understand art and literature of this period. While it operates across media, the documentary aesthetic is nonetheless rooted in the representation and rhetoric of authentic experience, structural analysis, and archival work. The gaps between experience, structure, and history—the failure of justice, equality, society, and family to nurture life—give documentary art its cutting edge, its potential to ignite a desire for a better world.

Documentary versus Postmodernism

One of the things that charting a history of the documentary aesthetic in the United States from the 1960s to the present reveals is an alternative history of contemporary aesthetics. This alternative is characterized less by familiar postmodern critiques of hierarchy, referentiality, and narrative than by attempts to frame structural conditions in relation to subjective experience. An early influential figure in this alternative history is Norman Mailer, who would help to define the New Journalism as a style in the 1960s and 1970s. In *The Presidential Papers* Mailer comments, "Once a newspaper touches a story, the facts are lost forever, even to the protagonists."[33] Mailer's critique of newspaper journalism pointedly uses the language of fiction; newspapers report "stories," not events, and those stories have "protagonists," not flesh-and-blood agents. Mailer's complaint seems to be less that newspapers willfully misrepresent facts than that newspapers can't tell stories that capture the desires, ambitions, social structures, and relational networks that would become the focus of Mailer's own documentary prose.

In a draft of his 1968 book *The Armies of the Night,* Mailer writes, "Phenomenologically speaking, a newspaper is a dull social novel with a new draft put out daily by a factory of mediocre novelists."[34] By failing in literary terms, newspaper journalism also fails to convey any facts to the reader. Facts and fiction are not exclusive categories in Mailer's estimation; they feel the same to a reader, for better or worse. If fiction is not factual, it's not a good story, and if facts are not arranged artfully, they lose their purchase on reality. This understanding of fiction's claim on reality becomes dominant in the late twentieth century, and while it led to an explosion of experimental documentary art from the 1960s to the present, the positing of reality as a social fiction was more often taken by critics to be a reason to focus on modes like metafiction rather than documentary. Indeed, it became a hallmark not just of literature but of art, architecture, music, and film to find in fluidity, malleability, and fictionality a utopian celebration of plasticity, a reason to believe that our relation to history and to the material world was a mere script, one that could be rewritten. From the 1982 film *Blade Runner*'s meditation on the indistinguishability of man and machine to the auto-tuned vocals of T-Pain and many others—which foreground the flatness of perfect pitch achieved through digital manipulation of voice—the triumph of postmodernism was registered in the embrace of constructedness. Whether through the social construction of categories like race and gender or the ubiquity of mediation, the mere fact that our understanding of any event comes through the media's spin machine became a hallmark insight of postmodernism.

By contrast, Mailer's critique of newspaper journalism calls not for more fictions but for more facts, represented more artfully. Perhaps because of the critique of representation associated with postmodernism—the idea that, per Mailer, facts are always fictions poorly told—nonfiction forms remained largely a footnote to the major periodizing and conceptualizing works that cataloged contemporary art, literature, film, and music from the 1960s onward. Hip hop, for example—a form saturated by autobiographical reflection and projection—has only recently been recognized with a Pulitzer Prize, for Kendrick Lamar's album *Damn* (2017). Even when major texts like Norman Mailer's *The Armies of the Night* (1968) and Truman Capote's *In Cold Blood* (1966) are excerpted in the "Fact Meets Fiction" section of the Norton anthology *Postmodern American Fiction*, their inclusion confirms rather than complicates the basic postmodernist thesis that reality becomes textual in the age of simulacrum.[35] And documentary film has never reached the kind of acclaim and recognition in contemporary venues that fiction film has despite its overwhelming prominence in our understanding of our relation to the world. Documentary forms have often registered as a kind of minor tradition within post-1960s American art and literature, something perhaps better served in departments of anthropology, communication, history, journalism, and sociology than in literary studies or art history.

In recent years, though, the kinds of literary forms popularized by the New Journalists—Truman Capote's "nonfiction novel," Hunter S. Thompson's "gonzo journalism," Joan Didion's memoiristic approach to reportage, Tom Wolfe's intertwining of immersion and critical distance—have become unmistakably influential in literary culture, and documentary, confessional, and autobiographical modes have become ubiquitous, even dominant to the point of parody, in fine art, music, film, and television. The conventions of reality television—the confessional room, the roving camera, the unscripted feel of dialogue—have become normalized in major sitcoms like *The Bernie Mac Show* (2001–6), *The Office* (2005–13), and *Modern Family* (2009–present). Drawing from long-standing traditions in blues and funk, autobiographical performances were central to the emergence of gangsta rap in the 1980s and 1990s, and they continue to be important in contemporary hip hop. Documentary projects also constitute some of the most celebrated art photography of recent years, from Edward Burtynsky's photographs of oil fields and manufacturing plants to Taryn Simon's photographs of both people wrongfully convicted of crimes and contraband seized at U.S. airports. As contemporary critics, writers, and artists have reevaluated the legacy of postmodernism and increasingly turned to more explicitly economic categories like neoliberalism to frame their thinking, the focus on lived experience and material reality emphasized in nonfiction and documentary forms, as opposed to the "history-as-text" and performative play of postmodernism, is due a reevaluation as a major aesthetic of our contemporary moment.[36]

This book is not alone in seeking alternatives to periodizing the immediate past and present as postmodern. Scholars like Mark McGurl have turned to longer modes of periodization that stem from deep time. Similarly, readings of contemporary literature, art, and culture through economic concepts such as debt, the creative economy, financialization, and neoliberalism more broadly have been put forth by a number of scholars, including Sarah Brouillette, Mitchum Huehls, Leigh Clare LaBerge, Annie McLanahan, and Rachel Greenwald Smith. These departures from postmodernism have emerged alongside attempts to rehabilitate the concept of postmodernism such as Jeffrey Nealon's "post-postmodernism" or Christian Moraru's "cosmodernism," as well as modes of criticism that engage with the problematic of the contemporary as a distinct category by scholars such as Amy Hungerford, Theodore Martin, and Terry Smith. These approaches all gesture to a need to revise our understanding of art, culture, and literature of the past fifty years, and this book is an attempt to do so.

The fact that the postmodern era is also the period of neoliberalism's emergence and dominance led me to consider how the documentary aesthetic functions as a major tradition in contemporary American art and literature, a tradition more concerned with material reality than the constructedness and malleability of history popularized under the headings of postmodernism. If our immediate history is no longer postmodern but neoliberal, then documentary matters as postwar art in a way that it never has before. Indeed, documentary artists have developed a number of conceptual modes through which to make visible and legible the structural changes brought to bear on everyday lives, public institutions, and labor by neoliberal culture and finance capitalism.

In the chapters that follow, I explore how documentary art since the 1960s represents the contradictions of our time. The chapters proceed thematically, charting major concepts, ideas, and structures that define the documentary aesthetic from the 1960s to the present. Chapter 1 focuses on the ways in which personal experience and structural realities differ in neoliberalism, first in Jeff Wall's photography and then in documentary works about music: D. A. Pennebaker's documentary film *Dont Look Back*, Charlie Ahearn's quasi-documentary film *Wild Style*, Kendrick Lamar's album *Good Kid, M.A.A.D. City*, and Ed Piskor's comics series *Hip Hop Family Tree*. All of these works position personal experience in tense relation to larger structures that are informed by, and sometime profit from, those personal experiences. In these documentary films, comics, and albums, personal craft functions in relation to collective belonging and structural exploitation, and these works thus envision a mode of survival and persistence from within our neoliberal moment. From Dylan's shift from folk balladeer to rock-and-roll icon, to Kendrick Lamar's narrative of street life and eventual rap fame, music is both bound to an immediate political context and also commodified in global markets.

Chapter 2 charts the emergence of the documentary aesthetic through an examination of works by the writer Joan Didion, the conceptual artist Hans Haacke, and the filmmaker Patricio Guzmán. The fragmentations of self and society occasioned by the emergence of finance capitalism and neoliberal economic policy become formally visible in their documentary projects. Didion, Haacke, and Guzmán's works provide a template for the emergence of the documentary aesthetic alongside, and in explanatory and affective response to, emergent neoliberal reforms in the American economy and in American foreign policy.

Chapter 3 details the figure of the hustler as an icon of neoliberal individualism in Jay-Z's autobiography *Decoded,* Alex Haley's *Autobiography of Malcom X,* and Hunter S. Thompson's "gonzo" journalism. The hustler embodies an ideal of neoliberal culture, a figure unfettered by traditional structures yet utterly determined by the conditions that have generated him. Because of this individualism and commitment to the marketplace, the hustler is a trope for thinking about enmeshment within neoliberalism, and also for fantasizing about rebellion against its social and economic norms.

Chapter 4 dwells on the "true crime" genre, one of the most prominent in our culture today. In a range of true crime documentaries, from bestsellers about Ted Bundy, Jeffrey MacDonald, and Charles Manson, to contemporary works by Maggie Nelson and Taryn Simon, I examine the ways that moral economies are substituted for structural explanations of crime, thus finding in criminals genre types rather than more complicated subjects. Since crime is a political structure, and one that has been a locus of racial and economic exploitation in the United States, narratives of crime and criminality are key sites where neoliberalism imagines transgressive and appropriately lawful subjecthood.

Chapter 5 traces the ways in which environmentalism is articulated in experimental, speculative documentaries, beginning with Rachel Carson's writings about the ocean and her iconic *Silent Spring,* and then moving to a cluster of later works including Allan Sekula's *Fish Story,* Werner Herzog's

Lessons of Darkness, Richard Misrach and Kate Orff's *Petrochemical America*, and A. Laurie Palmer's *In the Aura of a Hole: Exploring Sites of Material Extraction*. In these environmentalist documentaries, deep time and inhuman perspectives alternate with personal stories to provide a dual view of environmental harm and recuperative action. From within neoliberal culture, solutions to climate change seem impossible, for collective action cuts against the dominant currents of our value system. These speculative documentaries provide paths for imagining otherwise.

The book concludes with a chapter on the "memoir boom" in contemporary American culture, focusing particularly on memoirs by Joan Didion and Dave Eggers, as well as a range of works by the artists and writers Alison Bechdel, Phoebe Gloeckner, Sheila Heti, Miranda July, Adrian Nicole LeBlanc, Tao Lin, Jessamyn Lovell, Justin St. Germain, and Jesmyn Ward. Experimental memoirs offer ways of both focalizing and offsetting an individual voice, thus producing a representation of life within conditions of privatization. The memoir's first-person perspective dissolves in these works, emphasizing not the redemptive potential of self-realization so commonly associated with the memoir genre but instead the ways in which personhood is created through social structures.

While the chapters focus on some key works, they also address other works in passing or in conclusion, seeking to provide both a nuanced account of particular texts and the broader scope of the documentary aesthetic. The chapters progress from charting key facets of neoliberal culture—its economic patterns and their confusing relation to everyday experience, the tropes of entrepreneurial individualism, the moral economy of privatization—to modes of thinking within and beyond neoliberal culture, through artistic craft, speculative imaginaries, and revised senses of subjectivity.

The documentary aesthetic is prominent today, and has been prominent since the 1960s, as a way of making visible the systems structuring our world that often seem abstract and removed from our control. The fact that personal and subjective filters become distinctive in documentary art about neoliberal culture is no accident. It is perfectly neoliberal that we filter the world through our individual lenses, for that is the normative vantage point of free market economics. Documentary works can make visible the abstractions, detachments, and ironies that constitute our individuated lives. Along with this critical perspective, documentary works can also envision alternative modes of living, beyond the exploitative structures that surround us. It turns out these alternatives are everywhere if you know how to look.

1 / Money Trees

In *Postmodernism, or, the Cultural Logic of Late Capitalism,* Fredric Jameson famously uses the Bonaventure Hotel in Los Angeles as a metaphor for "the incapacity of our minds, at least at present, to map the great multinational and decentered communicational network in which we find ourselves caught as individual subjects."[1] Jameson seeks to make clear that the vertiginous experience evoked by the hotel's symmetrical towers, rounded lounges, and glassed elevators is not unique but instead an emblematic condition of postmodernism. To make this claim, he juxtaposes the Bonaventure Hotel with an account of helicopter flight from Michael Herr's 1977 work of literary journalism about the Vietnam War, *Dispatches.* In his reading of Herr, Jameson argues that the book's lexicon, which "fuses a whole range of contemporary collective idiolects, most notably rock language and black language," typifies the breakdown of narrative in the late twentieth century: "This first terrible postmodernist war cannot be told in any of the traditional paradigms of the war novel or movie—indeed, that breakdown of all previous narrative paradigms is, along with the breakdown of any shared language through which a veteran might convey such an experience, among the principal subjects of the book and may be said to open up the place of a whole new reflexivity."[2] Herr's refusal of fictional tropes gestures, in Jameson's account, to a proto-articulation of a "whole new reflexivity," later to be described as "something of the mystery of the new postmodernist space."[3] From our vantage point today, it seems rather clear what aesthetic form this "new reflexivity" has taken: documentary.

Dispatches opens with the abdication of objective journalistic standards: "We knew that the uses of most information were flexible, different pieces of ground told different stories to different people."[4] What this means is not that reality has no meaning, but instead that there is, in Herr's words, "not much chance anymore for history to go on unselfconsciously."[5] In his reflexive prose, Herr positions himself centrally among the soldiers he interviews and travels with, often juxtaposing official narratives released by the U.S. government about the war with the messy experiences of soldiers on the ground. This juxtaposition produces the book's own methodological rationale, an argument for the necessity of the documentary aesthetic in the 1960s and 1970s. As Herr notes, if "conventional journalism could no more reveal this war than conventional firepower could win it," then Herr's focus on personal experience and emotion strives to represent the war in its reflexive, mediated complexity.[6] Indeed, Herr describes his role as that of documentary storyteller: "So we have all been compelled to make our own movies, as many movies as there are correspondents, and this one is mine."[7] By blending techniques from film into prose, Herr captures the juxtapositions that define what we can now think of as a failed precursor to the more secretive U.S. military engagements of the 1970s and 1980s. Jameson's negative comparison of Herr's *Dispatches* to the "war novel or movie" only underlines what makes this reflexivity unique: in its combination of narrative breakdown, first-person experience, and vernacular language, and in its origins as long-form, impressionistic war reportage for *Esquire, Dispatches* is a work in the documentary aesthetic.[8]

That the category of "documentary" was not used by Jameson in the 1980s and early 1990s to describe postmodern aesthetics is understandable. After all, documentary was often critiqued during postmodernism as a naive, exploitative mode in photography and film.[9] Similarly, its literary equivalent of the period, in which Herr was often included, the New Journalism, seemed opposed to postmodernism in its sometimes archconservative politics and in its insistence on the role of the author as a major mediating force. Yet for Jameson, Herr's documentary prose marks something like an attempt at cognitive mapping through its collective vernacular, even if it ultimately represents less a totality than vertigo in his reading. Indeed, as Jameson's invocation of Herr implies but does not examine, a whole swath of documentary art from the 1960s to the present has aimed to create new modes of conceiving the relation of subject to structure, exploited to totality. Documentary art—ranging from works like Herr's *Dispatches* to conceptual artworks like Martha Rosler's *The Bowery in Two*

Inadequate Descriptive Systems (1974–75)—emerged to represent poverty, exploitation, and modes of being in the postwar United States while also using experimental modes to critique the older tradition of documentary that, as Rosler argued, "has been much more comfortable in the company of moralism than wedded to a rhetoric or program of revolutionary politics."[10] The "moralism" that Rosler points out is indicative of both New Deal–era documentary's polemic messaging and the logic of formal purity that came to be associated with modernist aesthetics. With Rosler and others working in the documentary aesthetic, documentary art moves beyond these origins and limits. Today, documentary experiments continue in an even more prominent fashion, including celebrated literary works such as Ben Lerner's *10:04* (2014), Claudia Rankine's *Citizen* (2014), and Maggie Nelson's *The Argonauts* (2015); photography projects like Trevor Paglen's *Invisible: Covert Operations and Classified Landscapes* (2010), Taryn Simon's *Paperwork and the Will of Capital* (2015), and Richard Misrach and Guillermo Galindo's *Border Cantos* (2016); installation art projects by Ann Hamilton and Fred Wilson; and digital documentaries like the video game *Kursk* (2018) by the Polish game studio Jujubee and the web-based *Offshore* (2013), an interactive documentary by Brenda Longfellow, Glenn Richards, and Helios Design Labs.

As Erika Balsom and Hila Peleg argue in their book *Documentary across Disciplines*: "Contemporary documentary practices reach across media and across disciplines to form a rich site marked by imperatives at once aesthetic and political. Far from any notion of 'fly-on-the-wall' immediacy or quasi-scientific aspirations to objectivity, such practices understand documentary not as the neutral picturing of reality, but as a way of coming to terms with reality by means of working with and through images and narrative."[11] If contemporary documentary art exists in an expanded field—no longer defined by medium specificity or simple binaries of truth and fiction—then it may be that documentary offers a framework for representing our immediate history and contemporary moment in a way that can make visible the structures of exploitation emblematic of the present.[12] When critics like Alberto Toscano and Jeff Kinkle or Walter Benn Michaels, in very different ways, find in film and photography a renewed assertion of cognitive mapping or aesthetic autonomy, what they may be noticing is less a commitment to the concepts of totality or autonomy than it is documentary form itself. The documentary aesthetic is newly prominent today but has a history of documenting both subjective experience and structures of exploitation that coincides with the emergence of finance capitalism in the 1960s.[13] Therefore many seemingly postmodern works might have different meanings if viewed as works in the documentary aesthetic.

For example, Jeff Wall's well-known 1982 photograph *Mimic* (fig. 3) would not be classified as documentary under traditional definitions, but by thinking of it as such, I hope to make the point that documentary form is a mode of artistic production today that surpasses its earlier, more rigid definitions. *Mimic* uses the aesthetic of a documentary genre, street photography, even though it is a posed and carefully composed photograph restaging an incident that Wall witnessed on a Vancouver street. Walter Benn Michaels has argued that this photograph represents the difference between individual feelings, ambitions, and expressions, and the economic system that, in his view, renders those sentiments irrelevant and even harmful to the pursuit of economic equality. The photograph represents an act of prejudice, a tense encounter between a white, seemingly

Figure 3. *Mimic,* Jeff Wall, 1982. Transparency in lightbox, 198 × 228.6 cm. (Courtesy of the artist)

working-class couple and an Asian man. The Asian man represents, here, a new, educated, upwardly mobile immigrant class, resented by the white man as his prospects point downward. Wall's photograph, for Michaels, asserts its autonomy as a photograph, and in turn the photograph's form "assert[s] the autonomy of structure in relation to affect."[14] Racial difference and class difference do not correspond and are indeed in an inverse relationship in the photograph. Yet the irreducibility of prejudice to exploitation is made available through the photograph's documentary presentation, through the use of a mode of photography that we expect to represent subjective experience as evidence of a structure of exploitation.

In Michaels's view, Wall rejects the generic conceits of street photography. This rejection makes it all the more compelling to read the photograph's form as a refinement of documentary aesthetics, a shift away from the familiar genre of street photography and toward a more rapacious documentary aesthetic. What has led critics to think of Wall's photograph as postmodern is how the subjective experience of prejudice, to borrow Douglas Crimp's phrasing in his landmark essay "The Photographic Activity of Postmodernism," is "a function not of presence but of absence."[15] That is, the racism expressed by the photograph's white male subject represents resentment and hate but does not immediately represent the economic and racial structures that have produced that feeling. As a restaging of an experience, *Mimic* documents an act of prejudice that becomes, in the photograph, evidence of a shift in economic relations, as the prospects of the white working class begin to dwindle as manufacturing and industry are reconfigured under globalization. Yet the value of the photograph as documentary is that it can only represent this structural condition by representing something else, a feeling produced by exploitation but one that exceeds its cause. The personal feelings and ambitions captured in the photograph are central to the project of documentary. Emotional and personal relations are not a false front for structural analysis to topple over. The feelings of the subjects in *Mimic* are visible alongside the structural relations of those very subjects, and the photograph captures this tension. Just as Herr's *Dispatches* places experience in relation to other, official discourses about the Vietnam War, *Mimic* juxtaposes feeling with structure, and in so doing it participates in the documentary aesthetic by presenting an account of the social world.

Documentary practices have expanded since the 1960s, and this expansion has been facilitated by the untethering of documentary from narrow constructions of political perspective, factuality, and medium specificity. Important documentary projects of our age cross media—they include journalistic writing classed under the headings of the New Journalism, literary journalism, and submersion journalism; conceptual and archival art practices that critique the museum as an institution and seek to break down the walls that separate the museum from society; memoirs that have populated bestseller lists from the 1990s on; major works of comics nonfiction like Art Spiegelman's *Maus* (1991) and Joe Sacco's *Palestine* (1996); and popular music across genres that trades in personal authenticity. Documentary produces a way of thinking of everyday life's distance from social structures as a site for aesthetic experimentation amid what seem to be intractably compromised conditions. Turning everyday life, real objects, and the structures that exploit and give them meaning into art through documentary form presents the contradictions of our contemporary moment as operating through both the unprecedented ubiquity of finance capital in everyday life and a surplus of subjective experience determined by, yet sometimes in excess of, those structures.

In this chapter, I will focus on works that foreground the tensions between individuality and systems beyond individuals in ways similar to Herr's *Dispatches* and Wall's *Mimic.* These works cross media forms, and they are particularly in sync with neoliberal culture, as they foreground the ties between personality and economy. In D. A. Pennebaker's documentary film *Dont Look Back,* Charlie Ahearn's fictionalized film about graffiti and hip-hop culture *Wild Style,* Ed Piskor's comics series *Hip Hop Family Tree,* and Kendrick Lamar's album *Good Kid, M.A.A.D. City,* individual styles are bounced off of consumer culture, collective imaginaries, corporate exploitation, and global capitalism. These works are part of rock and hip-hop cultures, arguably the now-universal languages of our time, and they capture how experience and structures work in a negative relation under finance capitalism.

Cultures of Resistance

D. A. Pennebaker's *Dont Look Back* chronicles Bob Dylan's 1965 tour in England. As a work of cinema vérité or "direct cinema," the film records overheard conversations rather than direct engagements with the camera or filmmaker. In one striking moment in the film, though, the agency of the filmmaker is more apparent than usual. Interviewed by a reporter from the BBC's African Service, Dylan is asked how he got started as a musician: "How did it all begin for you, Bob? What actually started you off?" Dylan responds with an "um," and then in an unprecedented bit of editing, the film cuts to a younger Dylan playing "Only a Pawn in Their Game," about the assassination of Medger Evers, in front of a group of African Americans in a rural setting. Keith Beattie details that this scene—"which was filmed in early 1963 during a voters' registration rally at Silas Mage's farm in Greenwood, Mississippi—was shot by Ed Emshwiller while working on a television programme dealing with civil rights."[16] The applause at the end of Dylan's performance behind a pick-up truck at this voter registration rally is blended into the cacophonous applause in a theatre in England, as Dylan begins playing "The Times They Are a-Changin'," alone on stage. This transition presents Dylan's career as one of stark contrasts. Notably, the interview sequence here differs from other media interviews in the film, where Dylan is often confrontational and prickly with reporters. As Jeanne Hall has noted of this scene, "Pennebaker's abrupt interruption of what might actually have been a productive (i.e., informative) interview is telling and perfectly in keeping with *Dont Look Back*'s systematic critique of the value of conventional reporting methods."[17] The documentary, then, presents a mode of filmmaking that is at once more personal and more abstract than conventional modes of representing personhood, especially in the case of Dylan, a figure who is beginning to refuse to participate in conventional ways with interviewers.

Once an overtly political songwriter, the Dylan of *Dont Look Back* has changed—his songs are more poetic, less political, and when he opens his concert with "The Times They Are a-Changin'," he looks visibly weary, his face unexpressive. What seemed like a moment of civil rights sympathy, even activism, in the jump cut to "Only a Pawn in Their Game," has become aloof obscurantism by 1965, in part because, the film implies, the wearying grind of media exposure has worn down Dylan's taste for sincerity. *Dont Look Back* charts the difference between Dylan's folk history and celebrity blankness. And in the film's final scene, when Dylan reads a review of his recent concert that claims he is an "anarchist," he jokes, "Give the anarchist a cigarette," and then after a pause says, "I don't think it's cool to be an anarchist." The camera lingers on his face. As he gazes through sunglasses out the car window, Dylan's personality is unavailable to us, the viewers. He is just as confusing to us as he is to the media that searches for ways to describe his politics after his shift into celebrity rock culture. The familiar politics of the progressive folk singer vanish, and as Dylan becomes a rock celebrity, cool and hip styles become the only explanations of his work, even if his work seems inexplicable without reference to personal experience and political commitments. *Dont Look Back* presents a vision of celebrity wherein politics become illegible and individual style becomes a kind of blank affect.

While *Dont Look Back* focuses on an iconic individual, *Wild Style* fuses individual style with collective events, gesturing not to the impersonal effects of celebrity culture but instead to ways in which artisanal crafts can help form a community. As Kimberley Bercov Monteyne has argued, the film is at once a documentary and a musical, and in his depiction of the South Bronx, *Wild Style*'s director Charlie Ahearn "underscores the power to be found in noncommercial spaces of creativity associated with early hip-hop and Black and Latino youth culture in the early '80s."[18] Tracking the life of the graffiti artist Zoro (played by the real-life graffiti artist Lee Quiñones), the film includes a number of musical sequences that feature early hip-hop groups, along with sequences of Quiñones at work with spray paint. While its overarching plot is fictional, *Wild Style* is filmed in the documentary aesthetic: it features musicians and cultural figures like Fab Five Freddy who play themselves, has largely improvised dialogue, and is shot on location in the Bronx. The film concludes with a large outdoor concert, performed in a bandshell that has been painted by Zoro. Initially frustrated by his vision for the bandshell, Zoro has to move beyond his romantic conception of the artist as a tortured, isolated individual: "I'm trying to paint this figure in the middle, and it's not even coming out right. I've already got the hands on the side, like the hands of doom, representing the city and the environment around this artist, and what I'm trying to draw is the artist in the middle. And he's like painting all by himself in his own world, and he don't care about nobody around him. And that's what the hands are, everybody around him." Upon hearing this, Rose (played in the film by Lady Pink, another real-life graffiti artist) responds with a critique of Zoro's individualized vision: "I don't like your mural. I don't like the idea. . . . You only worry about Zoro. Concentrate on what the whole thing is about. It's a jam. Rappers are gonna be coming down. They're gonna be the stars of this thing, not you." Zoro's face lights up after this, and he completes the mural, replacing the solitary artist with an electrified star at the center of the stage. Zoro imagines his graffiti star shooting lightning from the stage, no longer signifying resistance to oppressive forces in society but instead energizing a collective performance. This imagined electricity is paralleled by the concert itself, which features Busy Bee Starski and the Fantastic Freaks rapping in front of a large, dancing crowd. In a film about an illegal art form, graffiti, and a mode of musical performance that is intensely competitive, rap—one sequence in *Wild Style* features a rap song performed as a game of basketball—artistic craft is both individualized and collective. Graffiti artists and rappers alike are valued because of individualized styles that make them distinct. These styles emerge in the 1970s Bronx, a part of New York City decimated by the construction of the Cross Bronx Expressway from 1948 to 1972. A structure designed to facilitate the circulation of goods and workers—a hallmark of neoliberal capitalism's burgeoning logistics industry—the expressway produces a space for individual expression within exploitative conditions. Yet these styles achieve their full expression when artists participate in a collective environment.

The aesthetics of *Dont Look Back* and *Wild Style* solidify the terms of music documentary—on one hand, the history of popular music relies on iconic individuals whose personalities coextend with their styles, yet on the other hand, music is a collective enterprise, born of communities of craft. In our neoliberal culture, music functions as something of an exemplar of entrepreneurial individualism, yet it is also a mass form that can exceed commodification. In some instances, these individualized expressions facilitate pleasures and communities formed by craft. In these moments, one glimpses what it might be like to abandon isolated individualism for collaboration and collective work outside of familiar exploitative hierarchies. These valences of individual style, collaboration, and exploitation become even more apparent later in the twentieth century and into the twenty-first.

Documentary and Hip Hop, 1989

The year 1989 figures centrally in our histories of contemporary aesthetics. Not only does 1989 give us the convenient benchmark of the end of the Cold War, but it is also a point around which we can find an explosion of influential, experimental documentary. In 1988, Errol Morris's film *The Thin Blue Line* was released and Adrian Piper's influential performance/video work *Cornered* was first exhibited. Allan Sekula began his documentary art project *Fish Story* in 1989, and the second volume of Art Spiegelman's *Maus* was nearing the end of its serialization in *Raw,* to be published as a book in 1991. In more traditional media, Jeff Widener's 1989 "Tank Man" photograph at Tiananmen Square became another iconic work of photojournalism. More specifically, 1989 is a signal year for the history of hip-hop music. Public Enemy's anthem "Fight the Power," the opening song in Spike Lee's film *Do the Right Thing,* begins with Chuck D rapping, "1989, the number, another summer," and N.W.A.'s *Straight Outta Compton,* released in August of 1988, would appear on Billboard music charts in 1989 as well. Both groups trade in documentary tropes. Public Enemy's "Fight the Power" music video is a documentary work itself—a live performance and street gathering, intercut with archival footage of the civil rights movement. N.W.A.'s rap narratives include both street authenticity and structural analysis, as in their iconic anthem "Fuck the Police." As Jeff Chang, Joshua Clover, and Eithne Quinn have argued, the coincidence of Public Enemy's Black nationalism and N.W.A.'s gangsta lifestyle in 1989 represents a kind of fork in the road for hip-hop music.[19] As N.W.A.'s gangsta rap gained popularity, the Black nationalist politics and aesthetics of Public Enemy waned. In his history of hip-hop culture, Chang details this transition as a shift away from Reaganite messages of abstention, which dovetailed with Black nationalism's emphasis on self-discipline: "Reaganism had eliminated youth programs while bombarding youths with messages to desist and abstain; it was all about tough love and denial and getting used to having nothing. Even the East Coast utopians like Rakim and Chuck D talked control and discipline. By contrast, excess was the essence of N.W.A.'s appeal. These poets celebrated pushers, played bitches, killed enemies, and assassinated police. Fuck delayed gratification, they said, take it all now."[20] Joshua Clover characterizes this move from discipline to excess as "the internalization of struggle," a pivot from Black nationalism's vision of "a confrontation at the border of the ghetto and suburb" to gangsta's "spectacle of Black youth and a Black underclass ensnared (and even reveling) in a world of immanent violence that retreated from borders of geography, race, and class—and turned the violence on itself."[21] Eithne Quinn similarly finds in gangsta rap a turn away from the politics expressed by rappers like Chuck D and places the style squarely within the logic of neoliberalism: "Much of the timeliness and persisting resonance of gangsta rap derives from its dramatizing of reconfigured relations within the cultural marketplace, during an era in which profit was increasingly upheld as the only measure of worth."[22] As Quinn points out, what makes gangsta rap unique is not that it is a cultural commodity designed to turn a profit but that gangsta rappers themselves broadcast their profit-driven intentions as a central feature of the genre's expression.

Despite the initial public outcry against gangsta rap, N.W.A. and subsequently Dr. Dre's 1992 album *The Chronic* would recenter rap music around a gangsta, consumerist lifestyle, one that relies on aspirations to wealth and leisure as much as it does on first-person experience and authenticity as rhetorical poses. Writing about rap music during the summer of 1989, David Foster Wallace noted in *Signifying Rappers* that rap's commingling of the rhetoric of collective politics and the rhetoric of hustling and consuming positions it towards the kind of sincerity he would associate with the generation of writers to come after postmodernism in his well-known essay "E Unibus Pluram." In *Signifying Rappers,* Wallace writes, "Serious rap's the first music to begin creative work on the new, (post-)postmodern face the threat of economic inequality to American ideals is wearing: the dreadfully obvious one: viz., 'freedom' becomes not qualitative but quantitative, quantifiable, a cold logical function of where you are and what you have to exercise it on."[23] That is, in rap music, Wallace finds the departure from postmodern irony he would later predict in a generation of writers, like Dave Eggers, who would embrace the form of the memoir. Rap got there first.

In 1989, rap music was quickly becoming a mainstream form, signaled not only by a rising number of singles and albums on the Billboard charts, from Public Enemy and N.W.A. to Tone Loc's "Wild Thing," but also by *Yo! MTV Raps,* which began as a weekly show in 1988 and was converted to a daily after-school show in early 1989 because of its immense popularity. With this success, of course, rap also entered into finance capitalism, as a facet of the entertainment industry and as a way to make visible, and even heroic, the acquisitiveness and self-interested greed of the entrepreneurial individual so often associated with neoliberalism, removed from the politics of community building that lingered in Public Enemy's Black nationalism. *Village Voice* critic Greg Tate's 1993 poem "What is Hip-Hop?" seizes upon rap's imbrication within capitalism, its movement from regionally specific subcultures to popular culture:

> Hip-hop is the perverse logic of capitalism pursued by an artform
> Like capitalism, hip hop converts raw soul into store rack commodity
> Like capitalism, hip-hop has no morals, no conscience, and no ecological concern for the scavenged earth or the scavenged American minds it will wreck in its pursuit of new markets[24]

Tate's poem is critical, though it concludes with a recognition that hip hop constitutes a blues vernacular for the present, not despite but because of the form's imbrication with entrepreneurial pursuits. Because of this imbrication, then, hip hop is less a music form, or even a poetic form, than it is a multimedia mode, and one that is formed around documentary tropes. From its origins in the 1970s Bronx, alongside graffiti art and breakdancing, to its contemporary resonance as music, art, film, game, fashion, marketing category, and design template, hip hop has created and overwritten markets, while also remaining tied rhetorically, politically, and aesthetically to authenticity and reality.[25] This gritty "up-from-the-streets" authenticity is central to hip hop's appeal. As Adam Bradley has noted, autobiographical rap often strives to make "new meanings out of familiar circumstances," and along those lines, I view it as part of a larger swath of documentary art that emerges out of the increasingly privatized United States.[26] The dispersal and evacuation of public resources occasioned by privatization has a precursor in the environment from which hip hop emerges, the Bronx in the 1970s, and the depleted infrastructure found there would become more commonly experienced in the United States as privatization and the erosion of public resources became more prominent in the 1980s. In the Bronx, due to "white flight," plummeting property values, and high unemployment, all commonly attributed to the construction of the Cross Bronx Expressway, the distance between an economic system that promised wealth and everyday lives structured around poverty and dispossession became clear. Wealth was geographically proximate yet distant in reality, and the path out of poverty was no longer apparent. As documented in *Wild Style,* hip hop emerged out of that distance.

Hip Hop Family Tree's Archival Life

Like hip hop itself, Ed Piskor's *Hip Hop Family Tree* is a multimedia project. Initially serialized on the website Boing Boing starting in 2012, Piskor's series has been published serially as single-issue comic books and collected in four large treasury-edition books to date. Issue 12 of *Hip Hop Family Tree* also included an album, and Piskor designed Public Enemy action figures based on his illustrations of the iconic group for the media company Press Pop. *Hip Hop Family Tree* is a documentary comic, with a bibliography of both reference works and songs in the back of each volume. Yet unlike the comics journalism of Sarah Glidden or Joe Sacco, or the comics memoirs of Alison Bechdel, Marjane Satrapi, or Art Spiegelman, *Hip Hop Family Tree* is an appreciation. Hillary Chute argues that documentary comics about war and trauma tend to use "inventive textual practice to . . . express trauma ethically."[27] The documentary comics that Chute classifies in this way, like Spiegelman's *Maus* or Sacco's *Safe Area Goražde,* privilege an ethical mode of viewing, one that remains ambiguous and conflicted. Yet documentary can capture not just trauma but also exploitation, a process less prone to be punctuated by moments of astounding violence than constituted by something like Rob Nixon's concept of "slow violence" or David Harvey's "accumulation by dispossession," modes of exploitation that rely on subjects to produce wealth over long periods of time through predatory financial structures like disproportionately high rents and prices.[28] As the comic's original subtitle, *A Look into the Viral*

Propagation of a Culture, makes clear, *Hip Hop Family Tree* is less a record of tragedy and trauma than a documentation of how something like a collective style was fashioned by multiple agents in multiple places, often under conditions in which artists were not credited or compensated for their efforts. As the "family tree" in its title suggests, the comic proceeds episodically and generationally, moving from figure to figure, group to group, place to place as it tells the story of hip hop. There are flashpoints in the narrative where key figures are featured together on the same page, as in the dramatization of reactions to hearing the Sugarhill Gang's "Rapper's Delight" on the radio for the first time (fig. 4).[29] The structure of *Hip Hop Family Tree* is chronological and synchronic, a narrative that keeps a multitude of individuals, groups, and institutions in play over time.

Importantly for Piskor, hip hop and comics have an analogous relationship as popular media forms structured around the marketplace and shaped by exploitation of the very artists that defined, created, and refined those forms. One of the earliest strips published on Boing Boing, and one included in the back of book 1, is titled "The Hip Hop/Comics Connection."[30] As Piskor details on these pages, comics and hip hop have shared origins in poor neighborhoods in New York City, referencing the Yellow Kid, a street urchin in the *Hogan's Alley* comics published in both the *New York Journal* and the *New York World* in the 1890s, alongside the lyrics to the Bronx-based Grandmaster Flash and the Furious Five's 1982

Figure 4. Panels from *Hip Hop Family Tree, Book 1: 1970s–1981,* Ed Piskor, Fantagraphics, 2014. (Courtesy of the artist)

song "The Message" (fig. 5). Yet origins are only part of the connection. As Piskor notes, both forms are built upon transformation, the assumption of larger-than-life identities, and the importance of the battle and the team-up. The strip also makes clear that both hip hop and comics fandom share a pleasure in the archive, in tracking down rare singles, first appearances, and epic confrontations.

In *Hip Hop Family Tree,* this archival sensibility appears on the page through Piskor's illustration style, influenced by the graffiti art documented in films like *Wild Style* as well as by R. Crumb's portraits of obscure and mostly forgotten blues, jazz, and country musicians. The archive is also present in Piskor's references to video documentation of rap battles and performances, his citation of lyrics and interview segments, and, most important for "The Hip Hop/Comics Connection," his use of now archival cartooning techniques such as the Leroy lettering system and zipatone shading and his covers that mimic comics like *Tales from the Crypt,*

Figure 5. Panel from *Hip Hop Family Tree, Book 1: 1970s–1981,* Ed Piskor, Fantagraphics, 2014. (Courtesy of the artist)

Uncanny X-Men, and *Fantastic Four.* Piskor's use of actual ink and paper and the book's publication on thick, yellowed paper stock make material the archival impetus of the comic. *Hip Hop Family Tree* tells a history using historical forms, materials, and styles. This archival style makes the period documented in *Hip Hop Family Tree,* the 1970s and 1980s, present to the reader as a material object and as a narrative, transforming neoliberalism's past into neoliberalism's present.

Other moments in *Hip Hop Family Tree* depict how hip-hop music was molded by financial concerns from its very origins, at the same time as it was discounted as art. The first volume ends with an account of a *20/20* television news feature on hip hop, concluding with the broadcaster's voice-over: "Not everyone can sing, but anyone can rap!"[31] The easy, almost instinctive dismissal of the medium parallels the history of comics, viewed even as recently as MOMA's 1990 *High and Low* exhibit as mere raw material for the artistic practice of figures like Roy Lichtenstein. *Hip Hop Family Tree* champions the underdog persistence and over-the-top personae of early rappers. Like the unsung comics artists who toiled for publishers in the same period, their underground status makes their accomplishments all the more earth-shattering in Piskor's view. The dismissal of hip hop as a mere fad that requires no artistry is also countered by the comic's accounts of entrepreneurial visionaries like Sylvia Robinson, Rick Rubin, and Russell Simmons. Throughout *Hip Hop Family Tree,* Rick Rubin appears as a Tintin-like figure, a wealthy teenager interested in the style of the "Black punk rock" he encounters through a cassette recording of the Cold Crush Brothers.[32] In book 1, Rubin appears three times—in his "Richie Rick" introduction, at a Ramones concert at CBGB, and then performing with his own band the Pricks. In his concert performance, making a splash clearly trumps music, as he smashes a guitar over someone's head and then reads the newspaper the following day looking for a mention of his band's antics.[33] In later volumes, Rubin and Russell Simmons partner to promote Run-DMC, the Beastie Boys, and other groups, with Simmons taking lead when it comes to fashion. Their motives are always clearly poised between artistic vision and economic gain. Simmons raps on a b-side about "keep[ing] all the money," and Rubin stages a food fight with the Beastie Boys when he notices a lot of reporters around.[34] Management and publicity is part of the "viral propagation" of hip hop as it transitions to national distribution.

A recurring moment in the comic involves the making of rappers into celebrity musicians, often through the assumption of new names and looks. The utopian stylings in *Hip Hop Family Tree* make rap a magical transformation, akin to a superhero transitioning from alter ego to costumed titan. Yet within the comic's larger structure, those transformations are juxtaposed with economic realities. For example, Debbie Harry asks the Funky 4+1 to go on tour with Blondie. Sugarhill Records founder Sylvia Robinson threatens to replace any member of the group who leaves on tour, reminding them that "any of [them] can be fired from the group and replaced" according to the terms of their contract.[35] As Piskor then notes, "the 'Business' of Hip Hop has taken all the fun out of the culture," as Li'l Rodney C! and KK Rockwell decide to leave the group, breaking it up in 1983 before ever recording a studio album.[36]

What marks *Hip Hop Family Tree* as a work of documentary art, more than even its content, is its form. As I noted above, Piskor's art style synthesizes graffiti style and analog cartooning technology. And as in the bonus comic book included in the first boxed set of the series Piskor uses period styles from comics history to represent historical distance.[37] In the bonus comic, Piskor documents the connections between hip hop and superhero comics artist Rob Liefeld. Liefeld became a comics star in the 1990s after his influential runs on Marvel's *The New Mutants* and *X-Force.* He later left Marvel to cofound Image Comics, a creator-owned comics company in which artists and writers, rather than comics corporations, own their intellectual property. As Piskor details, Liefeld was featured in a Levi's commercial directed by Spike Lee in 1991, and he draws this moment in the style of Liefeld, featuring impossibly rippled muscles, narrow ankles, and form-fitting clothes. Then, the comic turns to Liefeld's brief meeting and planned collaboration with rapper Eazy-E, following Eazy's appearance at a comic shop signing. The comic concludes with Liefeld abusing artist Dan Fraga, paralleling the kind of exploitation Piskor also documents in the music industry. The economic cannot be divorced from the artistic and the personal—indeed, they coextend when personal relationships are defined through finance.

In this bonus comic, it becomes clear how *Hip Hop Family Tree* is a documentary that occupies an expanded field, meshing music history with comics history, using the visual language and historical specificity of comics illustration to produce a period style that captures artistic vitality, collective belonging, and economic exploitation. In his illustrations of rap battles, for example, Piskor's technique adapts the rhythm of rap to the form of the comics page, breaking the page up into multiple panels, often containing multiple word balloons with bold lettering announcing emphasized syllables. In book 1's documentation of Busy Bee Starski and

Kool Moe Dee's battle, Kool Moe Dee unquestionably wins. In hip hop history, this triumph has come to symbolize a departure from early "party rap" and a shift to harder-edged MCing. Piskor uses word balloons as a way to mark the interactivity of Starski's well-known routines (fig. 6), followed by Kool Moe Dee's commanding rap, large text blocks in word balloons with only an enraptured audience listening, not participating (fig. 7).[38] By using the comics form in this way, Piskor adapts an audio recording to a spatial design, making visual a historical event otherwise accessible today only through audio.

What *Hip Hop Family Tree* accomplishes, then, is the mediation of hip-hop history through comics, featuring stories of creative production within compromised circumstances. The comic's archival practice represents history as a site for enthusiastic recovery and artistry. Acknowledging how exploitation determines lives, *Hip Hop Family Tree*'s vision of art, craft, and style nonetheless makes clear the vital, self-taught, lo-fi history of our contemporary moment, in a way that also makes those lo-fi technologies accessible and understandable rather than obscure and

Figure 6. Panel from *Hip Hop Family Tree, Book 1: 1970s–1981,* Ed Piskor, Fantagraphics, 2014. (Courtesy of the artist)

Figure 7. Panels from *Hip Hop Family Tree, Book 1: 1970s–1981,* Ed Piskor, Fantagraphics, 2014. (Courtesy of the artist)

hidden. Exploitation, trauma, and tragedy are givens, the comic suggests. What is to be valued are moments when those givens are heroically suspended, when work sustains and nourishes life.

Good Kid, M.A.A.D. City's Tensions

Kendrick Lamar's 2012 album *Good Kid, M.A.A.D. City* bears the telling subtitle *A Short Film.* With the title written in black ink on what looks like a Polaroid snapshot, the album's cover art presents it as a visual artifact rather than a musical work (fig. 8). The album's gatefold, or the CD's booklet, contains more snapshots, displayed as if in a photo album. A short film titled *m.A.A.d.,* directed by Kahlil Joseph, uses a mix of the album as soundtrack and was installed as a two-screen video work at the Los Angeles Museum of Contemporary Art in 2015.[39] This filmic and photographic framework is in stark contrast to Lamar's 2013 tour partner Kanye West, whose 2013 album *Yeezus* calls attention to itself as audio media in its cover image of a blank CD and its abrasive use of synthesizers and voice, simplifying beats and rhymes to a one-man show. Lamar's "short film" of a record features many voices and is structured around a documentary aesthetic that casts the record as both a recovery memoir (in the tradition of both Malcolm X's autobiography and often-violent addiction memoirs like James Frey's fabricated *A Million Little Pieces*) and an inner-city gangsta film in the tradition of *Boyz in the Hood* or

Figure 8. Deluxe album cover, *Good Kid, M.A.A.D. City,* Kendrick Lamar, Aftermath Entertainment, Interscope Records, and Top Dawg Entertainment, 2012.

Menace II Society. This multifaceted formal structure—the record as family photo album, recovery memoir, and gangsta film—is nothing new in rap music. Indeed, the wedding of rap persona to the lived experience of the rapper was something of a cliché by the time Lamar's record appeared, with other contemporaries such as Danny Brown rhyming that he's "sick of all these niggas with their ten year old stories,"[40] or Pusha T embracing the cliché when he raps, "They ask why I'm still talking dope, why not?"[41] Lamar's record, though, reaches beyond either dismissal or bravado in its cyclical narrative framework.

Good Kid, M.A.A.D. City revolves around the minivan featured in the snapshot on the album's cover. On the album's first track, "Sherane a.k.a.

Master Splinter's Daughter," a tape starts playing, and Kendrick and some others pledge their lives to God and ask for forgiveness. Then the beat starts, and Kendrick tells us how he met a woman, Sherane, at a house party. They text back and forth until the present tense of the album, when Kendrick takes action: "Grab my momma's keys, hopped in the car, then oh boy / So now I'm down Rosecrans in a Caravan." Kendrick has borrowed his mother's Dodge Caravan, pictured on the album cover. When he arrives at Sherane's house, he is confronted by four men who ask him where he's from. The album then takes a flashback detour, detailing Kendrick's day prior to this confrontation, as he listens to music, freestyle raps in the backseat of another car, and robs a house with some friends. Then we return to the present tense of the album, as Kendrick is pulled out of the van in front of Sherane's house and beaten up. After this, Kendrick regroups with his friends, drinks, and returns to Sherane's house where his friends fire shots at those standing on the street. Kendrick and his friends later speak with a woman about God, saying the prayer that also begins the album. The album concludes with the anthem "Compton," featuring Dr. Dre, where Lamar celebrates the history of gangsta rap. Interestingly, though, the last moment on the album is Kendrick saying, "Mom, I'm fixin' to use the van real quick! Be back in fifteen minutes!," thus making the end a new beginning to this story about cycles of violence and redemption.

It becomes clear upon listening to the album and viewing *m.A.A.d.* that the snapshot of the minivan itself denotes its value to its owners in Los Angeles's car culture. The film features a number of aerial shots both of Compton and of the Los Angeles interstate system, alternating with point-of-view shots from within the backseats of moving cars, including a minivan like the one pictured on the album's cover. The car is both a site of mobility within Los Angeles and a secure vantage point from which to look at others and bond with friends. Yet also, in a telling detail shown in the video, the minivan is a family car, with family stick-figure decals on the rear windshield. On the voicemail that plays at the end of album's first track, Lamar's mother asks for the van: "Kendrick! Where you at? Head home! I'm sitting here waiting on my van. You told me you was gonna be back in fifteen minutes!" Later on the album, in another voicemail following the track "Real," Kendrick's mother again asks about the van and then reports that Top Dawg Records (one of the labels that released *Good Kid, M.A.A.D. City*) has called for her son. She concludes:

> If I don't hear from you by tomorrow, I hope you come back and learn from your mistakes. Come back a man, tell your story to these black and brown kids in Compton. Let them know you was just like them, but you still rose from that dark place of violence, becoming a positive person. But when you do make it, give back with your words of encouragement, and that's the best way to give back. To your city. And I love you Kendrick, if I don't hear you knocking on the door you know where I usually leave the key. Alright? Talk to you later, bye.

The temporal layering here is also a commentary on the record itself, as we experience the journey that establishes the record, that led to the rap persona of Kendrick Lamar. That rap persona is formed out of the very experiences that he is charged by his mother to escape from and return to. Lamar's rap persona is a figure of recurrence and repetition, endlessly replaying the experiences of a young man on the Compton streets, bound to the idealism of his family and the violence of his immediate surroundings.

This representation of life as cycle is also a representation of the structures of exploitation that underwrite life in the contemporary United States and that are most acutely felt and experienced in economically marginalized places like Compton. Indeed, cars like the minivan serve on the album as emblems of circulation, and circulation is both full of promise and constantly halted on the album. If the automobile offers mobility, a seemingly secure vantage point, a sign of family belonging, and also a space for homosocial commiseration, then the streets themselves promise a different kind of interaction. The contrast between the car and the street, as is made evident in the album's cover snapshot, is a difference between a commodity and a public space, a commodity valuable because it rides on top of, and through, the faulty infrastructure below, the cracked and poorly maintained street.

Yet on Lamar's album, that cracked infrastructure is the very place where value is created through exploitation and dispossession. As the song "Money Trees" with Jay Rock makes clear, Compton is lined with "money trees," yet getting "shaded by a money tree" in *Good Kid, M.A.A.D. City* comes from plundering one's own community, sticking up one's neighbors—"Go at a reverend for the revenue." The chorus of the track points to the limited possibilities in Kendrick's Compton—"It go Halle Berry, or Hallelujah / Pick your poison, tell me what you doing." The stark dichotomy that runs throughout the album is represented here through a familiar dyad, the female body as the material world versus the "Hallelujah" of the spiritual world, the fantasies of gangsta life versus the mother's call to "give back with your words of encouragement." The second verse of "Money Trees" makes the Halle Berry/Hallelujah dyad more explicitly a matter of capital:

> Dream of living life like rappers do
> Bump that new E-40 after school
> You know "Big ballin' with My Homies"
> Earl Stevens had us thinking rational
> Back to reality, we poor

The financial aspirations of the baller—figured in the lyrics by Earl Stevens, also known as the rapper E-40—are juxtaposed with the reality of structural poverty. The transition from the "rational" world of finance, sponsorship deals, and brand management occupied by Earl Stevens to the "poor" reality of Compton is abrupt, even caustic, in its juxtaposition of luxury and poverty. In "Money Trees," stick-ups and robbery emblematize the attempt to achieve wealth and also the quest for spiritual salvation: "Everybody gonna respect the shooter / But the one in front of the gun lives forever." Indeed, as Jill Leovy's book *Ghettoside* documents, homicide thrives in segregated neighborhoods with restricted mobility: "Indices of residential segregation are strong homicide predictors. Homicide thrives on intimacy, communal interactions, barter, and a shared sense of private rules. The intimacy part was also why homicide was so stubbornly intraracial. You had to be involved with people to want to kill them. You had to share space in a small, isolated world."[42] Locked in a binary, material gain and lasting value are produced at the same moment, the stick-up that can end in homicide. In "Money Trees," you are either the robber or the victim.

In the song, though, the neighborhood itself contains the promise of a solution: the "money trees" that line the streets, the high costs of living and high profits reaped from neighborhoods like Compton that are expropriated by landlords, retailers, and the privatized prison system. Indeed, as stated in a 2007 report, when compared to other ethnic demographics in Los Angeles, Black residents spend the highest percentage of their income on rent, 31 percent, and have the lowest homeownership rate, 38.1 percent.[43] The same report also makes clear how disproportionate prison time is for Black residents of Los Angeles—the 2003 felony arrest rate in Los Angeles was 3.7 percent for Blacks versus 1.4 percent for Latinos, 0.8 percent for Whites, and 0.5 percent for Asians.[44] During this same period, California was contracting with a private prison corporation, the Corrections Corporation of America, resulting in the company's revenues in California doubling between 2008 and 2012, the years leading up to the release of Lamar's album.[45] In Joseph's *m.A.A.d.,* Black male figures appear hanging from streetlights and storefronts, making literal the ways that the "money trees" that line Compton streets in Lamar's song are made up of exploited subjects, suffering from dispossession for the financial gain of the corporations and individuals who benefit from privatization. The "money tree" stands as a symbol of economic structures of exploitation that make a place like Compton function within Los Angeles as a site of exploitation through disproportionately high rents, high grocery costs, and participation in privatized organs like the state prison system and charter schools.

In "Money Trees," then, Lamar diagnoses the problem—the way that wealth is extracted from Compton and how that wealth seems attainable because it once belonged to the dispossessed. As Leovy notes, a change in legislation in Los Angeles has produced a decline in the homicide rate by renewing public infrastructure and support, the very systems eroded through privatization: "An eight-hundred-dollar-a-month check for an unemployed black ex-felon makes a big difference in his life. The risks and benefits of various hustles surely appear different to him. He can move, ditch his homeys, commit fewer crimes, walk away from more fights."[46] *Good Kid, M.A.A.D. City*'s documentary aesthetic positions this struggle as experientially cyclical yet also structural when viewed from a different vantage point. The album's closing anthem, "Compton," takes as its subject an overdetermined site for rap music that has become a synecdoche for a mythic gangsta lifestyle:

> Now we can all celebrate
> We can all harvest the rap artists of NWA
> America target our rap market, as controversy and hate
> Harsh realities we in made our music translate
> To the coke dealers, the hood rich
> And the broke niggas that play
> With them gorillas that know killers
> That know where you stay
> Roll that kush, crack that case, ten bottles of rosé
> This was brought to you by Dre
> Now every motherfucker in here say:

"Look who's responsible
For taking Compton international
I make 'em holla"

International Compton here signifies a way of thinking, a framework for understanding a global condition of limited possibilities, of stark dyads that offer no synthesis. The only way out of Compton, *Good Kid, M.A.A.D. City* argues, is to look at Compton from an elevated vantage point, signaled by the sweeping synthesizers of Jess Blaze's beat and the triumphalism of Lamar and Dr. Dre's lyrics. As Justin A. Williams has noted, the use of synthesizers on *Good Kid, M.A.A.D. City* creates an intertextual connection, invoking "early 1990s Compton under gang peace treaty, full of parties and barbecues, depicted in music videos from [Dr. Dre's] *The Chronic,*" and also serving as "a leitmotif for Compton that becomes attached to the horrors of the city and the anxieties of its inhabitants."[47] Indeed, as the view of the L.A. freeway suggests in *m.A.A.d.*, this elevated perspective signifies economic success, even as it remains focused on the same community and land that Lamar depicts as violent and anxious. This shift in perspective can be read as analogous to the abstracted view of finance capital, as homes, credit cards, education, and cars become not individual debts but instead bundled financial risks to be monetized and leveraged. Lamar's framing of these two levels signals a savvy negotiation of neoliberal culture. On one hand, Lamar and all of us live within a neoliberal economy, yet on the other hand, an awareness of the exploitation that underwrites that economy can lead one to desire an alternative system. As Tricia Rose remarks in her account of hip hop's cultural politics, even though "we live in this market economy, let's try not to let market value and personal profit rule over love, collective well-being, and sacrifice for the larger good."[48] Lamar's embrace of gangsta rap history leverages a neoliberal form toward a sense of collectivity and belonging, an awareness of exploitative conditions, and a vision of an alternative structure in which expropriated wealth remains with those who have been historically exploited.

As Ivan Ascher has argued in his account of the contemporary United States as a "portfolio society" increasingly structured around financial instruments that produce profits out of the debt of individuals: "On an ideological level, yes, ours may be a world where we are all investors, each of us taking and hedging risks as we see fit. But as the metaphor of the racetrack serves to remind us, the ideological cover provided by neoliberalism cannot entirely conceal the fact that investors depend on other investors in relations that are at once reciprocal and thoroughly asymmetrical."[49] This asymmetrical relation consists of two different frames or vantage points—one, the individual subject who takes out a loan, and who may or may not manage to make minimum payments on their debt; and two, the financial officers and investors who leverage bundled debts on the derivatives market. As Ascher writes: "It would seem to be a division between those who are free to run a race and those who are free to bet on its outcome. Or, to put it more generally yet, it would seem to be a division between those whose lives keep placing them at risk and having thus to seek protection (say, in the form of a loan or an insurance policy) and those whose position of relative security, by contrast, gives them the opportunity to take risks—say, by lending to others or betting on the probability of default."[50] Subject to the operations of the derivatives market, an individual's loan has a financial life that extracts profit from everyday life, in a way that remains largely invisible to the debtor except insofar as monthly payments or the failure to make monthly payments both make profit for the diversified portfolios of investors.

The story of hip-hop music coincides with the increasing exploitation and infrastructural dispossession that we now routinely associate with our era of finance capitalism. The postures, rhetoric, modes of empowerment, and economic success of hip-hop style have in turn produced an attractive vision of the hustler as entrepreneur that has proven flexible and exportable across the globe. What Lamar's album does is represent the gaps and fissures, the economic structures that produce both a vision of the individual as hustling entrepreneur and a palpable anxiety that alternates between desperation and hopelessness in the face of rampant poverty amid massive accumulation by the wealthy. His invocation of tradition and his autobiographical reflections present cycles of violence and poverty as designs, mediated through tropes in gangsta rap and consumer culture. In an article about rap moguls' relationships to Occupy Wall Street, Eithne Quinn warns against "neoliberal determinism—affording too much agency to neoliberalism—in explanations of how individuals operate within rampant capitalist dynamics."[51] Lamar's album and its artistry only make sense if one heeds Quinn's warning. It is at once a piece of neoliberal culture, fashioned around hustler tropes and a narrative of individual development, and at the same time a call to recognize a cycle of violence and poverty as a structural condition, reproduced through cultural tropes of wealth and hustle.

If Kendrick Lamar's *Good Kid, M.A.A.D. City* presents a vision of the individual rapper, poised between street authenticity and the entertainment industry, everyday Compton and International Compton, structures of exploitation and a vision of collectivity, then Ed Piskor's *Hip Hop Family Tree* celebrates the street culture out of which hip hop grew, finding nostalgic comforts in old media and collectivity. What these two very different kinds of texts—a concept album that calls itself a film and a comics series that calls itself a family tree—have in common is their documentary aesthetic. This documentary aesthetic engages an expanded field, across media forms, to represent modes of dispossession and exploitation amplified by finance capitalism from the 1960s to our present moment. *Dont Look Back*'s Dylan poised between folk authenticity and theater-packing celebrity and *Wild Style*'s collective yet individually styled artists capture both the promise and capitulation of politics and performance during neoliberal culture's emergence. In Lamar's *Good Kid, M.A.A.D. City* and Piskor's *Hip Hop Family Tree,* structures of exploitation and individual exertion are distant, even invisible to each other. This is less a problem of cognitive mapping than an indication of a truth of our moment—that financial structures have become abstracted from the social relations they exploit, perhaps all the better for them to topple and for those relations to be reformed from outside of finance's channels. In both Lamar's and Piskor's documentary works, history is a site of conflict, a place to recover crafts that can both diagnose and point beyond neoliberal culture.

2 / Emergence in Retrospect

One of the most prominent forms of the documentary aesthetic was the New Journalism. While the music documentaries in the previous chapter articulate neoliberal structures and subjectivities and the possibilities beyond them, the New Journalism often focused on the dissolution of postwar liberalism and civil society. New Journalists both embrace and mourn the political changes underway during the counterculture's increasing centrality to American culture and neoliberalism's shift from intellectual project to public policy from the 1960s to the 1980s. Indeed, for many New Journalists writing in the 1960s and 1970s such as Norman Mailer and Hunter S. Thompson, literary nonfiction fused countercultural aesthetics with politics. This connection was a kind of survival mechanism, as many New Journalists and their readers witnessed the increasing failures of the New Left to produce the changes that it envisioned in the face of rising conservativism and increasing neoliberal reforms in the United States and internationally. And while the New Journalism typically refers to a group of writers who published important nonfiction works about the drug culture, antiwar movement, and hippies of the 1960s and 1970s, it is just one of many documentary movements prominent from the postwar era to the present. There are also conceptual art projects fueled by documentary methods, such as Hans Haacke's *Shapolsky et al. Manhattan Real Holdings, A Real-Time Social System, as of May 1, 1971,* discussed later in this chapter. Photography played a significant role in this emerging aesthetic, from street photography to large-format landscape photography. Then there are the popular memoirs, hip-hop autobiographies, and documentary films, such as Patricio Guzmán's *Chile, Obstinate Memory,* with which I conclude this chapter. In short, the documentary aesthetic that I am tracing is an aesthetic because it traverses media forms yet retains a singular focus on linking subjective experience to structural conditions through experimental modes of nonfiction writing and image making. The documentary aesthetic modifies and recalibrates all manner of media, in response to the erosion of New Left utopianism and the coterminous emergence of the neoliberal fragmentation of collective imaginaries. This chapter explores how Joan Didion, Hans Haacke, Patricio Guzmán, and Milton and Rose D. Friedman represent the emergence of neoliberal culture, broadly, and neoliberal U.S. foreign policy, more particularly, across documentary media forms.

Joan Didion, Fragmentation, and Neoliberal Policy

Perhaps no New Journalist better exemplifies the fragmentation that emergent neoliberalism generated than Joan Didion. In what seems by now to be a ubiquitous postmodern gesture, but one that is also an elegant encapsulation of the New Journalist's role as survivor and witness, Joan Didion's essay "The White Album" begins with the assertion, "We tell ourselves stories in order to live."[1] Following this general statement about the narrative construction of reality, Didion narrows her scope to the personal, shifting from the plural pronoun "we" to the singular "I" and detailing her own experience: "I began to doubt the premises of all the stories I had ever told myself, a common condition but one I found troubling. I suppose this period began around 1966 and continued until 1971."[2] This introduction foregrounds narrative, the author's voice, and the breakdown of language's hold on reality, all central to Didion's prose.[3] "The White Album" was published in the 1979 collection of Didion's journalism of the same name, and the essay itself was a compilation of shorter fragments, mostly essays published in the Points West column that Didion shared with her husband, John Gregory Dunne, in the *Saturday Evening Post.* One of Didion's most well-known essays, "The White Album" reproduces these *Saturday Evening Post* columns along with other autobiographical fragments. In the collage essay, Didion juxtaposes memoiristic passages about her vertigo and personal life with fragments of reportage, as she covers, among other things, Huey P. Newton's 1968 trial for the shooting of John Frey, the Manson murders, the Doors recording their third album, *Waiting for the Sun,* and the 1968 student strike at San Francisco State College. Complimenting this focus on the breakdown of narrative is Didion's account of her own vertigo and nausea, which connects the author's body to the text and the larger world that it represents. What interests me about "The White Album" is the way that Didion periodizes her vertigo—1966 to 1971. While this might lead the reader to guess that Didion somehow comes to terms with her experiences and develops a narrative that can explain and account for all of these disparate fragments by the 1970s, her own prose does not bear that out. Instead, Didion develops cultural disorientation, physical ailment, fragmentation of experience, and lack of narrative into a narrative itself. "The White Album" chronicles the specific disorientation induced by the events of the late 1960s and early 1970s at the same time as it accounts for the emergence of Didion's own literary style as she seizes upon fragmentation as a documentary form.

When critics write about Didion, the question of style inevitably comes up. For Deborah Nelson in her book *Tough Enough,* Didion is a writer who is poised between two modes: emotional identification and ironic detachment: "Her reputation now alternates between two diametrically opposed characterizations: one as an anxious and emotionally fragile sensitive and the other as an unsentimental, ironic, and unsympathetic critic."[4] Part of this opposition has to do with how Didion represents emotion. What seems or even feels personal is often represented in Didion's works as part of a larger structure. As Nelson puts it, Didion often represents feelings in a way that is "depersonalized and exteriorized, less her own than a part of the social effluvia, something ambient, shared between and passed from individual to individual, community to community."[5] With Didion, we see the world through her ironic and critical distance, yet we also inhabit the same landscape and its attendant structures. That is, we identify with Didion, just as we see the world through her detached perspective, stoic and hardened. What Nelson does not account for, in her formalist explication of Didion's style, is the broader cultural and historical role that Didion's writings—and by extension Didion as a persona—have played in postwar American culture. To understand what Didion and documentary art more generally offer us today, I will focus on the intricate workings of her prose style, as well as the larger structures that her style connects to and makes visible.

As was made evident in the announcement and subsequent coverage of the fashion company Céline's 2015 ad campaign featuring Didion and iconic Didion photographic poses, Didion's style is not just a matter of diction and syntax. It is also a matter of subject position and embodiment. Writing about the ad campaign in *Vogue,* Alessandra Codinha captures the attachment to Didion's style: "Let's talk about Céline's just-debuted ad campaign featuring French dancer Marie-Agnes Gillot, model Freya Lawrence, and none other than immortal intellectual-and-otherwise dream girl Joan Didion. Well, did you just feel the collective intake of breath shared by every cool girl you know? Did you feel the pulse-quickening vibrations of every recent college grad and literature fan? Did you sense the earth trembling beneath your feet? *Do you have two eyes and a heart?*"[6] Didion serves, today, as a relay for connecting the past to the present, the 1960s to the twenty-first century, the self-styled outsider perspective to the toughness and resolve of internet culture's self-help visions of femininity. Even in ads that didn't feature Didion, some of her iconic poses and accessories, like her Corvette Stingray, are replicated. Yet, as Didion pointed out to the *New York Times,* 2015 was not her first fashion campaign.[7] She appeared in a 1989 Gap campaign with her daughter Quintana Roo, photographed by celebrity photographer Annie Leibovitz. Didion has been iconic for some time, and she encapsulates a curious interplay between cool detachment and intimate identification in our time. This dualistic function is emblematic of the cultural history she has documented since the 1960s: the emergence of neoliberalism and the emergence of a distinctly post-1960s documentary aesthetic.

Fragmentation works in Didion's prose in a number of ways. First of all, fragmentation operates at the level of content. Her work as a journalist includes essays about disparate topics, as my above summary of "The White Album" suggests, and her fiction draws upon her journalism quite explicitly, be it in the meditations on California highway and water systems in *Play It as It Lays* (1970), the descriptions of the renamed Salvadoran setting, Boca Grande, of *A Book of Common Prayer* (1977), or the dramatization of the CIA presence in Vietnam in *Democracy* (1984). In keeping with the first-person style of many New Journalists, Didion details her own life as a journalist in her nonfiction, as she bounces from city to city and country to country on assignment and as the only stable places in the United States and beyond become nonplaces such as hotel bars and airport lounges. Similarly, her fiction is written in the first person, with a female narrator who is consciously writing the story being read, often troubled by her inability to make sense of the events and relationships that she is narrating. Both Didion's journalism and her fiction can then be read as experiential guides to U.S. culture and U.S. international entanglements in the late twentieth century, from San Francisco, Malibu, and Miami to Bogota, San Salvador, and Saigon. The interconnectedness of her fiction and nonfiction shatters any conventional literary taxonomy that would make a distinction between the real and the imaginative, the journalistic and the novelistic. Secondly, fragmentation informs her literary style and the form of her prose as an organizing principle, bouncing between images and moments, denying the reader any singular or totalizing framework or explanation. This pastiche might produce a sense of totality within fragmentation, perhaps, but Didion leaves the resolution of the fragments to the reader. Lastly, her nonfiction prose circulated originally as single essays, published in glossy magazines or literary reviews and only later collected in book form. The unifying principle that underlies all of these varied types of fragmentation is literary style, the first-person voice that Didion adopts in both her journalism and fiction. This tension between style and fragmentation, between a unified, coherent narrative voice and that voice's dissolution as it articulates disparate and irresolute events, produces a literary form that captures key facets of neoliberalism: the privileging of entrepreneurial individualism, the privatization of public resources, and the proliferation of new, niche markets. In its complication of traditional literary taxonomies, its fragmentary pastiche, and its origin in magazine features, Didion's writings helped to establish the documentary aesthetic in prose.

By reading Didion in this way, I hope to demonstrate how we can think broadly of the postwar era, and especially art and literature from the late 1960s to the present, as the era of the documentary aesthetic, and concurrently as shaped by finance capitalism and neoliberal culture. Briefly, neoliberalism is free market ideology, a set of economic, political, and social policies that limit government regulation of the economy, endorse the privatization of public services, and seek to dismantle the modern welfare state in the name of efficient markets. As noted earlier, neoliberalism was developed by Austrian economist Friedrich A. Hayek during and after World War II, and later by the economists of the Chicago School, especially in the influential works of Milton Friedman. Its baggy confederation of intellectual commitments to the free market was championed by the United States and European nations from the 1970s to the present day, though our current wave of populist nationalism seems to be complicating the long-standing neoliberal consensus across major political parties in the U.S. and around the globe. As such, neoliberalism names the economic and political worldview of major economic institutions such as the World Bank and International Monetary Fund.[8] It has led to a widespread erosion of government institutions that provide public services, the reduction of financial regulations, and the waning of labor unions and other forms of worker's rights in the name of the free market. Moreover, neoliberalism is more than a cluster of policy positions. As

Philip Mirowski has chronicled, neoliberalism is a plural enterprise, and its flexibility makes it both difficult to define across national and historical contexts and also powerful as a worldview that reshaped business and society in the late twentieth century: "Neoliberalism cannot be easily defined on a set of 3 by 5 cards and needs to be understood as a pluralist organism striving to distinguish itself from its three primary foes: laissez-faire classical liberalism, social welfare liberalism, and socialism. . . . Neoliberal intellectuals understood this general goal to imply a comprehensive long-term reform effort at retatting the entire fabric of society, not excluding the corporate world."[9] In her journalism, Didion records a series of fragments that can be read as a literary genealogy of neoliberalism and its rupturing of categories like the state, the nation, and the subject, from the 1960s counterculture in the United States to the neoliberal reforms implemented in Central America in the 1980s and 1990s.

In her nonfiction, Didion explicates the radical revisions to the way in which the individual is privileged as the basic unit of economic and social life under neoliberalism, as well as the ways in which neoliberal economic and political reforms collapse space not by connecting it through communication networks, transportation systems, and global finance but instead by fragmenting it. In her prose, Didion articulates how space and time are broken in the late twentieth century, in ways that lead not to homogeneity or totality, multiculturalism or trickle-down prosperity, but to the collapse of sense and meaning. The individual ascends, while society wanes. Didion's prose grapples with this zero-sum game, a game that we can identify now, retrospectively, as neoliberalism.

Like many New Journalists, Didion privileges impression over fact, though she denies the kinds of analyses, interpretations, and summaries of events common to Norman Mailer and Hunter S. Thompson, both of whom had political aspirations. Mailer ran for mayor of New York City, Thompson for Sheriff of Aspen County, Colorado. In *The Armies of the Night,* for example, Mailer compares the 1967 March on the Pentagon to a Mathew Brady photograph of a Civil War battlefield. In *Fear and Loathing in Las Vegas* (1972), Thompson likens Las Vegas's Circus Circus casino to what the world would look like if Hitler had won World War II. These comparisons are meant to orient the reader historically and politically. They interpellate the reader into the left conservative or libertarian-on-mescaline positions adopted by Mailer and Thompson, respectively. In contrast, Didion's prose resolves little and privileges a meditative production of disparate figures. Didion focuses on how the inexplicability of an event constitutes the meaning of that event. For example, in her essay "Slouching Towards Bethlehem," Didion explains her move to San Francisco in 1967: "All that seemed clear was that at some point we had aborted ourselves and butchered the job, and because nothing else seemed so relevant I decided to go to San Francisco. San Francisco was where the social hemorrhaging was showing up. San Francisco was where the missing children were gathering and calling themselves 'hippies.' When I first went to San Francisco in that cold late spring of 1967 I did not even know what I wanted to find out, and so I just stayed around a while, and made a few friends."[10] This situatedness without purpose carries the rest of the essay and much of Didion's writings about the counterculture. The open-endedness of her account, though, is complicated when one looks at the context in which her writings, and especially "Slouching Towards Bethlehem," originally appeared.

In its original published form, as a feature article on the "hippie generation" with accompanying photographs in the September 23, 1967, issue of the *Saturday Evening Post,* the essay has an immediate context that overwrites Didion's ambivalence about the counterculture. In this feature article form, "Slouching Towards Bethlehem" is an exposé in the magazine that is perhaps best known for its iconic 1950s Norman Rockwell covers, though the *Post* was using photographs on its covers by the 1960s when Didion became a regular contributor. In the *Saturday Evening Post,* Didion's "Slouching Towards Bethlehem" appears alongside advertisements for washer-dryer machines, an album titled *Anthony Newley Sings Songs from Doctor Dolittle,* hemorrhoid cream, and denture glue. The essay serves a clear documentary function, capturing the reality of the younger generation for what is clearly an older, more conservative readership. The photographs by magazine photojournalist Ted Streshinsky that accompany the essay feature members of the hippie generation, with long hair and John Lennon–style round glasses; many of them are long exposures with blurry subjects, connoting the marijuana and LSD hazes through which the hippies perceive the world. The essay concludes with one of a series of anecdotes, about a mother named Sue Ann who is yelling at her toddler when she catches him chewing on an electrical cord, while everyone else in the house is "in the kitchen trying to retrieve some very good Moroccan hash which had dropped down through a floorboard damaged in the fire" caused that same morning by the toddler.[11] In the essay's original magazine context, reinforced by a photograph in the feature article of a mother and toddler at a dance club (fig. 9), the essay's closing

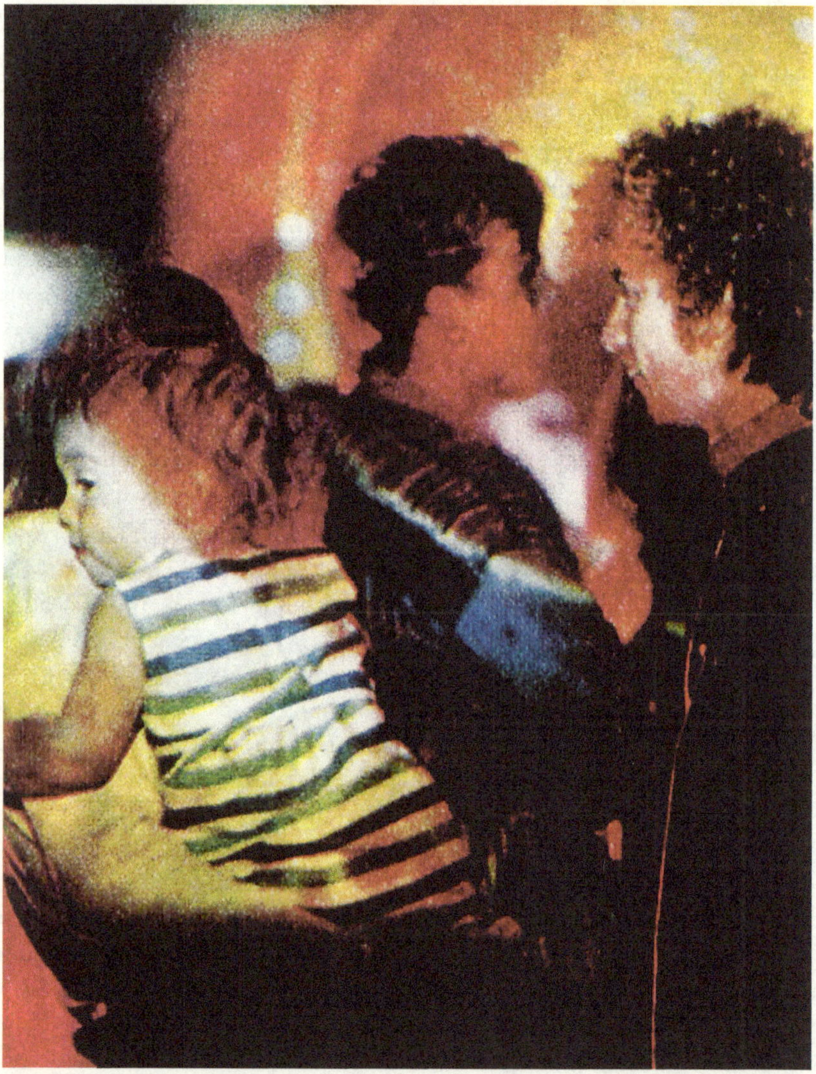

Figure 9. From "Slouching Toward Bethlehem," Ted Streshinsky, *Saturday Evening Post*, September 23, 1967. (Photograph © SEPS licensed by Curtis Licensing Indianapolis, IN; all rights reserved)

account of a child in danger while most of the adults search the kitchen for Moroccan hash seems typical of an exposé of all that is wrong with the hippie generation.

This moralism, though, is complicated when the essay is taken out of that context and repackaged, without the accompanying photographs, in the 1968 collection of Didion's essays also titled *Slouching Towards Bethlehem.* There, the final paragraph resonates differently, as a moment of negligence and misguided values, to be sure, but also as a moment of possibility. As Didion remarks earlier in the essay, what captivates her about the hippie generation is the way in which it stages rebellion without a clear sense of what that rebellion will entail, without a language to express their rebellion: "This was not a traditional generational rebellion. At some point between 1945 and 1967 we had somehow neglected to tell these children the rules of the game we happened to be playing. . . . These were children who grew up cut loose from the web of cousins and great-aunts and family doctors and lifelong neighbors who had traditionally suggested and enforced the society's values. . . . They are sixteen, fifteen, fourteen years old, younger all the time, an army of children waiting to be given the words."[12] In this light, Didion is writing less of an expose and more of a meditation on the possibilities and challenges of the younger generation. Here, the child chewing on the electrical cord is less the sign of the hippie generations' immaturity and irresponsibility than their troubled search for a way to articulate rebellion. The child is the hippie generation's failure and its possibility, an image of danger and neglect but also of curiosity and a willingness to pursue threatening agency. This juxtaposition of potential harm and naive action is left deliberately unresolved at the essay's conclusion. This irresolution registers with Susan Sontag's account of what she called the "new sensibility" in a 1965 essay in *Mademoiselle,* later collected in *Against Interpretation and Other Essays* (1966). In the essay, Sontag claims that the "new art," which ranges from Samuel Beckett, William S. Burroughs, and Robert Rauschenberg to the Supremes, Budd Boetticher, and Jean-Luc Godard, "demands less 'content' in art, and is more open to the pleasures of 'form' and style," making it "less snobbish, less moralistic—in that it does not demand that pleasure in art necessarily be associated with edification."[13] What Sontag details in her essay as 1960s art's rejection of a genteel aesthetic sensibility is, I think, central to understanding not only Didion but also the documentary aesthetic.

Didion's deeply ambivalent and uncertain representation of the hippie generation is part of Sontag's new sensibility, which ignores or even critiques edification and moralism in art of all sorts, from literature and painting to film and music. What is curious, though, is the way in which postmodernism has been codified as precisely the opposite of what Sontag claims in 1965, an early moment in the formation of postmodern styles and theories. From Linda Hutcheon's "historiographical metafiction" to Jameson's "third-world allegory," postwar literature—and especially the postwar novel—has been read either as moral, in its production, for example, of hybrid figures that destabilize systems of oppression, or as becoming incoherent, paranoid, or nostalgic in the face of late capitalism, and thus registering moral resentment at the losses of identity, home, and history.[14] These losses and possible recovery from them become the moral center of postmodern literature, whether present as textuality or absent and therefore the object of paranoiac speculation. Didion provides an alternative view, as she represents not what was and what will be (or, at least, the struggle to imagine the latter in light of the former) but instead the possibilities of her own situation and the limitations of her own historical moment. The way that Didion represents fragmented space and experience documents emergent neoliberalism, and the privileged perspective afforded to the individual in her essays about the counterculture—not to mention the individual's own simultaneous involvement in and skeptical detachment from the events that she witnesses—allegorizes the role of the individual in a neoliberal order where national identities and state sovereignty have broken down.

This is particularly evident in Didion's 1983 *Salvador,* a nonfiction account of the Salvadoran Civil War. The Salvadoran Civil War began with a leftist coup d'état in 1979 and concluded with the Chapultepec Peace Accords in 1992. Didion's trip to San Salvador took place during the "reign of terror" period of the Civil War between 1981 and 1983, a period when the conflict was at its most violent. As Paul Almeida notes in his study of resistance movements in El Salvador, "between 1979 and 1983, some thirty thousand to forty thousand civilians fell victim to government and/or paramilitary groups—a veritable genocide."[15] Didion's *Salvador* was originally published in three parts in the *New York Review of Books* during November and December 1982, then packaged together as a small book in 1983. In *Salvador,* Didion examines how the Salvadoran Civil War produces a sense of terror that isolates the individual, and in the text, Didion becomes an interlocutor who can account only for absences and unevenness rather than totality. The strength of neoliberalism's emergence, then, as Didion's *Salvador* emphasizes, lies in its presence in absence, its subsumption within fragments rather than its coherence as an ideology. Mary Louise Pratt has placed Didion's *Salvador* in the long tradition of imperialist travel writing, yet she notes: "The grand aspirations of the imperial powers reduce here to a bureaucratized wish for 'management.' Welcome to the 1980s!"[16] Didion's vision of El Salvador, and the Salvadoran Civil War itself, marks a shift from older imperial models of colonization to a neoliberal focus on management. This neoliberal rationality was difficult to understand and criticize in the 1980s, even though it was operative. Largely a series of policy decisions made behind closed doors, neoliberal reforms in El Salvador would only begin to be singled out by activists in the country as a problem in the late 1990s. By then, it was difficult to roll back measures recommended and, indeed, mandated by international organizations like the International Monetary Fund, with whom the Salvadoran government signed its first accord in 1982, resulting in wage freezes and a devaluation of Salvadoran currency.[17] Neoliberalism remade everyday life before it could be named in everyday life; neoliberalism is an ideology that could only be recognized as such after the fact.

Didion's *Salvador* begins in the El Salvador International Airport, which is forty miles from San Salvador and designed to feed tourists into a resort district that was never completed. Didion reads the airport and its surroundings as a vertiginous space, like the Bonaventure Hotel in Fredric Jameson's famous account of postmodernism,[18] that repeats the same patterns over and over again yet might also reverse or change its structure at any moment: "In the general absence of tourists these [Salvadoran resort] hotels have since been abandoned, ghost resorts on the empty Pacific beaches, and to land at this airport built to service them is to plunge directly into a state in which no ground is solid, no depth of field reliable, no perception so definite that it might not dissolve into its reverse."[19] The play on the word "state" here invokes both Didion's subjective experience of being in El Salvador during the Civil War and the evaporation of the "state" itself as the U.S.-backed Salvadoran military and ruling party, consolidated into ARENA, fought against the FMLN, the guerilla leftist group that had, at the time, retreated to the countryside after being driven back from San Salvador. The evaporation of the "state" registers in *Salvador* uniquely. It had been widely reported in the U.S. that the Salvadoran security forces, many officers of which had been trained in the United States or in El Salvador by the CIA, had formed unofficial "death squads" that had committed a number of brutal crimes. The two most notable, for Didion and others, were the assassination of leftist leader Archbishop Romero and the murder of four American missionaries, both taking place in 1980. What registers here, then, is the dissolution of the state of El Salvador, but also the state of the United States, as Reagan continued to support the Salvadoran security forces despite these widely reported crimes, undermining Cold War rhetoric that made the United States' support of democracy worldwide a centerpiece of foreign policy. The trip to El Salvador also plunges Didion into "a state" that allows her to witness the dissolution of liberalism for the sake of destabilization and privatization. From our contemporary vantage point, it is clear that *Salvador* chronicles how Reagan's anticommunism was also, at the same time, emergent neoliberalism, and how the Salvadoran Civil War allowed for the production of individualism outside of any identifiable state, the kind of free-market ego idealized in neoliberal thought.

Didion describes El Salvador, at times, as entirely foreign and other. She even uses an excerpt from Joseph Conrad's *Heart of Darkness* (1899) as the book's epigraph. The famous passage about Kurtz's report to the International Society for the Suppression of Savage Customs ends with Kurtz's "scrawled" note: "Exterminate all the brutes!" This quotation resonates, in the early 1980s, with Francis Ford Coppola's 1979 film *Apocalypse Now,* adapted from *Heart of Darkness* to the context of the Vietnam War, and with Hunter S. Thompson's 1966 *Hell's Angels,* a New Journalist account of the infamous motorcycle club, which concludes with the same quotation. In *Apocalypse Now* and *Hell's Angels,* Kurtz's scrawl becomes the American response to both international and domestic threats, the spread of communism and the challenges of the counterculture. What, for Conrad, was a maddening engagement with the other in Africa becomes, in the context of Didion's *Salvador* and this chain of citations, a realization that the other and the self have folded in on one another. The difference between El Salvador and the United Sates, leftist revolutionaries and the Hell's Angels, a military dictatorship and the Reagan administration, blurs. As Didion remarks in "Insider Baseball," an essay on the 1988 presidential race, the categories that we use to understand the world lose their meaning as they are continually redefined by powerful elites toward "the invention of a public narrative based at no point on observable reality."[20] The connection Didion draws between El Salvador and the U.S. is often elided in critiques of *Salvador,* which, as Patricia Stuelke points out, tend to fault Didion for the detached mode through which she approaches "the problem of representation confronting 1980s solidarity activists and artists, the question of which affective modes could ethically and effectively inspire solidarity with Central Americans struggling against US-backed dictatorships and death squads."[21] Didion's detachment, though, does allow her to register neoliberalism's emergence, as an impersonal force that binds the United States to El Salvador at the level of economic policy if not at the level of political solidarity.

Because of the Civil War and because, as Didion claims, "terror is the given of the place," El Salvador is not only in flux but without a past or future.[22] Instead of seeing ruins or museums, Didion learns to see details that matter in the war-torn environment, adjusting her perceptions: "These are the details—the models and colors of armored vehicles, the makes and calibers of weapons, the particular methods of dismemberment and decapitation used in particular instances—on which the visitor to Salvador learns immediately to concentrate, to the exclusion of past or future concerns, as in a prolonged amnesiac fugue."[23] This perpetual present—the "amnesiac fugue"—undoes not just historical context but also individual security. Didion, for example, describes having dinner while watching two armed strangers across the street: "Nothing came of this, but I did not forget the sensation of having been in a single instant demoralized, undone, humiliated by fear."[24] This debasement of personal security is the "mechanism of terror" in the Salvadoran Civil War, and it is also symptomatic of the broader stripping away of security, that is, the protections of the welfare state, under neoliberalism. During Didion's stay in El Salvador, the president was Álvaro Magaña, who, Didion notes, "studied in the United States, at Chicago."[25] The University of Chicago was the crucible for the development of neoliberalism in postwar America, and the mention of Magaña's alma mater is followed by an interview with an unnamed Salvadoran elite. Didion writes: "'Don't say I said this, but there are no issues here,' I was told by a high-placed Salvadoran. 'There are only ambitions.' . . . That this man saw *la situacion* as only one more realignment of power among the entitled, a conflict of 'ambitions' rather than 'issues,' was, I recognized, what many people would call a conventional bourgeois view of civil conflict, and offered no solutions, but the people with solutions to offer were mainly somewhere else, in Mexico or Panama or Washington."[26] The book's final clause clarifies where these solutions lie: "The State Department announced that the Reagan administration believed that it had 'turned the corner' in its campaign for political stability in Central America."[27] Didion's account positions the Salvadoran Civil War as a conflict between elites, educated and trained in the United States, yet also as a conflict that has no clear political stakes because of this orchestration. It is a contest between individual ambitions rather than political viewpoints—a contest that Paul Almeida identifies as the first stage of neoliberal reform in El Salvador, followed by a wave of privatization, national debt, and mandated government austerity measures.[28] Moreover, this privileging of the individual over politics, ambition over policy, is a transformation that Didion associates with the 1960s and that accompanies and facilitates neoliberalism. First-person narration and individual subjectivity are the only available frameworks to experience the world, and even that journalistic subjectivity is incapable of organizing, analyzing, and packaging events into historical coherence. Didion's documentary prose elevates the individual only to demonstrate the individual's tentative and fleeting hold on a reality that itself lacks any coherence, as categories like "state," "nation," and "citizen" lose their referents.

In "On the Morning after the Sixties," an essay originally published as "A Generation Not for Barricades" in the June 5, 1970, issue of *Life* and collected in *The White Album,* Didion catalogs the remains of the 1960s. She identifies the sixties as a failure but one that she is unable to leave behind. According to Didion, the central idea of the sixties was radical personality: "We were all very personal then, sometimes relentlessly so, and, at that point where we either act or do not act, most of us are still. I suppose I am talking about just that: the ambiguity of belonging to a generation distrustful of political highs, the historical irrelevancy of growing up convinced that the heart of darkness lay not in some error of social organization but in man's own blood."[29] When this passage is read alongside *Salvador,* Didion's historical perspective becomes clearer. The radical individualism of sixties politics results in stillness, in inaction, in "historical irrelevancy." This individualism is also fostered by neoliberal reform, which emerged as a theory and practice of the United States in the era that Didion is writing about—and, especially, as foreign policy by the early 1980s, when Didion wrote *Salvador.* Through her New Journalistic style, Didion struggles with the fact that the individual is all that we are left with, yet the individual is rendered meaningless not by social institutions but by their erosion. For Didion, those who experienced the 1960s "are survivors of a peculiar and inward time."[30] Her journalism is an attempt to recognize the losses that allowed for the survival of the personal. These varied, multiple losses—of society, of politics, of utopia—are registered through the persistence of the New Journalism, as personal style becomes, in a privatized, neoliberal culture, both hegemonic and the only available tool of critique.

Hans Haacke, Finance, and Juxtaposition

Similar to Didion's representation of life and experience in pieces, Hans Haacke's *Shapolsky et al. Manhattan Real Estate Holding, a Real-Time Social System, as of May 1, 1971* solidifies the difference and incompatibility of experience and structure, life and history. However, it does so in a way that inverts Didion's privileging of fragmented experience. Haacke's conceptual art installation emphasizes structure and system, capturing the fluidity yet monopoly of ownership in the New York real estate market. Haacke's *Shapolsky et al.* consists of two large maps, 142 photographs of properties in New York with accompanying text descriptions, and six charts tracking business transactions (fig. 10). All of the materials in the work chart the real estate holdings and transactions of the Harry Shapolsky family, from roughly 1951 to 1971. Haacke chose to document the Shapolsky family because, as he states, "They represented the largest concentration of real estate under the control of a single group. They were owned by about seventy corporations and were frequently sold and mortgaged among them."[31] Haacke's accompanying text describes Shapolsky's legal troubles, which include a 1959 conviction for rent gouging, an indictment for bribing building inspectors, and, in the words of a New York assistant district attorney, "ruthlessly exploit[ing] the shortage of housing space" in Manhattan.[32] Infamously, the Guggenheim Museum rejected Haacke's *Shapolsky et al.* and cancelled an exhibition of the artist's work in 1971, six weeks before the show's planned opening. According to then-director of the Guggenheim Thomas Messer, Haacke's documentary work was not art. Messer described the installation as "an alien substance that had entered the art museum organism."[33] As Messer stated elsewhere, Haacke's work "reduce[d] the work of art from its potential metaphoric level to a form of photo journalism concerned with topical statements rather than with symbolic expression."[34]

While the Guggenheim Museum's objection to Haacke's *Shapolsky et al.* branded the work mere journalism and therefore not art, Haacke's reception since 1971 has proven otherwise. Indeed, *Shapolsky et al.* has been cast by Benjamin Buchloh as an important work of sculpture, one that is ultimately valuable not because of its documentary framing but instead because it "contest[s] the transhistorical validity of the traditional sculptural aesthetic of 'pure' materials and process."[35] While this argument is compelling insofar as it places *Shapolsky et al.* in the context of conceptual art, this focus on sculpture as a medium displaces the work's political

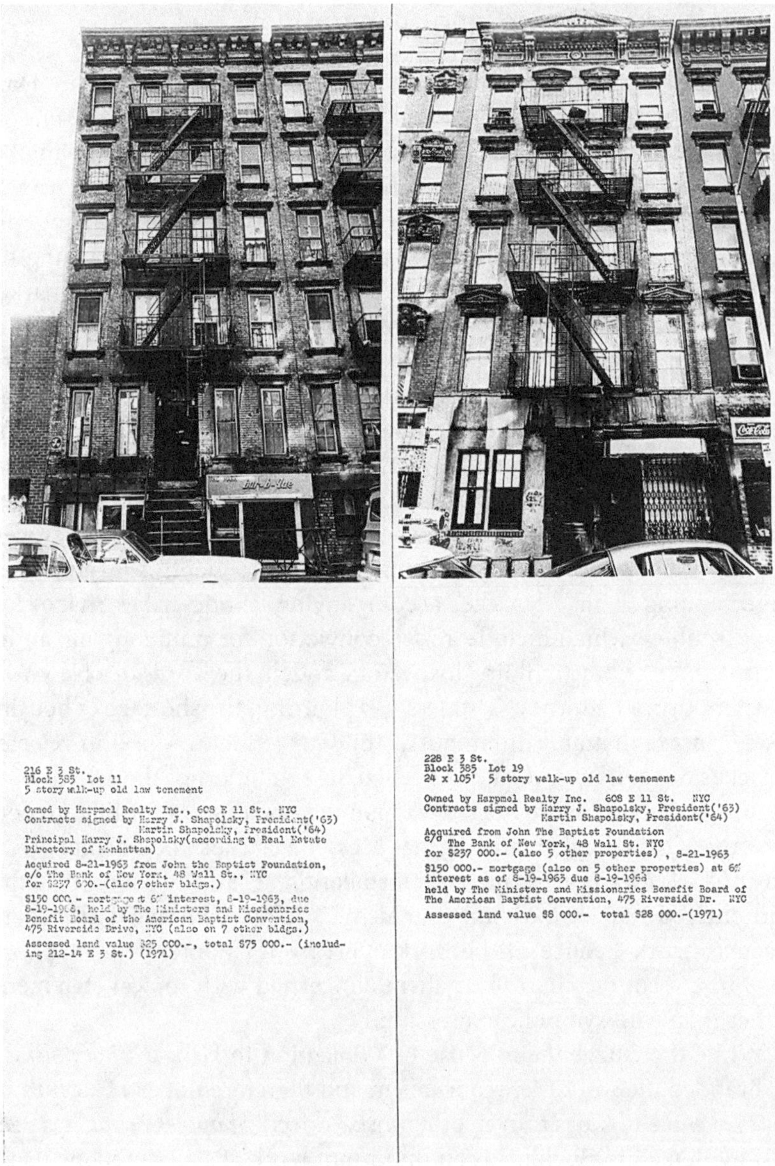

Figure 10. Detail from *Shapolsky et al. Manhattan Real Estate Holdings, a Real-Time Social System, as of May 1, 1971*, Hans Haacke, 1971. Two maps (photo-enlargements), black and white photographs, 142 typewritten sheets, 6 charts, one explanatory panel. (© Hans Haacke/Artists Rights Society (ARS), New York/VG Bild-Kunst, Bonn; courtesy the artist and Paula Cooper Gallery, New York)

and social critique with the rarefied status of a traditional art medium. It is hard to imagine how a work about the financialization of real estate could not figure as being about economic realities just as much, if not more, than it is about the idea of sculpture. Contrary to Buchloh, Rosalyn Deutsche has argued that Haacke's work made visible the "economic and social conflicts" that undergird the art museum. Moreover, as Deutsche argues, Haacke's photographs of buildings and vacant lots in *Shapolsky et al.* undo any romantic conception of tenement photography that museumgoers might expect from an exposé of a slumlord. Instead, they "reinforce at the level of individual structures the impression of the city as an economic product. Shot from street level, looking up at the buildings, the photographs have borders that coincide with property lines, emphatically refusing compositional devices that might identify the buildings as historically or aesthetically interesting structures rather than as real estate."[36] The 142 identically sized photographs tell the viewer nothing about the experience of living in one of those buildings. Instead, the photographs display with seeming indifference the building's front, sometimes with a parked car, trash cans, or passing pedestrians out front. The photographer did not even wait for the scene to be clear. These survey-like photographs, then, are mere documents, interesting not because of their composition but because of the absence of aesthetic qualities. Accordingly, the work as a whole is where Haacke's documentary aesthetic is to be found. In the conceptual linkage and presentation of mere buildings as commodity values to be swapped, mortgaged, refinanced, and swapped again through the Shapolsky family's many shell corporations, the buildings are important not as buildings but as the material traces of increasingly abstract financial dealings, dealings that Haacke makes visible in the six charts in *Shapolsky et al.* that trace the family's shell corporations and mortgage operations.

First exhibited in the United States at the University of Rochester in 1972 and then exhibited as part of Haacke's "Unfinished Business" retrospective in 1986 at the New Museum, *Shapolsky et al.* was also shown as part of the opening exhibit at the new Whitney Museum of American Art in 2015, an exhibition fittingly titled "America Is Hard to See." This title is fitting because Haacke's *Shapolsky et al* is a work of art that hinges on the elision of experience and feeling and the replacement of familiar modes of engaging with corruption and crime by systemic analysis and investigative documentary. Reviewing the Whitney's show in the *Nation,* Barry Schwabsky took Haacke's work as an occasion to reflect on the Lower East Side, where many of Shapolsky's holdings were located:

> I couldn't help noticing that many of the buildings Haacke pictured were in my own neighborhood, the Lower East Side, so I decided to make an expedition around my environs to see what had become of those buildings over the last 44 years. The Lower East Side is a very different place than it was in the 1970s and '80s. . . . In fact, some of the buildings featured in Haacke's piece no longer exist: There's a school playground where 216 and 218 Stanton Street must have been; 209 and 211 Eldridge Street were replaced in 1988 by a New York City Housing Authority project called Lower East Side I Infill. At the same time, many of the properties look—at least from the outside—as if they've risen in the world, and some of them have upscale bars and cafes on their ground floors. But such appearances can be deceiving: 42 Rivington Street is the site of a charming little French restaurant and wine bar where I've whiled away a happy hour or two; but the entrance to the apartments above it is filled with graffiti, and a "no trespassing" sign posted by the Manhattan district attorney's office suggests that there's been serious trouble recently. A Google search turns up many recent violations, including reports of no heat or hot water.[37]

Schwabsky's response to Haacke's work is to embrace the role of flâneur, to walk his neighborhood and see what has changed, what hasn't. Yet this leaves the art critic a bit at a loss:

> It's hard to know what goes on behind the facade of a building, today or back in 1971 when Haacke was making *Shapolsky et al.* The piece takes a documentary form, but only to remind you that it is really a formal exercise revealing how little a work of art—or the name of a building's owners—can reveal. Haacke's piece exposes a fraudulent real-estate system, according to the Whitney's accompanying wall text, but not really. Rather, it exposes a system of ownership that lacks transparency, but as to what end that opacity was cultivated we can only speculate. And it tells nothing about the lives of the people who lived in those buildings.[38]

Schwabsky views Haacke's work, then, as failing to have any content. Instead, it is a "formal" exercise, a conceptual work, about meaning and the work of art. Yet this formal exercise is much more than that if we expect documentary art to provide not a transparent account of subjectivity but instead an account of the tensions and gaps between subjectivity and structure. Indeed, Haacke's *Shapolsky et al.* does not neglect experience so much as it presents a system of financial transactions that cannot be experienced, that elide explanation. After all, even after studying Haacke's documents, it is not really clear how the Shapolsky family operates, how they make money, how the shell corporations and mortgage swaps produce profit. And it's not clear that any of those financial transactions have anything to do with the buildings themselves, with the leases and maintenance needs that the Shapolsky family also exploited for profit.

The Structure of Neoliberalism's Emergence

The gap between experience and system is indicative of how neoliberalism operates in our own age and how it operated from its emergence in postwar America. In Haacke's 1974 work *Solomon R. Guggenheim Museum Board of Trustees,* the relation between finance, art, and neoliberalism is made even clearer. In this work, consisting of seven printed panels, Haacke traces the connections between the Guggenheim family, the Guggenheim Museum's board of trustees, and their shared interests and roles in corporations. As Rosalyn Deutsche details: "For the multinational Kennecott Copper Corporation—which counted a Guggenheim family member and two museum trustees on its board of directors—Haacke presented information about the company's investments in Chile and included a statement by the country's deposed and murdered president Salvador Allende. . . . Kennecott was later named in hearings on the destabilization of the Allende democracy by United States interests."[39] Like El Salvador, Chile was one of the countries in which the United States would test out neoliberal economic and political policies under the secrecy provided by the Cold War. What Haacke's documentary art and what Didion's first-person reportage make visible, then, is not the reality of neoliberal culture's emergence but instead the ways in which that emergence was not visible. Today, after the 2008 financial crisis, we remain in the same relation to economic and political structures, unable to understand the ways in which economic models failed in what Phillip Mirowski has described as the "conceptual debacle" that resulted in the retrenchment of neoliberal policies and neoclassical economic models in the twenty-first century.[40]

This curious retrospective relation to neoliberalism's emergence is captured in Patricio Guzmán's 1997 documentary film *Chile, Obstinate Memory.* In the film, Guzmán returns to Chile after fleeing during the 1973 military coup that included the assassination of Salvador Allende. In its conclusion, Guzmán screens his 1979 documentary *The Battle of Chile* for people who participated in Allende's movement and a group of college students who were small children during the coup. After watching the film, they respond, often in tears, and reflect on the terrible violence of the coup. One man says, through tears, "I was a child. I remember the 11th September [1973, the date of the military coup]. I was on my bed, happy not to have to go to school. Having seen that [the film], I don't understand how people can be so barbaric. Killing a family because it doesn't think like you. You understand. Would you kill the dreams of history because you don't like art?" The painful juxtaposition here, between a childhood memory of happiness and a realization of the violence that occasioned that happiness, is transformed in his reflection to an account of ideological struggle. "Art" and the "dreams of history" are conjoined, as *The Battle of Chile* seems to capture the utopian imaginary of Allende and his supporters as well as its brutal suppression by military forces in the service of early neoliberal policies propagated by the United States. *Chile, Obstinate Memory* documents not the "dreams of history" but instead the relation between those past dreams and the present, the distance between experience and the structures that facilitated that experience.

The film's framing is echoed in Milton and Rose Friedman's memoir *Two Lucky People*, in which they document how the "Chicago Boys," a group of economists from the University of Chicago, served as economic advisers to the Pinochet regime. The memoir represents Milton Friedman's visit to Chile as fleeting. That his trip resulted in protests against him for supporting a military junta is the subject of some bemusement: "I never could decide whether to be more amused or more annoyed by the charge that I was running the Chilean economy from my office in Chicago."[41] Yet the Friedmans also view Chile as proof positive of free market economics' beneficent effect on society. Ignoring the human rights violations committed by the Pinochet regime—according to the Valech Commission, the number of "recognized victims" is 40,018[42]—the Friedmans instead view Chile as a triumph: "More than twenty years after the Chicago Boys were given authority . . . real income per capita multiplied more than two-and-a-half fold, inflation fell from 500 percent per year to 8 percent, the infant mortality rate per 1,000 live births fell from 66 to 13, and life expectancy at birth rose from 64 years to 73 years. And authentic political freedom has been restored with the turnover of power by the junta to a freely elected government."[43] For the purposes of this book, what is interesting in the Friedmans' account isn't the accuracy of their claims but, instead, the framework that they use to make them and the elisions they are constructed around. On one hand, the Friedmans defer to their own experience to claim that Milton Friedman did not, in fact, control the Pinochet regime's economic policy. He is personally baffled by that claim and recounts meeting Pinochet only once "in a session that lasted perhaps three-quarters of an hour or so and in which I had to communicate through interpreters."[44] Yet Chile's economic and political history over twenty years is, at the same time, evidence that Friedman and his colleagues held valid ideas that were put into practice in Chile. The Friedmans both aren't personally responsible for the Pinochet regime and are responsible for the structural changes to the Chilean economy and society. What the Friedmans ignore is precisely the accounting of trauma and violence that Guzmán's documentary names "obstinate." In keeping with their neoliberal ideology, the Friedmans view Chile as both a personal experience and a theoretical exercise. The costs to civil society and to 40,018 humans is ignored in a framework that cannot connect personal experience to the realities of structural change, that can only think in either the terms of personal experience or structural abstractions.

This disjunction between system and experience, structure and history, is the reality that we live in, and it is one with which works in the documentary aesthetic grapple. Since the 1960s, works in the documentary aesthetic have sought to make sense of both experience and systems. Our neoliberal moment has made this a feat that requires art to make reality newly visible as a project of collective making. Yet, as Didion's signature style makes clear, the project of collective imagination is complicated by our neoliberal culture's privileging of personal experience and individual will as the barometer of value. In Haacke's conceptual art and Guzmán's reflection on neoliberal reforms in Chile, the documentary aesthetic makes visible the distance between economics and subjectivity, the ways in which our subjective frames are determined by structures that we can understand, perhaps, only retrospectively. Yet that backwards glance opens up the possibility of an interruption. The next chapter further explores the valences of neoliberal individualism and political possibility.

3 / Neoliberal Style

In the song "Diamonds from Sierra Leone (Remix)," Jay-Z puns, "I'm not a businessman / I'm a business, man."[1] This line brilliantly illuminates the ideal subject of neoliberal economics—the entrepreneurial individual, unfettered from any organization or regulation.[2] The "businessman," the company man, is outmoded in a world where the individual is, him- or herself, the business. In the years following Bob Dylan's shift from folk activist to rock icon, personality in general has also shifted into an increasingly economic logic, as, for example, in the concept of "personal branding" so central to social media. Jay-Z captures this logic and represents its cultural power in the elaboration of a multicultural society stratified by the free market and the abandonment of collective bargaining, organization, and agitation.[3] As Jay-Z indicates in his autobiography, *Decoded,* his own career and the history of rap music more generally have developed by documenting life stories through the trope of the hustler—a stylized narrative of an individual accumulating wealth outside of regulated markets.[4] The hustler's reach into hip hop and, by extension, contemporary global culture, is vast. As Tricia Rose remarks of hip-hop culture, "Being a hustler is *the* central model of success."[5]

In the afterword to the paperback edition of *Decoded,* Jay-Z places his memoir in the context of literary culture, though he does so through an interlocutor, the poet Kathleen Norris. He recounts:

> A month before the hardcover edition of *Decoded* hit the shelves, a poet named Kathleen Norris saw unbound pages of the book . . .

> lying on the desk of my publisher. She picked them up out of curiosity and started reading. Norris isn't exactly part of the hip-hop generation: She's an award-winning poet who has spent much of her adult life in South Dakota, and her most famous books are meditations on the spiritual life, based on her experiences in a monastery in North Dakota. I'm not sure she knew who I was at all when she started reading those pages. . . . But her response was humbling and gratifying—the first suggestion that maybe the book would achieve what we'd set out to accomplish.[6]

Norris's response to the book, also reproduced in the afterword, dwells on how Jay-Z's lyrics and his discussions of them reminded her of Emily Dickinson's "bending" of language and the endnotes to T. S. Eliot's *The Waste Land*. But, she writes, "Most of all, this book has reconnected me with *The Autobiography of Malcolm X*. A teenage hustler in jail, realizing that his vocabulary is limited to street slang, sets out to learn English by reading the dictionary! It's really the story of a life saved, and a book written so that other kids that our society considers 'throwaways' might find a way out, another way to live."[7] Norris's chain of literary associations—Emily Dickinson's poetry, T. S. Eliot's notes to *The Waste Land*, and Malcolm X's autobiography—place Jay-Z's book in both an aesthetic and a social context. Resonant with traditional literary values—the use and manipulation of language, the construction of a tradition in which a contemporary work exists—the nonfiction work also has an overtly social and political meaning: it imagines and articulates an alternative to social norms, "another way to live." This twinned formal compulsion—aesthetic and activist—is precisely what Jay-Z is after.[8] Following Norris's email, Jay-Z remarks,

> For her, the book wasn't a passive, one-way experience. She left it hungry to make *more* connections. That was all I'd hoped for when I first decided to write a book. When my publisher sent me Norris's email, I emailed them back: Take the books off the shelves, I'm good.
>
> Of course, I didn't mean that literally.[9]

The joke that concludes Jay-Z's citation of Norris replaces aesthetic and political values with individualized, economic value. Since *Decoded* pleased an established poet, who then placed it in a luminary literary context, Jay-Z asks to have the book taken "off the shelves," humorously implying that the book's economic function is subordinate to its aesthetic and political meaning. To the contrary, the joke emphasizes, the book's economic value is inextricably connected to its literary value. The saturation of art by economics is even more apparent in the music video for Jay-Z's 2013 song "Picasso Baby," titled *Picasso Baby: A Performance Art Film*. The video was filmed at New York's Pace Gallery over the course of a six-hour performance, during which Jay-Z performed with marquee artists and provocateurs like Marina Abramović and Andres Serrano. In the video, Jay-Z registers in the rarefied world of fine art as a sign of multiculturalism's success and the free market's meritocratic operation.[10] Economic agency in "Picasso Baby" is equivalent to art making—the ability to buy a Picasso is evidence of Jay-Z's own aesthetic production: "House like the Louvre or the Tate Modern . . . / . . . I'm the modern day Pablo, Picasso, baby." Jay-Z's joke in *Decoded*—that he "didn't mean that literally," that his book shouldn't actually be taken off the shelves because Norris praised it—likewise makes clear that economic value coextends with aesthetic value, rather than differing from it.[11] Jay-Z's text posits that the work of nonfiction has aesthetic, economic, and political functions—it aims to be art, to sell, and to incite the reader to make new connections with others—yet economic rationality and the entrepreneurial figure of the hustler determine the circulation and presentation of the work. As in "Picasso Baby" and his larger body of work, Jay-Z is both speaker and subject, rapping about his experiences and their value as models both of entrepreneurial individualism and of the commodification of life. Perhaps the greatest aesthetic theorist of our time, Jay-Z writes and raps in neoliberal style.

As Norris's comparison of *Decoded* to *The Autobiography of Malcolm X* suggests, Jay-Z's brand of overblown, neoliberal individualism can be traced back to literary nonfiction about African American culture and the drug culture of the 1960s and 1970s, and the above, brief reading of *Decoded* and "Picasso Baby" establishes the basic terms, as well as the contemporary relevance, of this chapter's genealogical analysis of Alex Haley, *The Autobiography of Malcolm X*, and Hunter S. Thompson's gonzo journalism. Haley and Thompson each documented radical politics and the drug culture for major magazines, and they consistently used the first-person voice in their nonfiction. The modes of nonfiction narration used by Haley and Thompson in their reportage about the 1960s and 1970s and their privileging of the first-person perspective of the hustler, the activist, the radical, and the drug fiend constitute a neoliberal style through which countercultural and revolutionary politics in the United States and beyond become ways not of contesting capitalism but of possessing rebellious individuality within it.[12] As Wendy Brown has noted, the privatization and free market logic that have become dominant under neoliberalism led to a thorough instrumentalization of personhood, as humans are thought of not as subjects whose lives extend beyond the economy but instead as "human capital," whose total existence is comprised of economic relations: "Neoliberal rationality recognizes and interpellates the subject only as a speck of human capital, making incoherent the idea of an engaged citizen, an educated public, or education for a public life."[13] Neoliberal style functions as a counter and compliment to this neoliberal rationality, as a "structure of feeling" that allows the subject to imagine individualized agency yet projects agency in political and social terms that neoliberalism renders increasingly moot as they are incorporated into market logic.[14] In *A Brief History of Neoliberalism,* David Harvey explicates the ways in which all social relations are rationalized as economic relations under neoliberalism. Harvey remarks, "The cultural consequences of the dominance of such a market ethic are legion."[15] Similar to Ferdinand de Saussure's aside in *Course in General Linguistics* that the consequences of the arbitrary nature of the sign "are numberless"—a provocation that can be mapped onto the rise of literary theory—Harvey's claim points to the vast cultural consequences of neoliberalism, a charge that has been taken up by a number of scholars in anthropology, geography, literary studies, and philosophy.[16] Indeed, as the ideology of finance capitalism, neoliberalism has influenced the subjective mode of the documentary aesthetic. In nonfiction prose about African American culture and the drug culture, neoliberal style presents radical, countercultural politics as individualized and personalized, and in the context of nascent and emergent neoliberalism in the 1960s and 1970s, this individualization functions to obscure the collective promise of countercultural politics and to outfit resistance as an attractive posture for the neoliberal subject.

Haley's and Thompson's writings about the counterculture and their publication histories demonstrate the coextension of 1960s radicalism and emergent neoliberalism. As the "embedded liberalism" that Harvey notes as dominant in the post-1945 United States and Europe broke down in the 1960s and came into crisis in the 1970s, neoliberal policies were unevenly adopted and exported throughout the world over decades.[17] While neoliberalism "only converged as a new orthodoxy with the 'Washington Consensus' in the 1990s," the "capitalist world stumbled toward neoliberalization" during the decades in which Haley and Thompson produced their major works.[18] In these decades, the high growth rates following World War II began to stall out, spurring on neoliberal strategies of privatization and deregulation.[19]

Aside from their shared historical moment, Haley and Thompson have, on the surface, very little in common. Haley is a commercial writer with moderate politics. He built his career publishing in mainstream magazines like *Playboy, Reader's Digest,* and the *Saturday Evening Post,* coauthored *The Autobiography of Malcolm X,* and published a massive best-seller, *Roots.* Thompson, by contrast, rose to prominence writing for *Rolling Stone* about drug use, Freak Power, and Brown Power. In both cases, though with different valences and implications, Haley's and Thompson's first-person, nonfiction prose transforms political opposition into neoliberal style, an individualized, rebellious lifestyle ethic that inflects the subject's imbrication in the free market. By naming and providing this genealogy of neoliberal style in first-person prose about 1960s and 1970s countercultures, I seek to name neoliberal style as a style and thus point to the ideological stakes of style in neoliberalism. As D. A. Miller notes, "Though style has never exactly been an art that conceals *art,* it has certainly been an art that tries hard to conceal *labor.*"[20] The labor underneath neoliberal style is both the labor of Haley and Thompson as nonfiction stylists, as writers who struggle to articulate political positions through first-person prose, and the labor of neoliberal reforms, the increasing construction of the first-person perspective as a hegemonic subjectivity, determined by economic rationality. In his lectures on biopolitics and neoliberalism, Michel Foucault captures Fredrich A. Hayek's neoliberal philosophy when he remarks that in order for subjects in neoliberalism to believe that free market logic produces "the greatest good . . . for the greatest number of people, not only is it possible, but it is also necessary that each actor be blind with regard to this totality. . . . Being in the dark and the blindness of all the economic agents are absolutely necessary."[21] In *Playboy* interviews, *The Autobiography of Malcolm X,* and writings for *Rolling Stone,* despite their different politics and personas, Haley and Thompson use a mode of narration, neoliberal style, that is focalized through the first-person perspective of successful celebrities or charismatic activists associated with eroding political projects, thus finding in personal experience both the myopia that Foucault deems "necessary" to neoliberalism and also the promise and appeal of individual success and individual charisma as the only values remaining after the failure of collective movements. Because of their subjective form and content, Haley's and Thompson's writings produce a neoliberal style that comes to dominate life narratives and, not insignificantly, left politics under neoliberalism.[22]

In neoliberal culture, as all activity is rendered in economic terms, it is clear why Malcolm X can be a footnote reference to Jay-Z's lyric "I got a hustler spirit."[23] Malcom X's politics recede from view, as an economic understanding of Malcolm X as an agent in the free market, rather than an activist in society, becomes the hegemonic way of reading not just him but all subjects. In Haley's and Thompson's prose, the figure of the hustler is both a villain and a hero, a criminal and an icon of the rapacious ambition both writers themselves possessed and found in their subjects. For Haley, the transformation of the hustler "Detroit Red" into the activist and intellectual Malcolm X revised a classic American narrative of individual development. For Thompson, the figure of the hustler identifies not those at the bottom of America's class structure but those in places of power: "[Henry] Kissinger is a slippery little devil, a world-class hustler with a thick German accent and a very keen eye for weak spots at the top of the power structure. Nixon was one of those, and Super K exploited him mercilessly, all the way to the end."[24] Whether Detroit Red or Henry Kissinger, the hustler finds a way to thrive and control his circumstances, and Haley and Thompson admire this drive—Kissinger even becomes "Super K." Haley's and Thompson's documentary prose offers a formal, stylistic presentation of the individualized hustler, the production of neoliberal style.

The Hustler and the Handshake

The figure of the hustler is famously central to *The Autobiography of Malcolm X*, a collaboration between Malcolm X and Alex Haley. Haley is a somewhat neglected figure in American literary history. He is excluded from Henry Louis Gates Jr.'s *Norton Anthology of African American Literature* despite being one of the most influential and successful writers of the 1960s and 1970s.[25] Haley pioneered the *Playboy* interview in the early 1960s and would become a celebrity with the publication of *Roots* in 1976, adapted into the landmark TV miniseries in 1977. Ranging from articles like "Mr. Muhammad Speaks" in *Reader's Digest* in 1960 to his *Playboy* interviews with Cassius Clay, Miles Davis, Malcolm X, and Martin Luther King Jr., Haley's work would represent African Americans and, especially, the Nation of Islam in mass-market magazines and in *The Autobiography of Malcolm X*, which Haley completed after Malcolm X's assassination in 1965. The distillation of Malcolm X into the figure of the "hustler" is one of the ultimate results of Haley's work in the 1960s, in which he wrote about radical politics for a largely white readership and, in so doing, explained them away as radical positions that would inevitably be tempered and folded into American democracy. As Roderick Ferguson describes this process, neoliberalism thrives as "a means of using difference to foster capitalist distribution while curtailing social redistribution for underrepresented folks."[26] In what follows, I read Haley's work as a way of promulgating racial difference within and as complementary to mainstream politics and nascent neoliberal economics, thus replacing redistributive justice and structural critique with the promise of agency in the free market.

The production of difference as a facilitator of rather than an inhibitor to the spread of the free market is perhaps best seen in Haley's work as an interviewer for *Playboy*. Haley's first interview published in *Playboy* was with Miles Davis, and it would be the model for the *Playboy* interview feature still running in the magazine today. In the interview, the unnamed interviewer, Haley, opens by asking Davis to comment on his "reputation for bad temper and rudeness to [his] audiences," a question that addresses one of the major features of *Playboy*, the marketing of jazz, stereos, cocktails, and fashion to white males under the banner of the "hip."[27] Davis's response both reassures the white consumer of jazz and educates him about the proper, cool attitude to take when listening to the music: "Look, man, I like people. I *love* people! I'm not going around telling everybody that. I try to say that my way—with my horn."[28] As suggested by the advertisement for Brookfield clothes that ran alongside the Miles Davis interview in the September 1962 issue of the magazine, *Playboy* attracted a youthful, white male readership who increasingly turned to jazz and African American styles—two of the three styles offered by Brookfield, "Ivy, Jivey, and Cats," connote racialized hipness (fig. 11). Moreover, as Elizabeth Fraterrigo argues in her study of *Playboy*, the magazine actively reported on and took a liberal stance toward the civil rights movement in keeping with its editorial focus on the "rights of an individual in a free society," even if, ultimately, "*Playboy* cared more about the status line than the color line."[29]

Haley's interview with Miles Davis focuses on what can now be described as emergent multiculturalism, especially when it comes to Davis's account of race in music, television, and film:

> If movies and TV are supposed to reflect this country, and this country's supposed to be democratic, then why don't they do it? Let's see all kinds of people dancing and acting. I see all kinds of kids downtown at the schools of dancing and acting, but from what I see in the movies and TV, it's just the white ones that are getting any work. . . . Look, man, right in music you got the same thing happening. I got this album, 'Someday My Prince Will Come,' and

Figure 11. Brookfield Clothes Advertisement, *Playboy,* September 1962.

> you know who's on the jacket cover? My wife—Frances. I just got to thinking that as many record albums as Negroes buy, I hadn't ever seen a Negro girl on a major album cover unless she was the artist. There wasn't any harm meant—they just automatically thought about a white model and ordered one. It was my album and I'm Frances' prince, so I suggested they use her for a model, and they did it.[30]

Davis's interest in representation is coupled in the interview with his emphasis on individual artistry. As he remarks when Haley asks how he would rank other trumpet players: "Trumpet players, like anybody else, are individualized by their different ideas and styles. The thing to judge in any jazz artist is does the man project, and does he have ideas."[31] Haley then shifts the interview away from Davis's aesthetics—the above rationale for why Davis plays with his back turned to the audience as a refusal to be considered a paid performer, a refusal of the tradition of minstrelsy—to a discussion of how "hip" consumers can modify their habits of consumption according to Davis's desires. Fittingly, the interview concludes with Haley asking Davis if he is indeed "one of the financially best-off popular musicians," to which Davis responds by discussing his "good portfolio of stock investments," his house, "worth into six figures," and his Ferrari.[32] In the interview, Davis's resistance to commodification and resistance to the marketing of jazz music rests comfortably next to his financial success. As the Brookfield ad demonstrates, printed alongside Davis's statement of aesthetic principles and discussion of his stock portfolio, Davis's individualized aesthetic commitments are both what make his music attractive as a hip commodity and unrelated to the marketing of jazz music and the jazz musician as a commodity for *Playboy*'s readers. Individual determination and perseverance would remain key to Haley's representations of race in America, a mode of difference compatible with free market ideology as long as one's individual commitments remain individual, not collective. This emphasis on the individual meshes with the consumerist logic of *Playboy* and the withering of modes of collective belonging under nascent neoliberalism, with which Davis's view that prejudice obstructs the individual artist is entirely compatible.

A good portion of Haley's other journalism from this period, including later *Playboy* interviews, would deal more directly with political figures. Alongside *Playboy* interviews with Malcolm X and Martin Luther King Jr., Haley would also work on articles on the Nation of Islam for *Reader's Digest* and the *Saturday Evening Post*. In these articles and ultimately in *The*

Autobiography of Malcolm X, Haley would position the Nation of Islam as an extreme in relation to a more universalist and less separatist racial politics. For example, published in the *Saturday Evening Post* in 1963, "Black Merchants of Hate" was cowritten by Alfred Balk and Haley. According to Manning Marable's definitive biography of Malcolm X, Haley's coauthor was fed information by the FBI,[33] and the article explicitly critiques the Nation of Islam as a threatening, radical group: "The Muslims' mass rallies are perhaps the most spectacular and frightening events they stage, reminiscent in some way of the huge meetings at which Hitler screamed his doctrines of Aryan supremacy. We attended their latest rally in Philadelphia last October. Three hours before meeting time at the Philadelphia Arena a vanguard of 40 charter buses and caravans of cars began arriving from as far away as Boston and Atlanta. Most passengers wore the Muslim 'uniform'—for men, dark suits and dark shoes; for women, Arabic-type white robes and kerchiefs."[34] The overt parallel between the Nazi Party and the Nation of Islam here casts the Nation of Islam in starkly negative terms, bizarrely erasing racial difference, and in so doing, Balk and Haley present other civil rights groups and strategies as beneficent in comparison. Alongside this portrait of the Nation of Islam as a kind of African American Nazi Party, the article also amplified Malcolm X's role in the Nation of Islam—Malcolm X is introduced as a "lanky, energetic, good-looking man," and the article devotes five paragraphs to outlining his life story, detailing his childhood, his young adulthood as the small-time hustler "Detroit Red," named after his reddish hair, and incarceration for larceny.[35] The article positions Malcolm X as an imminent threat to the Nation of Islam organization: "While Muhammad appears to be training his son Wallace to succeed him when he retires or dies, many Muslims feel that Malcolm is too powerful to be denied the leadership if he wants it."[36] Malcolm X's history as the hustler Detroit Red and his conversion in prison would become key events in the *Autobiography*, which would soon get underway following Haley's subsequent interview with Malcolm X in *Playboy*'s May 1963 issue. "Black Merchants of Hate" begins to narrate Malcolm X's difference from the Nation of Islam and the power of his life story to resonate with others as both "remarkable and typical," unusually interesting yet full of possibilities for identification. Haley would go on to expand on this in the *Autobiography*, a work whose potential audience is made clear in the early excerpt published in the *Saturday Evening Post* titled "I'm Talking to You, White Man."[37]

If Haley's interview with Miles Davis foregrounds the ways in which multiculturalism is compatible with free market ideals, Haley's reporting on the Nation of Islam positions the separatist group as a foil, to propose and advocate for integrationist reform against the specter of fundamentalist, even fascist collectivity. Malcolm X would become the chief figure through which Haley would develop his advocacy of integration, and Haley's own political perspective would be largely articulated in autobiographical form, giving the *Autobiography* its neoliberal style. Published in 1965, just months after Malcolm X's assassination, the *Autobiography* is one of the most important texts in late twentieth-century American literature and culture. As Loren Glass has shown in his history of the *Autobiography*'s original publisher, the Grove Press, the book "was in the vanguard of the curricular revisions that transformed American education" from the 1960s to the present.[38] The political becomes the personal in the *Autobiography*, especially insofar as the political recedes in the face of the personal. By casting Malcolm X as a man in perpetual conversion, ultimately arriving at a moderate racial politics, Haley expresses his attachment to the Cold War ideology of humanistic belonging.[39] What the history of this attachment and the collapse of radical politics into identity make clear, though, is that a commitment to humanist belonging leads to the production of the individual consumer as the ultimate arbiter of politics, culture, and society. By making Malcolm X accessible and heroic to a wide audience, the *Autobiography* takes radical politics and turns them into life narrative, thus making any substantive political change seem unrelated to the more pressing issue of self-actualization. The structure, here, is one similar to what Lauren Berlant has described as "cruel optimism"—an affective attachment to an object that promises to further one's political goals but in fact obstructs them.[40]

One of the most compelling and influential figures in the *Autobiography* is, of course, the hustler. Late in the *Autobiography*, Malcolm X reflects on his ability to speak to so many different audiences:

> The point I am making is that, as a "leader," I could talk over the ABC, CBS, or NBC microphones, at Harvard or at Tuskegee; I could talk with the so-called "middle-class" Negro and with the ghetto blacks (whom all the other leaders just talked about). And because I had been a hustler, I knew better than all whites knew, and better than nearly all of the black "leaders" knew, that actually the most dangerous black man in America was the ghetto hustler. . . . The ghetto hustler is internally restrained by nothing. He has no religion, no concept of morality, no civic responsibility, no fear—nothing. . . . The ghetto hustler is forever frustrated,

> restless, and anxious for some "action." Whatever he undertakes, he commits himself to it fully, absolutely.[41]

The transformation of the hustler into the political leader and the co-extension of the two entails notable omissions, mainly the elision of the collective belonging and advocacy so central to the Nation of Islam. Importantly, this hustler mentality is articulated in the *Autobiography* when Malcolm X is on the cusp of his full break with the Nation of Islam and his shift toward a more inclusive politics: "In the past, yes, I have made sweeping indictments of *all* white people. I will never be guilty of that again—as I know now that some white people *are* truly sincere, that some truly are capable of being brotherly toward a black man."[42] This speech is followed with a brief scene in which a white couple in a car pull up at a traffic light next to Malcolm X. The white man in the opposite car asks, "Do you mind shaking hands with a white man?" And Malcolm X narrates, "Imagine that! Just as the traffic light turned green, I told him, 'I don't mind shaking hands with human beings. Are you one?'"[43] It is left unsaid, of course, if the handshake actually happens, and that is key to the *Autobiography*, a text published mere months after Malcolm X's assassination. The *Autobiography*'s opening chapter contains the following predictive sentences in a stand-alone paragraph, foreshadowing what the reader already knows to have happened: "It has always been my belief that I, too, will die by violence. I have done all that I can to be prepared."[44] In his epilogue, Haley concludes with the following paragraph, sealing Malcolm X's reputation through the book contract: "After signing the contract for this book, Malcolm X looked at me hard. 'A writer is what I want, not an interpreter.' I tried to be a dispassionate chronicler. But he was the most electric personality I have ever met, and I still can't quite conceive him dead. It still feels to me as if he has just gone into some next chapter, to be written by historians."[45] The unrealized handshake functions as a metonym of Haley's own engagement in crafting Malcolm X's story and the legacy that Haley imagines here. By casting Malcolm X as a radical turned moderate, a separatist turned universalist, a criminal hustler turned political hustler, Haley's epilogue mourns the death of the leader who could have been, the man that Malcolm X is projected to be on the way to becoming. The handshake between Malcolm X and the white man, African American radicalism's transition to a less threatening, more moderate politics, never happens, but Haley stages it as a formal possibility. The "next chapter" that Haley wishes could be written about Malcolm X's life would come to be occupied by Haley's own pilgrimage not to Mecca but to Gambia, where he would construct his own ancestry through the figure of Kunta Kinte in *Roots*. Neoliberal style, then, offers not just a way to retain political beliefs as an individual, rather than part of a collective, but also a transformation of the past into a deeply personal genealogy, one that culminates in the late twentieth-century neoliberal subject.

Gonzo Journalism's Freak Power

While *The Autobiography of Malcolm X* personalizes radical politics by undermining political difference in the name of universalism, thus positioning the desire for collective politics as a compliment to, rather than a potential disruptor of, the free market, Hunter S. Thompson's "gonzo journalism" takes a different approach. Rather than occupying the position of moderate in relation to radicals, Thompson in the 1970s occupies the position of the radical, a position shared with Chicano lawyer and "Brown Power" activist Oscar Zeta Acosta, who appears in *Fear and Loathing in Las Vegas* as "Dr. Gonzo."[46] Thompson's gonzo journalism documents the perpetual derailing and failure of radical politics in the 1970s, as emergent neoliberalism accommodates the drug culture as consumerism rather than resistance to American hegemony. As in Haley's and Jay-Z's first-person texts, Thompson's prose uses neoliberal style to present a charismatic, rebellious individual, a subject who speaks as a political radical yet is ultimately isolated.

In his first contribution to *Rolling Stone* in October 1970, "The Battle of Aspen: Freak Power in the Rockies," Thompson details his involvement in candidate Joe Edwards's mayoral race, as well as his own run for sheriff of Aspen County. Thompson begins the essay by explaining his Freak Power party's strategy of registering young people to vote, a difficult pitch to members of the drug culture: "The central problem that we had grappled with last fall is the gap that separates the Head Culture from activist politics. Somewhere in the nightmare of failure that gripped America between 1965 and 1970, the old Berkeley-born notion of beating the System by fighting it gave way to a sort of numb conviction that it made more sense in the long run to Flee, or even to simply hide, than to fight the bastards on anything even vaguely resembling their own terms."[47] Balancing the desire for individual freedom with the commitment to political activism is the tension that motivates Thompson's writing from the 1960s to his death in 2005, and that tension would often register the triumph of consumer choice over and against political change. Of course, Thompson immediately brings to mind hedonistic abandon and drug-fueled depravity—these famous paragraphs from *Fear and Loathing in Las Vegas,* originally published in *Rolling Stone* in 1971, speak to this mad accumulation of pleasure and goods:

> The sporting editors had also given me $300 in cash, most of which was already spent on extremely dangerous drugs. The trunk of the car looked like a mobile police narcotics lab. We had two bags of grass, seventy-five pellets of mescaline, five sheets of high-powered blotter acid, a salt shaker half full of cocaine, and a whole galaxy of mutli-colored uppers, downers, screamers, laughers . . . and also a quart of tequila, a quart of rum, a case of Budweiser, a pint of raw ether and two dozen amyls.
>
> All this we had rounded up the night before, in a frenzy of high-speed driving all over Los Angeles County—from Topanga to Watts, we picked up everything we could get our hands on. Not that we *needed* all that for the trip, but once you get locked into a serious drug collection, the tendency is to push it as far as you can.[48]

The shopping spree that opens *Fear and Loathing in Las Vegas* stands out as a hyperbolic example of the consumerist side of Thompson's individualism. Pushed to its limits—by buying illegal drugs, and in such quantities—consumerism becomes less a progressive facet of modern life, as it is in *Playboy*'s association of consumerism with integration, and more of a dangerous, threatening violation of conventional morality and the self. The massive consumption of drugs—especially, in *Fear and Loathing,* ether——pushes individual consumption into the dissolution of the individual: "There is nothing more helpless and irresponsible and depraved than a man in the depths of an ether binge."[49] This hyperindividualism that then dissolves the individual is where politics emerge in Thompson's writing.

In "The Battle of Aspen," published a year before *Fear and Loathing in Las Vegas,* Thompson describes his Freak Power party's platform. Freak Power advocates for large-scale action against real estate developers: "Our program, basically, was to drive the real estate goons completely out of the valley: to prevent the State Highway Department from bringing a four-lane highway into the town and, in fact, *to ban all auto traffic from every downtown street.* Turn them all into grassy malls where everybody, even freaks, could do whatever's right. . . . Fuck the tourists, dead-end the highway, zone the greedheads out of existence, and in general create a town where people could live like human beings, instead of slaves to some bogus sense of Progress that is driving us all mad."[50] Thompson's idea of open space now conjures up visions of open-air pedestrian malls, popularized from the 1960s to the present as vital to urban renewal. Freak Power's platform was launched against real estate developers and was articulated through the drug culture, a mode of consumption that is outside of sanctioned consumerism. Thompson's vision is nevertheless coextensive with emergent "community-minded" real estate development, which equates personal freedom with the ability to shop, to consume, to purchase. That is, once the illegality and resistance of the drug culture is stripped away, Freak Power's platform looks like a more acerbic version of urban renewal—the production of a community organized around the fusion of working, shopping, and consuming, rather than an alternative to the lifestyles produced from within free market ideology.

The tenuous fusion of individual liberty and the collective good imagined by Thompson would be the focus of his next article for *Rolling Stone,* too, published in the April 29, 1971, issue. "Strange Rumblings in Aztlan" details the murder of journalist Ruben Salazar by the LAPD—he was shot in the head with a tear-gas canister—and its galvanizing effect on the Chicano movement in Los Angeles:

> Within twenty-four hours, the very mention of the name Ruben Salazar was enough to provoke tears and a fist-shaking tirade . . . all over East L.A.
>
> Middle-aged housewives who had never thought of themselves as anything but lame-status 'Mexican-Americans' just trying to get by in a mean Gringo world they never made suddenly found themselves shouting 'Viva La Raza' *in public.* And their husbands—quiet Safeway clerks and lawn-care salesmen, the lowest and most expendable cadres in the Great Gabacho economic machine—were volunteering to *testify;* yes, to stand up in court, wherever, and calling themselves Chicanos. The term 'Mexican-American' fell massively out of favor with all but the old and conservative—and the rich.[51]

These articles on Freak Power and Brown Power articulate consciousness-raising not as an act of self-realization but as an act of self-revision, and for both Thompson and Acosta, that revision of self was facilitated by massive drug use, which led to the dissolution and reconstitution of the self. Thompson's political vision here is quite different than Haley's—for Haley, a focus on life narrative signals a universal, liberal sense of belonging and community. For Thompson, the personal pronoun "I" leads to the formation of an oppositional block, a utopian collective founded on Truth and Power.

In an editorial note published in *Rolling Stone* in 1971, Thompson rails against the recent popularity of born-again Christianity: "A generation of failed dingbats and closet-junkies should under no circumstances be allowed to foul our lines of communication. . . . We have serious business to deal with, and these fuckers will only be in the way."[52] Thompson's political aspirations, at this point, combined the rhetorical style of the counterculture with the pragmatics of political party organization, namely, the construction of a party platform and voter registration efforts. His neoliberal style both relies on and belies collective organization—he aspires to a great collective good on some level, but, at the same time, the forceful, foul-mouthed Thompson's tone is so distinctive, so stylistically personalized, that it is incapable of being collectivized, of being imagined as the voice of a group rather than the voice of an individual.

Only a few months later in 1971, Thompson would begin to mourn this politics in his well-known quasijournalistic *Fear and Loathing in Las Vegas*. Ostensibly in Las Vegas to report on the Mint 400 Off-Road Motorcycle Race, Thompson's alter ego, Raoul Duke, and his attorney, Dr. Gonzo (Acosta), turn their trip into a drug-fueled quest for the American Dream. As Duke and Gonzo arrive at the Desert Inn to see Debbie Reynolds in concert, Thompson's narration contrasts the glamour associated with Las Vegas with its tacky reality: "This was Bob Hope's turf. Frank Sinatra's. Spiro Agnew's. The lobby fairly reeked of high-grade formica and plastic palm trees—it was clearly a high class refuge for Big Spenders. . . . The moment we got inside we lost control. The tension had been too great. Debbie Reynolds was yukking across the stage in a silver Afro wig . . . to the tune of 'Sergeant Pepper,' from the golden trumpet of Harry James. 'Jesus creeping shit!' said my attorney. 'We've wandered into a time capsule!'"[53] Debbie Reynolds jumbles signifiers of the 1960s counterculture—the afro, the Beatles—into a middle-class performance for Las Vegas tourists drawn to the casinos because of their classy connotations and plastic luxury. As Duke meditates later in their journey, Las Vegas comes to represent the death of the American Dream, yet this recognition also entails, as Marianne DeKoven notes, a "muted identification with Las Vegas," a troubling sense that Duke's own rabid consumption is not, ultimately, that different from the middle-class consumerism on display at the Debbie Reynolds concert.[54] Looking out the window and thinking about his life in San Francisco during the 1960s, Duke thinks about "that sense of inevitable victory over the forces of Old and Evil" that he had, that feeling of "riding the crest of a high and beautiful wave."[55] In Las Vegas, Duke realizes that he has found its endpoint: "So now, less than five years later, you can go up on a steep hill in Las Vegas and look West, and with the right kind of eyes you can almost see the high-water mark—that place where the wave finally broke and rolled back."[56] Thompson's countercultural hopes are thwarted by Las Vegas, which represents middle-class consumerism, the appropriation of countercultural styles by mainstream America, and conservative politics. Las Vegas consumerism would also, of course, come to symbolize postmodern simulacra and excess, the completely commercial landscape where form follows economic function, or as it was stated in the influential architectural book *Learning from Las Vegas,* where "buildings are also signs."[57] Individualism, then, becomes not a mode of redemption and universalization, as it is for Haley in his representation of Malcolm X's break with the Nation of Islam, but a paradox—the only place left to go during neoliberalism, but also the place that has been created to contain and neutralize what once counted as political alternatives. In its dramatization of charismatic individuals who have already failed to realize collectivity, whether in Malcolm X's potentially universalist political activism or Thompson's Freak Power party, neoliberal style leaves one trapped within an individualized subject position, from which any kind of collective belonging has been preemptively stripped away.

Fear and Loathing was published in *Rolling Stone* the same year that the United States, under what is called the "Nixon Shock," ended the convertibility of U.S. currency to gold, effectively shifting the global economy away from fixed exchange rates and toward a growing consensus against any form of protection from the vicissitudes of the free market.[58] *Fear and Loathing,* then, signals a dirge-like retreat from politics to the personal, from collectivity to consumerism, from the protections of the welfare state to the privatizations of neoliberalism. Indeed, in one of Thompson's last columns, written for ESPN in 2003, he writes:

> The American nation is in the worst condition I can remember in my lifetime, and our prospects for the immediate future are even worse. I am surprised and embarrassed to be a part of the first American generation to leave the country in far worse shape than it was when we first came into it. Our highway system is crumbling, our police are dishonest, our children are poor, our vaunted Social Security, once the envy of the world, has been looted and neglected and destroyed. . . . The Stock Market will never come back, our Armies will never again be Number One, and our children will

> drink filthy water for the rest of our lives. . . . Big Darkness, soon come.[59]

Thompson's adopted role—Raoul Duke, the cartoonish drug- and alcohol-fueled prophet of doom and despair—functions as a formal device for registering the displacement of political aspirations onto neoliberal style. It is an inversion of the handshake in *The Autobiography of Malcolm X* that never happens—a formal placeholder that marks the gap, ever widening, between personal experience and material conditions. That gap and its ever-widening expanse is the cultural force of neoliberalism, a force made visible through documentary.

When read as neoliberal stylists, Haley and Thompson document how personal experience and charismatic personae become the source of our political investments, just at the historical moment when entrepreneurial individualism emerges as the ideal subject of neoliberalism. Evident in the hustler trope ubiquitous in rap music, neoliberal style has also shaped the documentary aesthetic more generally: in the memoir boom starting in the early 1990s, in the "new sincerity" of contemporary writers, in the way that Errol Morris's Interrotron presents interview subjects as speaking directly to the viewer, and in the focus on "presence" in performance art by Marina Abramović, Carolee Schneemann, and others. It is also evident how racial differences in the United States have been the site both of fantasy projection for someone like Thompson, who finds in Oscar Zeta Acosta his rampaging, drug-fueled id, and of personal empowerment for writers like Haley and Jay-Z, for whom documenting the history of Black activism and art creates a path for future generations to follow. In neoliberal culture, these racialized modes become individualized even when they address or exploit collective experiences. Naming neoliberal style as a style and tracing its emergence in documentary narratives about countercultures is one way to begin charting the promises and the limits of entrepreneurial individualism and to become more attentive to modes of representation that cast neoliberal subjecthood against the exploitative structures that produce it.

4 / True Crime

The first essay in Joan Didion's celebrated 1968 collection of nonfiction *Slouching Towards Bethlehem* is a true crime story. Titled "Some Dreamers of the Golden Dream" in the book, the essay focuses on Lucille Miller, who was convicted of burning her husband to death in the San Bernardino Valley in 1964. Didion recounts the crime as an event inspired by media narratives—about success, about manipulative and aspirational housewives, about California and upward mobility. The land itself seems to be more of an agent, even, than the people who inhabit it:

> This is the California where it is possible to live and die without ever eating an artichoke, without ever meeting a Catholic or a Jew. This is the California where it is easy to Dial-a-Devotion but hard to buy a book. This is the country in which a belief in the literal interpretation of Genesis has slipped imperceptibly into a belief in the literal interpretation of *Double Indemnity,* the country of the teased hair and the Capris and the girls for whom all life's promise comes down to a waltz-length white wedding dress and the birth of a Kimberly or a Sherry or a Debbi and a Tijuana divorce and a return to hairdressers' school. "We were just crazy kids," they say without regret, and look to the future. The future always looks good in the golden land, because no one remembers the past.[1]

In this country, Didion writes, Lucille Miller is a "tabloid monument."[2] Her criminal conviction—she would serve seven years of a life sentence, then be granted parole in 1972—was based on a "curiously predictable story."[3] Miller's recorded phone conversations sound like dialogue from a film noir, like *Double Indemnity,* and in her story, Didion finds "the revelation that the dream was teaching the dreamers how to live."[4] That is, life in this middle-class, aspirational country was removed from history—no one remembers the past, everyone looks to the future—and therefore their lives are determined by narratives, tropes, and styles from popular culture. Reality follows a script.

"Some Dreamers of the Golden Dream" was originally published in 1966 as an article in the *Saturday Evening Post,* with the title "How Can I Tell Them There's Nothing Left?" The article's title is a quote from Lucille Miller at the scene of the crime, as she thinks about what she will tell her children about their father. The article partook of the "true crime" genre that was then, as it is now, in vogue. Just months before, Truman Capote's "nonfiction novel" *In Cold Blood* was published to much critical and popular acclaim. This coincidence was not lost on Dan Wakefield in his review of *Slouching Towards Bethlehem* in the *New York Times.* He noted, "Now that Truman Capote has pronounced that such work may achieve the stature of 'art,' perhaps it is possible for [Didion's writing] to be recognized as it should be: not as a better or worse example of what some people call 'mere journalism,' but as a rich display of the best prose written today in this country."[5] While the book collection elevated the work beyond "mere journalism," Didion's article appeared in the *Saturday Evening Post* with familiar journalistic attributes. The article was printed alongside a photograph of the Miller's suburban home and burned-up car.

On the magazine article's subsequent pages, Lucille Miller's wedding photo and mugshot as well as action shots from the courtroom conventionally frame the story with visual references. Yet unlike the typical true crime stories to which we've been accustomed—which focus on, in Capote's case, the complex life stories that lead up to criminal activity or, in works like the documentary podcast *Dirty John* (2017) or the documentary television series *Surviving R. Kelly* (2019), the patterns of serial offenders—Didion casts the crime of Lucille Miller as part of a larger cultural narrative of ambition, dreaming, and selfishness, a feature of the American landscape more so than a reflection of an individual psychology. The essay concludes with an iconic Didion sentence, which makes a metaphor of a fashion accessory. The man with whom Lucille was having an affair, and for whom, it was believed, she killed her husband, gets married to "his children's pretty governess, Wenche Berg." Of their wedding day, Didion writes: "The bride wore a long white *peau de soie* dress and carried a shower bouquet of sweetheart roses with stephanotis streamers.

A coronet of seed pearls held her illusion veil."[6] The "illusion veil" is, on one hand, a mere description, following Didion's careful and precise accounting of the bridal outfit. On the other hand, though, the illusion veil is metaphorical. The image concludes the essay with an ironic flourish, as the "dreamers" in the San Bernardino Valley continue to dream their golden dream, continue to live in a perpetual present where the future is full of promise and individual aspirations are felt to be individual, not the clichés that Didion points them out to be.

The illusion veil of ahistorical individual ambition is a definitive feature of neoliberal culture, in which individual drive is both an ideal of free market subjecthood and a rationale for success or failure. Attaining happiness is a sign of individual drive and determination marked by the acquisition of wealth, property, and the moving target of wellness monetized by gym memberships, spa treatments, and time away from work. Failing to achieve these goals is evidence of a personal shortcoming, a lack of entrepreneurial determination and discipline. And it is not only individual subjects who are viewed through this framework. We increasingly view inhuman structures—governments, corporations, educational institutions, multinational brands—as individuals that succeed or fail on personal terms. For example, the 2003 documentary film *The Corporation* concludes that given the history of corporate abuses of workers, consumers, and the environment, any contemporary corporation analyzed as a person would be a psychopath. While the entrepreneurial individual is venerated in neoliberal culture, that figure is also subject to critique, as in *The Corporation,* for violating the public good that, paradoxically, neoliberal reforms often turn into matters of private responsibility. By documenting and diagnosing the corporation in this way, the film uses tropes common to the "true crime" story. In true crime narratives, the moral conservatism of neoliberal culture becomes apparent, making clear that the twinned discourses of entrepreneurialism and personal responsibility serve a policing function, one that homes in on individuals while neglecting structural forces.

An iconic example of the true crime genre is the 1974 bestseller *Helter Skelter: The True Story of the Manson Murders.* In the book, Vincent Bugliosi and Curt Gentry represent Charles Manson as a master manipulator: "Manson created his own band of schizophrenics. . . . He brought to the surface their latent hatred, their inherent penchant for sadistic violence, focusing it on a common enemy, the establishment. He depersonalized the victims by making them symbols. It is easier to stab a symbol than a person."[7] Bugliosi's account emphasizes the power Manson exerted over his "family" and focuses on noirish details about Manson's cruelty and depravity, such as when he notes that "at the same time the LaBiancas were being murdered, the man who had ordered their deaths [Manson] was sipping a milk shake."[8] In another true crime best seller, *The Stranger Beside Me,* Ann Rule chronicles her own relationship with the serial killer Ted Bundy as well as the brutal murders he committed. In the book, Bundy is repeatedly flagged by both Rule and Bundy's fiancée as a suspect in a rash of disappearances and murders, yet Rule emphasizes how unlike a criminal Bundy seemed: "I could not believe he was guilty."[9] Different from Manson, whom Bugliosi and Gentry describe as projecting cultish charisma, Bundy nonetheless shares a key element with him. Both are represented as masterminds, seeking to undo the very social fabric that makes individuals feel safe. Bundy, for example is described as playing "some kind of perverse game of challenge . . . as if, each time [he abducted a woman], he would come a little further out of the shadows, take more chances, to prove that he could do what he wanted and still not be caught, or even seen."[10]

This vision of crime—as a predominantly egotistic endeavor, a kind of entrepreneurial individualism gone astray—folds neatly into both the shifts in policing and the emergence of family-values politics that have defined much of neoliberal culture. As Christopher Wilson has argued, policing has increasingly come to rely upon citizens and self-policing in the neoliberal era, which coincides with moves toward the privatization of the public sphere. Since the 1960s, we have come to view crime as a matter to be addressed through risk management, a logic that "has actually abandoned any genuinely collective (or macro) sense of a greater good" and instead privileges responsible and affluent individuals as the core constituents to whom safety is a consumer good, not a public good.[11] Moreover, American politics under neoliberalism has increasingly sought to maintain the sanctity and moral centrality of the nuclear family in American society. As Melinda Cooper has argued, "In a somewhat paradoxical fashion, private family responsibility would become the guiding principle of [neoliberal] social policy."[12] True crime books like *Helter Skelter* and *The Stranger Beside Me* function much like the antidrug public programming undertaken by the Reagan administration in the 1980s. They publicize the dangers individuals and, more importantly, individual choices pose to the neoliberal culture that nurtures that very individualized conception of social life.

This chapter will focus on how true crime narratives and our fascination with them place individual subjects in relation to structures and institutions, beginning with psychological accounts of criminality in genre-defining works. True crime is a unique documentary genre, not only because it is so ubiquitous across media forms, from television and films to prose and podcasts, but because it is a genre that so clearly engages with formulaic narrative tropes. Following an exploration of works that develop those tropes, I will explore how a contemporary writer, Maggie Nelson, and a contemporary photographer, Taryn Simon, have sought to represent crime in a way that avoids the genre tropes so common in true crime. Nelson's *The Red Parts* and Simon's *The Innocents* develop modes of interrogating the often gendered and racial types that have become concretized in true crime and have had real effects in the criminal justice system. In so doing, Nelson and Simon both build on the history of documentary experimentation since the 1960s and refine their documentary styles to emphasize not the reader- or viewer-centered moralism we usually expect from true crime but the uncertainty and open-endedness that result both from crime and from the uneven, often unjust processes of the justice system. In their documentary works, victims, criminals, and innocents are represented not as types to be grounded in the rhetoric of journalistic truth but as lives rewritten, overwritten, and exploited by crime. True crime, then, is undone by documentary aesthetics, thus staging the relation between subjective experience and the impersonal structures that give shape to contemporary experience in more complex ways.

Moral Economy

As with any genre, true crime traffics in tropes—the murderous husband, the young woman under the spell of a charismatic killer, the manipulative wife, the alienated heartthrob, and more. These tropes have been refined in a number of nonfiction bestsellers such as *Helter Skelter, The Stranger Beside Me, In Cold Blood,* Norman Mailer's *The Executioner's Song* (1979), and Joe McGinnis's *Fatal Vision* (1983), as well as on television programs such as *20/20, American Justice,* and *Forensic Files.* As Janet Malcolm influentially argued in the late 1980s, true crime journalism is particularly vulnerable to embellishment. In her account, a journalist like Joe McGinnis operates as "a kind of confidence man, preying on people's vanity, ignorance, or loneliness," and when one of his subjects is not "a ready-made literary figure," the journalist must "fashion a Raskolnikov" from an otherwise mundane person.[13] Indeed, even in her critique of true crime journalism in *The Journalist and the Murderer,* Malcolm uses the very genre tropes that she argues overdetermine the journalist-subject relation, "seduction and betrayal."[14] In true crime narrative, genre precedes reality.

Along with the character tropes and genre conceits that often preoccupy narrative accounts of crime, there are structuring principles that often ground true crime stories. In Joe McGinnis's *Fatal Vision,* for example, the author posits that the suspected, and later convicted, murderer Jeffrey MacDonald could have committed violent acts because of his use of diet pills. "With the amphetamines swelling the rage to flood tide," McGinnis asks, "would it be too much to suggest that in that one instant . . . a critical mass had been achieved . . . and that by 3:40 A.M. of February 17, 1970, the ensuing explosion of rage had destroyed not only Jeffrey MacDonald's wife and daughters, but all that he had sought to make of his life?"[15] This kind of forensic hypothesis, supported by expert testimony, offers the comfort of plausibility. It makes sense of what might otherwise seem a chaotic tragedy.

In his more recent book about Jeffrey MacDonald, *A Wilderness of Error,* Errol Morris finds holes in the prosecution's and McGinnis's case against the convicted murderer. Like Janet Malcolm, Morris sees in McGinnis a writer who chose to craft a story about "a truly demonic figure," rather than "MacDonald as an innocent man . . . not a terribly compelling figure."[16] Eschewing psychological and toxicological explanations of MacDonald's possible motivations, Morris instead is interested in the "totality of the evidence," which he staunchly believes was never properly considered because MacDonald was suspected early on in the police's investigation.[17] Yet, as one of MacDonald's lawyers, Bernard Segal, argued in court in 1979, "Physical evidence doesn't say a darn thing. . . . The only thing that is speaking is not the physical evidence, but it is the interpreter speaking. Who is the interpreter of the evidence for you?"[18] Morris's emphasis on the "totality of evidence" is demonstrated even in the design of his book on MacDonald, which features full-page line drawings of objects in between each of the book's sixty-five chapters, as well as reproductions of maps, letters, photographs, and official documents. The book was illustrated by the Pentagram design firm to further its argument. The design firm's description of that collaboration captures the significance of the illustrated objects throughout the book: "Early on in the design process, simply to create a visual inventory, the designers reduced the objects to simple line drawings. Morris was so struck with the deadpan quality of the drawings that he suggested the designers create even more, and further, . . . make them a significant visual element of the book. Reversed out of black, they seem both childlike and sinister, and serve as guideposts as Morris leads the reader through the evidence. At the same time, the simplicity of the images complements the straightforward nature of Morris's analysis."[19] As in the line drawing of the overturned coffee table at the scene of the crime (fig. 12), the illustrations throughout Morris's book offer a kind of minimalist clarity in comparison to what he describes as the "wilderness" of problems that bother him about MacDonald's trials. On one hand, Morris's *A Wilderness of Error* emphasizes how evidence can be selectively used to construct a narrative. On the other, the book relies on material evidence in its very design to emphasize the indexical power of objects and documents. This is a seeming contradiction that can be resolved if we place this book in the context of neoliberal culture. The official narrative about MacDonald's guilt is to be distrusted, as it was crafted both by institutions, the district attorney's office and the police, and an author chasing a bestselling story. Institutions, and especially government institutions, are unreliable and hostile to individual interests in our neoliberal imaginary. Instead, the mute objects and documents placed in front of the reader by Morris resonate as reliable precisely because the individual reader/viewer and the independent documentarian are the arbiters of the evidence. The "totality of evidence" can only be weighed by individuals. Thus, Morris does not solve the crime anew but merely displays alternatives and gaps, leaving a collection of objects and documents for each individual to weigh. Instead of legal decisions and procedures, we are left with a moral imperative to decide for ourselves. Dismissing true crime tropes and toxicological speculations about an individual run amok, Morris designs a narrative about the evidentiary capabilities of objects and the interpretive sway of forensic analysts. Both McGinnis's and Morris's approaches share in neoliberal conceits, through their disinterest in social systems and their individualized imaginaries. In McGinnis, the murderer is a failed individual, lacking the willpower and determination to continue living a normal domestic life, and in Morris, the individual reader and not the judicial system should be the final arbiter of justice. Neither account leaves much room, if any, for a social conception of crime and violence.

Recently, the narrative tactic of hypothetical explanation employed by McGinnis has appeared in the podcast *S Town*, produced by *This American Life* in 2017. *S Town* is an investigation into the life and death of John B. McLemore, an idiosyncratic clock restorer in rural Alabama. McLemore committed suicide, and alongside his history of discussing suicide and persistent depression, the podcast presents mercury poisoning from "fire-gilding" old clocks as a potential overarching explanation of

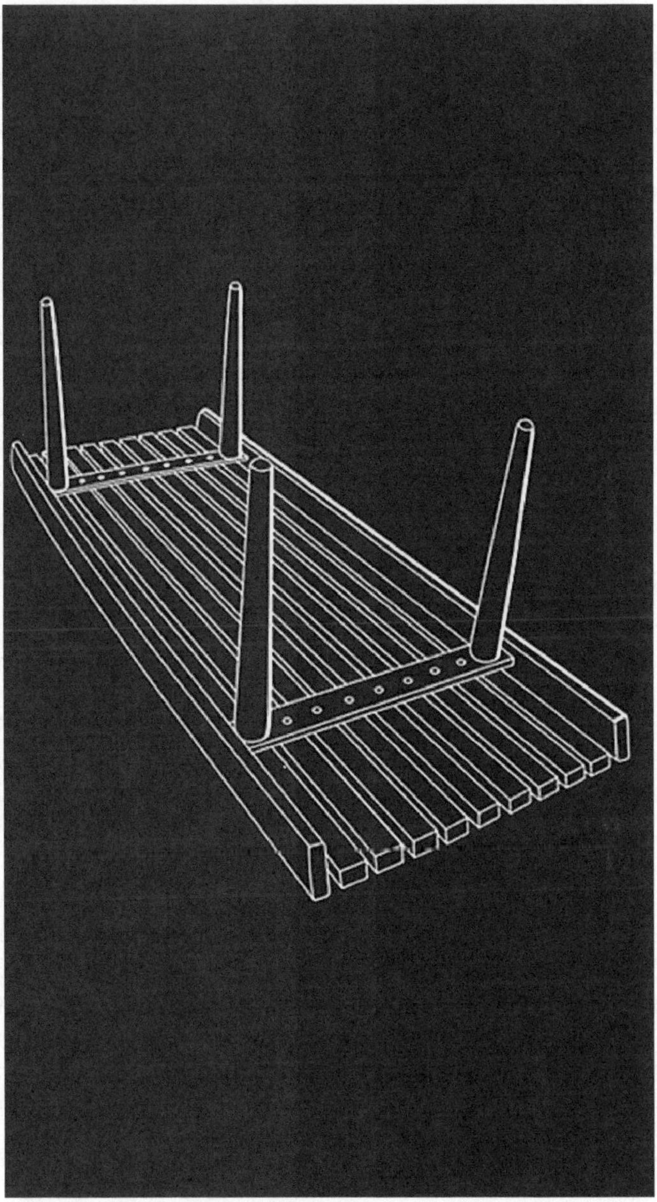

Figure 12. Illustration by Pentagram from *A Wilderness of Error: The Trials of Jeffrey Macdonald,* Errol Morris. (© 2012 by Errol Morris; used by permission of Penguin Press, an imprint of Penguin Publishing Group, a division of Penguin Random House LLC; all rights reserved)

McLemore's behavior and mental state. Similar to McGinnis's invocation of amphetamine use, *S Town*'s presentation of mercury poisoning posits narrative closure as a possibility for the reader or listener: "Doctors and scientists who are experienced in dealing with mercury, when my researcher or I have described John's fire-gilding practices, they say judging from that alone, it's almost inconceivable that he wouldn't have some level of mercury poisoning. Then when they hear about John's symptoms, the physical ones, plus the anxiety, the depression, the paranoia, the fact that he committed suicide, that all makes them even more confident that he was suffering mercury poisoning. One expert said, you'd almost have to prove that he didn't have it."[20] Whether it is mercury poisoning or amphetamine abuse, these explanations produce closure through a representation of a failed individual. The purview of the true crime story shrinks, homing in on individual choices that can serve as moral signposts.

In documentary films about crime, form follows individual closure, often with close-ups that narrow the field of vision to individual agents and the evidence that damns them. Examples of this kind of structure include the Maysles brothers iconic 1970 documentary *Gimme Shelter*, in which footage of Meredith Hunter's murder by Hell's Angel Alan Passaro during the Rolling Stones' concert at Altamont features prominently. The documentary unfolds chronologically, yet when Hunter is stabbed during the concert, the film cuts to an editing room. In the editing room, Mick Jagger asks to have the tape played back. The event of Hunter's murder is replayed in slow motion, with both Hunter's pistol and Passaro's knife pointed out. Jagger looks at the replay solemnly, saying, "So horrible." After this interlude in the editing room, the film returns to the Altamont concert, where the Rolling Stones play "Street Fighting Man" and then leave on a helicopter. Following their escape, the film cuts back to the editing room, where Jagger says "See y'all later" and gets up to leave. The film then freezes on Jagger's face and zooms in, with filmmaker David Maysles visible behind him. In her review of the film for the *New Yorker*, Pauline Kael compared *Gimme Shelter* to the Zapruder film of President John F. Kennedy's assassination and found the scenes of Jagger in the editing room to be evidence of the documentary's contrivance:

> When Mick Jagger is seen in *Gimme Shelter* pensively looking at the Altamont footage—run for him by the Maysles brothers—and wondering how it all happened, this is disingenuous movie-making. . . . *Gimme Shelter* has been shaped so as to whitewash the Rolling Stones and the film-makers for the thoughtless, careless way the

> concert was arranged, and especially for the cut-rate approach to keeping order. The Hell's Angels, known for their violence, but cheap and photogenic, were hired as guards for five hundred dollar's worth of beer. This took less time and trouble than arranging for unarmed marshals, and the Hell's Angels must have seemed the appropriate guards for Their Satanic Majesties, the Stones.[21]

Kael's critique of the film hinges on the ethical complicity of the filmmakers and musicians who, in part, created the spectacle of the Altamont concert. In the editing room close-up on Jagger's somber face, the film seems to stage that complicity, as well. The close-up and zoom-in on Jagger's face leads the viewer to look for something, an emotional response, a spontaneous reaction of some kind—he says only "So horrible" and "See y'all later," and his face is not expressive, especially in comparison to the high-energy dancing and singing during the concert footage that surrounds the editing room scenes. By focusing on Jagger as the moral center of the film, *Gimme Shelter* presents a charismatic individual as the ultimate barometer of crime, yet Jagger's impassive face offers less a way to feel about Hunter's death than a face on which to project whatever the viewer feels. The structures that led to Hunter's death—the poor planning of the event, the decision to hire Hell's Angels as security, even the rock-and-roll outlaw image of the Rolling Stones—are outside the frame.

Gimme Shelter represents crime as something to be witnessed and responded to emotionally by individuals. That focus on individual responsibility channeled through evidence is also a prominent feature of Errol Morris's 1988 documentary *The Thin Blue Line*. The film concludes with a tape recording of David Ray Harris confessing to the murder of a police officer, a crime for which Randall Adams had been convicted. On screen, the viewer sees a tape recorder playing Morris's interview with Harris:

> *Errol Morris:* Well, what do you think about whether or not he's innocent?
> *David Harris:* I'm sure he is.
> *Errol Morris:* How can you be sure?
> *David Harris:* Because I'm the one that knows.

The documentary concludes with text, explaining that Adams was, at the time, still in prison for murder (he was exonerated and released from prison in 1989, shortly after *The Thin Blue Line*'s release in 1988). The tape recorder serves as a marker of the evidentiary quality of Harris's confession yet also as a clear marker of the filmmaker's presence and role as interlocutor. Grounded in the materiality of the tape recorder, the indexical crackle of the audio recording serves to persuade the viewer of Adams's innocence and Harris's guilt, while artfully leaving open a chasm between the visual and the verbal, a space in which the viewer serves as ultimate analyst of the material presented in the film. As in our neoliberal culture and its moral economy of policing, the individual is imagined as the final arbiter of crime. Justice is left out of the hands of institutions and placed in the domain of individual subjects, neoliberalism's ideal barometer of right and wrong.

Similar to *The Thin Blue Line,* Andrew Jarecki's 2015 documentary series *The Jinx* concludes with an audio recording of Robert Durst seemingly confessing to murder while in the restroom. On the screen, the viewer sees the empty conference room where Durst was being interviewed by Jarecki, while audio and subtitles record Durst in the adjacent bathroom, muttering: "What did I do? . . . Killed them all, of course."[22] The episode concludes as the lights are turned off in the conference room, and then the credits begin to roll. Durst's bathroom recording is the documentary's final moment, left without context or analysis of any kind, yet the visual and audio disconnect of the final sequence leaves open an interpretive chasm. On one hand, the viewer is left to decide what Durst's words mean. On the other, the ambient tension in the empty conference room resonates as Jarecki's own presence as filmmaker, as the empty room he provides for the interview is the stage on which Durst's guilt is made evident. *The Jinx* concludes with both Durst's confession of guilt and a lack of analysis that leaves it to the viewer to decide guilt or innocence.

These uses of evidence—toxicological speculation, tape-recorded confessions, slow-motion and zoomed-in video—serve to ground a true crime documentary in some kind of certainty, though it is a certainty left in the audience's hands. The crime is solved, the event is made visible, the criminal is compelled to admit the crime, the individual viewer can weigh the evidence and reach a verdict. Yet this kind of closure is often at odds with how crime and violence function, as both structural conditions of exploitation that target the poor and as traumatic events that cannot be resolved or achieve closure. As Mark Seltzer has argued about true crime, media representations of crime reproduce violence as a condition of public life, a matter of statistical fact that makes bodies equivalent to other objects that circulate according to economic flows in our "pathological public sphere."[23] If the true crime genre is evidence of the ways in which documentary art has permeated popular culture, then modes of true crime documentary that resist or depart from true crime's ubiquitous tropes also demonstrate how documentary art can make crime visible as a complex structural, economic, and psychological form of discipline in neoliberal culture.

Outside Genre

In Taryn Simon's photographic project *The Innocents*, individuals who were wrongfully convicted of crimes and exonerated are photographed at sites related to the crime they didn't commit. Some subjects are photographed at the scene of the crime—a place that they may never have visited before being photographed there for this project—while others are photographed at the site where they were arrested. Simon's posed, large-format photographs give the wrongfully convicted a seeming agency, as they revisit (or visit for the first time) these sites under their own volition. They pose looking at the camera, turning the location of the portrait into a kind of stage for their presentations of self and the narrative of the crime. In her photograph of Troy Webb, for example, he stands at the scene of a sexual assault of which he was convicted and later exonerated, after serving seven years of a forty-seven-year sentence (fig. 13). In the photograph, Webb wears a suit, asserting professional, human dignity from within the muddy pine grove in which he stands. The height and number of the pine trees make him seem small, even hard to notice, in the photograph, which resonates with the series' larger conceptual argument: individuals and their actual guilt or innocence are irrelevant to the structures of criminal justice in the neoliberal United States.

The text that accompanies each photograph details the crime for which the subject was sentenced to prison, as well as information about their arrest and release. The text that accompanies Simon's photograph of Larry Mayes at the scene of his arrest, posed as he was found by the police "hiding beneath a mattress in his room" at the Royal Inn in Gary, Indiana (fig. 14), reads: "In October 1980, two assailants entered a gas station in Hammond, Indiana, threatened the clerk with a gun, demanded money, and forced her to leave with them. The victim was beaten with the gun and raped by both assailants before being released." Details of Mayes's conviction follow: "The victim identified Mayes as the smaller assailant in a photographic array, but only after failing to identify him in two live lineup procedures. At some point in this process, without the knowledge of prosecutors or defense lawyers, the victim was hypnotized. None of the fingerprints collected from the scene belonged to Mayes. Serological

Figure 13. From *The Innocents,* Taryn Simon, 2002. "Troy Webb / Scene of the crime, The Pines, / Virginia Beach, Virginia / Served 7 years of a 47-year sentence for Rape, Kidnapping and Robbery." (Courtesy of the artist)

testing was performed on semen found on the vaginal swabs and underwear collected from the victim, but the results were not useful for identification."[24] The text concludes with Mayes's account in quotes: "There's so many guys in there that are innocent but can't get a chance. They take us, put us in cages, and leave us there. You go there. The whole cell house is nothing but black dudes. It'll always be that way."

Larry Mayes served eighteen and a half years of an eighty-year sentence before being released after DNA testing exonerated him. The fifty individuals (forty-nine men, one woman) in Simon's project are given their subjecthood back through photographic portraiture. This return to civil society is balanced by the presence of the "scene of the crime" as an irreversible past, something outside of which these subjects can never step. One of the interesting conceptual turns in *The Innocents* is the revision of what the "scene of the crime" means. Instead of being a site to be analyzed by a detective—as in so many forensic procedurals today, or in true crime books that reprint maps and blueprints of crime scenes—the

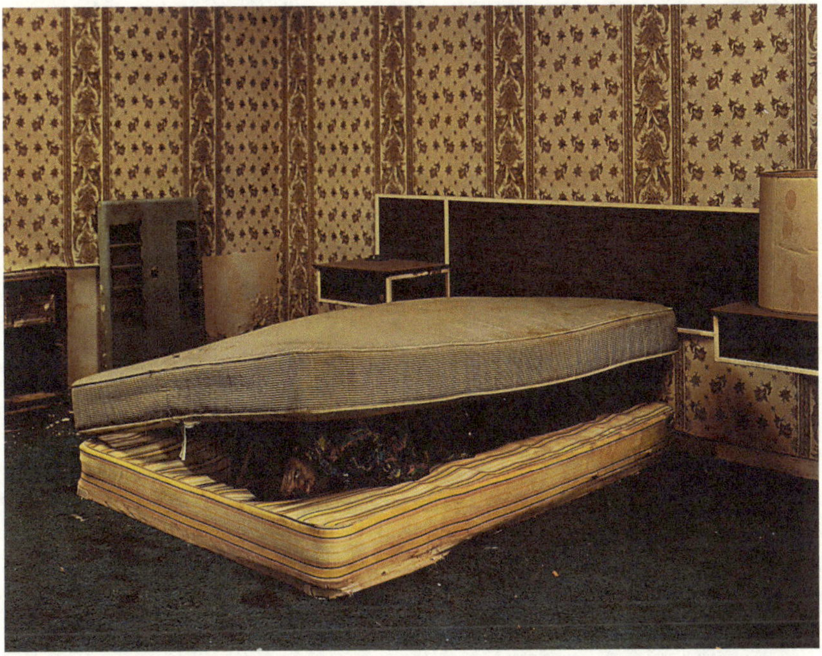

Figure 14. From *The Innocents,* Taryn Simon, 2002. "Larry Mayes / Scene of arrest, The Royal Inn, Gary, Indiana / Police found Mayes hiding beneath a mattress in this room / Served 18.5 years of an 80-year sentence for Rape, Robbery and Unlawful Deviate Conduct." (Courtesy of the artist)

scene of the crime in *The Innocents* represents both the originary crime itself, described in text, and the site of wrongful conviction and imprisonment. In *The Innocents,* the unjustly imprisoned look at you. The true crime genre's commitment to presenting evidence of guilt or innocence for the reader or viewer to judge is inverted, and its reliance on forensic technology to attain a degree of certainty is revealed to be fallible and, in most of the cases included in the project, racially biased. Our fascination with true crime narrative is made visible as a potentially, and in practice clearly, reckless impulse, one that turns innocents into victims, one that multiplies rather than resolves crime.

Simon's *The Innocents* returns to the scene of the crime, to produce a jarring juxtaposition of a violent setting with a different kind of victimized subject than is typical in true crime documentary. Similarly, Maggie Nelson's *The Red Parts* returns to a crime and revises its meanings and resonances. *The Red Parts* is a sequel of sorts. Nelson's book of experimental poetry *Jane: A Murder* deals with the murder of her aunt Jane Mixer in 1969. The murder happened before Nelson was born, and the poetry volume tries, in Nelson's own words, to account for "how one might live—how my family lived, how I lived—under the shadow of the death of a family member who had clearly died horribly and fearfully, but under circumstances that would always remain unknown, unknowable."[25] As Nelson was finishing *Jane: A Murder*, she learned that her aunt's murder case had been reopened due to new DNA tests and that an arrest was eminent. Her attempt to reach a kind of closure around unknowability is then complicated by the looming chance of knowledge, of closure through investigation and trial.

But, the memoir posits, what might this pending closure accomplish? Nelson cites a passage from D. W. Winnicott that becomes something of a conceptual framework for her thinking about the trial and conviction that occupies the bulk of the memoir:

> In one of his last psychoanalytic papers, D. W. Winnicott wrote: *Fear of breakdown is the fear of a breakdown that has already been experienced.* This statement has always been a source of great comfort to me. For years I took it to mean that the other shoe has already dropped, that you've already been to the place you fear the most, that you've already come back from it.
>
> It's only lately that I've realized that Winnicott is not suggesting that breakdowns do not recur. Now I see that he may be suggesting just the opposite: that a fear of breakdown in our past may be precisely what causes it to repeat in our future.[26]

This shift from a future-oriented to a past-oriented understanding of breakdown, from a sense that breakdowns have been overcome and therefore exist as specters to a sense that breakdowns repeat rather than resolve, moves the trial away from a sense of impending closure and to a sense of recurrence, repetition, and continued revisitation.

Nelson explicitly rejects the idea that justice can provide some kind of closure, and she does so by making clear that the closure offered by justice promises an impossible synthesis of the viscerally passionate and the idealistic:

> I find the grammar of justice maddening. It's always "rendered," "served," or "done." It always swoops down from on high—from God, from the state—like a bolt of lightning, a flaming sword come to separate the righteous from the wicked in Earth's final hour. It

> is not, apparently, something we can give to one other, something we can make happen, something we can create together down here in the muck. The problem may also lie in the word itself, as for millennia "justice" has meant both "retribution" and "equality," as if a gaping chasm did not separate the two.[27]

Another way of describing this "chasm" within justice is to say that the narrative conceits of true crime trade on retribution, and they do so precisely by undoing equality through the use of conventional genre tropes.

When she is being interviewed for the pulpy TV program *48 Hours Mystery* about her aunt's murder and the 2005 trial, Nelson is told by the TV interviewer that she doesn't need makeup: "They wouldn't be filming me if I didn't look good. . . . *This is primetime,* she winks. *No black people, no bad teeth.*"[28] Nelson is taken aback by this, and questions what she is doing talking to this TV program: "Am I sitting here so that Jane Mixer can join JonBenét Ramsey, Elizabeth Smart, Laci Peterson, Chandra Levy, Natalee Holloway, in the dead-white-girl-of-the-week club? . . . I'm sitting here because I wanted—I still want—Jane's life to 'matter.' But I don't want it to matter more than others."[29] This shift from the singular to the collective, to an individual life mattering as a way for all lives to matter equally, marks a kind of chasm, one that is linked to the difference between justice as retribution and justice as equality. The goal of justice as equality is to ensure that everyone cares for all, that those harmed have a way, however undefined, of "mattering." Nelson strives to balance that equality with a recognition of real harm, and it becomes a question about her motive as a writer offering a true crime narrative of her own:

> Am I sitting here now, in Los Angeles, writing all this down, because I want *my* life to matter? Maybe so. But I don't want it to matter more than others.
>
> I want to remember, or to learn, how to live as if it matters, as if they all matter, even if they don't.[30]

Nelson's revision from "remembering" to "learning" how life matters returns to Winnicott's understanding of breakdowns. An understanding of equality entails a breakdown of sorts, a breaking down of the narrative structures that present crime and justice to us. A breakdown that removes us from the reality of our culture—where some lives matter and some don't—to an equal world where systemic oppression and exploitation don't turn the ideal of blind justice into a tool for unequal retribution and the extraction of profits.

Nelson's invocation of photographs relates to this insofar as she denies sensationalism. Throughout the memoir, Nelson includes italicized descriptions of photographs presented as evidence during the trial rather than including the actual photographs. These text descriptions serve to distance the reader from the images, just as Nelson and her family struggle with whether or not to look at the crime scene and autopsy photographs as they are projected in the courtroom. After being advised that they might not want to view a particularly gruesome photograph of Jane's body in the coroner's office, Nelson serves as a lookout for her mother, who turns her head and closes her eyes:

> Each time an image appears I look at it quickly, opening and closing my eyes like a shutter. Then I look a little longer, in increments, until my eyes can stay open. I know the image will stay on the screen for some time, until the attorneys and their witnesses have said everything about it that needs to be said. So there's no rush. You can acclimate to it slowly. And the thing is, you do acclimate.
>
> *Well?* my mother whispers from her bent-over pose.
>
> *It's not so bad,* I whisper back, *but you might as well not look.*[31]

Nelson's detailed description of both the forensic photographs and her viewing of those photographs offers a kind of depletion of affect, a flatness that counters the righteous retribution and comeuppance tropes of true crime.

This flat idealism, coupled with the chasm that separates it from our genre-soaked reality, is made apparent in the memoir's coda. It concludes with two funeral home viewings—Nelson's mother recounts viewing Jane's body, and Nelson herself remembers viewing her father's body after his death. Nelson's mother finds the funeral home viewing of Jane in 1969 to be jarring: "By the time she saw her sister at the funeral home Jane didn't look like herself. She had that strange, bloated, alien look of the several-days dead." Yet the autopsy photos that she sees in 2005 have a different effect on her: "But in this photo, taken within hours of her murder, she recognizes [Jane]. Even with the dark bullet holes, even with her hair matted with wet and dried blood, even with the stocking buried unutterably deeply in her neck, she recognizes her. She says she is glad to see her again. She says she is glad to see, finally, what was done."[32] Nelson then concludes the memoir with an account of viewing her father's body before it is cremated: "He was wearing his glasses, which seemed right but odd, as I knew he did not need them anymore. His hands were folded on his chest and his fingers were dark purple at the tips. He looked like he was trying to keep a straight face, but was about to jump up and call the whole thing off. *I am immortal until proven not!* I looked at him long enough to be sure this was not the case. Then I told him I loved him, kissed his face, and walked out of the room."[33] This moment seems like closure, but it is more like preservation. Her father's own words—"I am immoral until proven not!"—remain somewhat ambiguous here. Nelson is "sure this was not the case," yet it's not clear if she's sure he's not immortal or sure that his immortality hasn't been disproven. Similarly, Nelson's mother is "glad to see [Jane] again," over thirty years after her murder. The memoir's title itself, *The Red Parts,* refers to red letter editions of the Bible, in which the words spoken by Jesus during his life are printed in red. Nelson's memoir uses italics, not red type, yet also presents the dead as still visible, still around, parallel to the photographs that are presented in court that conjure the dead back into our vision. The breakdowns that we fear, *The Red Parts* seems to posit, are also the breakdowns that allow us to see what equality might look like, in both death and life. Nelson's mother opens all of the windows in the house, Nelson leaves her father's body to re-enter the world. The breakdown of the distinction between death and life makes it apparent that the justice system cannot provide closure, cannot make wrongs right. Significantly, the initial charge brought against Jane's soon-to-be convicted murderer is "open murder." Nelson writes, "It means, essentially, murder without a story." The lack of a story makes the trial and Gary Leiterman's sentencing seem less like retribution and more like a reckoning of facts. As Nelson notes, "The incoherence of the act, the suffering it caused—these things are not negotiable."[34] And this, ultimately, is what makes Nelson's memoir interesting as a work in the documentary aesthetic. It avoids sentimentality in its presentation of violence and suffering as "not negotiable," and in so doing, Nelson's own understanding of the trial—rather than that of the detectives, the lawyers, true crime television, even the court system—emphasizes the process as abstract, impersonal where the murderer is concerned. All things equal, suffering is not negotiable, and "the dead are the dead. Presumably they have finished with their wanting."[35] *The Red Parts* strives to make the trial both intensely personal and abstract, both about Jane Mixer and not at all about Jane and her family.[36]

In *The Beauty of a Social Problem,* Walter Benn Michaels notes that art strives to make clear the distance between its form and reality, thus making the difference between our feelings about something and the thing itself clear. In his reading of Nelson's experimental work of poetry about her aunt, *Jane: A Murder,* Michaels argues that Nelson attempts to achieve a kind of aesthetic perfection, one that renders Jane a formal device rather than a person about whom we might have feelings. This is, he argues, a conceptual way of thinking about how "the cultural moment of increasing equality has been a financial moment of increasing inequality," as Jane comes to matter as a contemporary work of art rather than a person who can represent the feminist past.[37] In light of this, *The Red Parts* signals an attempt to reconcile aesthetic distance with the immanence of the artist, writer, and subject in the systems and structures of which art strives to gain some distant view. In Simon's photographs and Nelson's memoir, crime connects us to the world and to the systems of exploitation that determine us. Rather than occupy a negative relation to the world, these works engage it and produce in its materials something like survival. These works imagine survival within compromised conditions, the desire for a viewer and a reader, the marking of time spent, the making out of the past a reason to act differently in the present, not because of yourself, but because and in spite of the structures that make yourself meaningful. These works make apparent the relation of subject to structure, in ways that foreground how structures that promise closure oppress and exploit.

In our contemporary moment, it is becoming ever more pressing to realize how tropes around crime in the United States reinforce and affirm structural racism and exploitation. As Patrisse Khan-Cullors and asha bandele posit in *When They Call You a Terrorist: A Black Lives Matter Memoir,* the experience of growing up black in the United States feels like living in "a world we did not make and did not know we had the power to unmake."[38] Realizing that the world can be unmade entails realizing that "the service we have offered to people, systems, and structures that did not love, respect or honor us" can be withheld or redirected, in ways that produce not more exploitation but a revision of belonging in the world.[39]

5 / Speculative Ecology

As the last chapter demonstrated, works in the documentary aesthetic can complicate an individualized understanding of life, morality, crime, and even death in our neoliberal culture. In this chapter, I focus on how documentary works can reorient our understanding of time, in ways that can make different relations to the environment possible. For example, the conceptual artist Hans Haacke's 1975 work *On Social Grease* is a series of photoengraved magnesium plates. Each plate reproduces a statement about supporting the arts from a corporate executive or U.S. politician who sits on the board of a major museum or cultural institution. The plaques document the way in which art is a social asset for petroleum corporations, a way to embed oil into everyday life not through the pump but through the more rarefied air of the art museum. The work's title is a play on how art is used by corporate interests as a way to ease the opening up of new markets, especially in urban centers. One plaque, in particular, uses the overt metaphor of "lubrication" to connect fossil fuels with markets (fig. 15):

> EXXON's support of the arts serves the arts as a social lubricant.
> And if business is to continue in big cities, it needs a more lubricated environment.[1]

This vision of smooth circulation, perhaps with undertones of sexual intercourse between Exxon and "the arts," implies that oil is both the medium through which we view works of art and the environment in which economic relations take place. That is, our fossil fuel economy is imagined

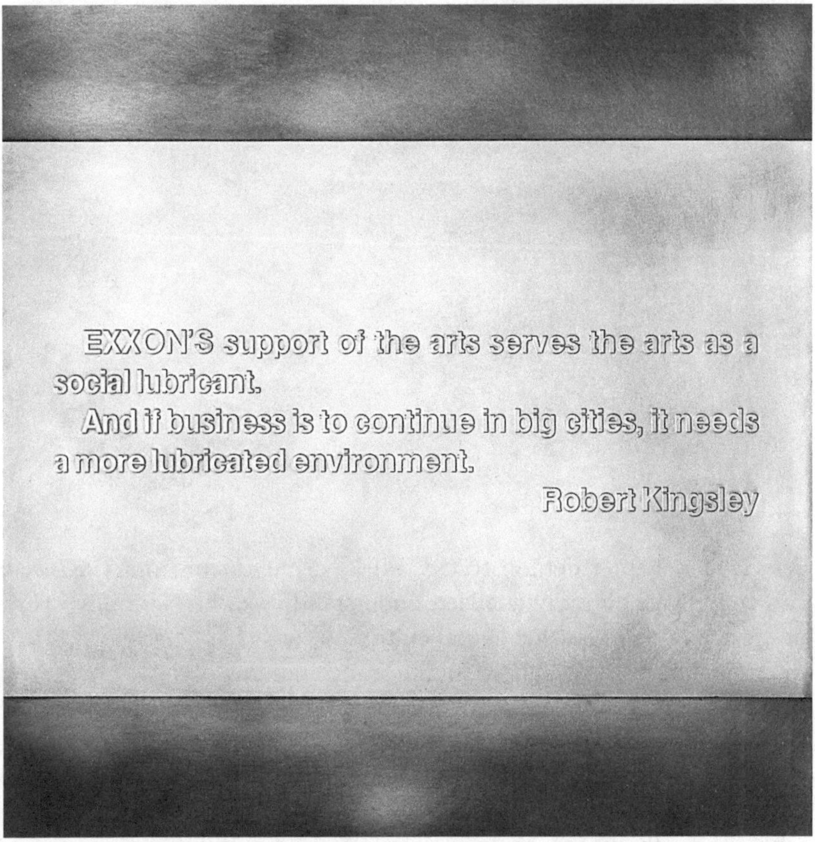

Figure 15. Detail from *On Social Grease*, Hans Haacke, 1975. Six photo-engraved magnesium plates mounted on aluminum, 76 × 76 cm each. (Photo: Walter Russell; © Hans Haacke/Artists Rights Society (ARS), New York/VG Bild-Kunst, Bonn; courtesy of the artist and Paula Cooper Gallery, New York)

here as constituting the horizon of aesthetic and economic activity. The metal plaque's appearance as a kind of permanent marker also gestures toward a possible future where this sentiment has become historical. The plaque functions as a future memorial to days past, even as it documents the present.

Taking this plaque as a starting point, this chapter will explore how documentary works like Haacke's have seized upon the intertwinement of nature and culture as a site of contestation in finance capitalism and the expansive time of environmental crisis that has accompanied it. If the coming struggles, as Joshua Clover has argued, are going to be about circulation within finance capitalism, then the ways of life and visions of futurity premised on a future of plentiful oil, of smooth circulation, provide a place to raise questions, to form resistance, to make more viscous the "lubricated environment" that allows for the uneven distribution of food, housing, and clothes.[2] As climate change produces a more erratic environment, the modes of circulation that have defined wealthy and even middle-class existence under neoliberalism must be transformed, and our global reliance on extractive resources must transition to other modes. Documentary art can both make visible the exploitative nature of our relation to the environment and posit speculative paths forward, beyond neoliberal "fixes" to climate change that would not change the exploitative structure of fossil-fueled life but merely afford an increasingly privatized zone of energy-dependent comfort for those who can afford it. In focusing on documentary forms about the environment, this chapter aims to account for how works in the documentary aesthetic approach, on one hand, the economic and ecological reality of climate change and, on the other hand, the possibility of imagining a future beyond our current economic regime's reliance on fossil fuels.[3]

Like most of the previous chapters, this one begins with a documentary text published during the period of neoliberal culture's emergence, in this case Rachel Carson's 1962 *Silent Spring.* Carson provided a speculative approach to environmentalism that became a template for future environmentalist documentaries, just as her work was also distilled into a set of positions that allowed neoliberal policies to adopt the rhetoric of environmentalism without advocating for the necessary changes to exploitative structures that have led to our current environmental crises. Carson's work of literary nonfiction straddles the New Deal era of programmatic documentary and the 1960s era of the documentary aesthetic. The book is often celebrated for its legislative effect. As is frequently noted, Carson's book documenting the harmful effects of DDT and other pesticides was central to the creation of the Environmental Protection Agency by executive order of Richard Nixon in 1970 and the nationwide ban on the use of DDT in 1972. The immediate reception of *Silent Spring* as a pressing work of activist documentary has just as much to do with the work's speculative imaginings as it does with its more traditional journalistic content. Though primarily lauded as the origin point of modern environmental legislation, *Silent Spring* is part of a larger trajectory in Carson's documentary writings about nature, one that is concerned not just with regulating chemicals like DDT but also with a broader reorientation of our relation to the environment in a way that can make visible, and therefore allow us to begin to think of alternatives to, the structural conditions of environmental harm that have led to the crisis of climate change. Carson's prose blends nature writing, science writing, investigative reporting, and lyrical imagining into a mode that I will describe as speculative documentary. This mode blends traditional documentary modes with visions of economic and environmental futures, both to emphasize the "slow violence" of pollution and climate change and to ground that violence and its long-term effects in our everyday lives.[4]

Silent Spring consolidates New Deal–era documentary forms aimed at a broad public with a more speculative imaginary emergent in Carson's earlier writings. Carson's lyrical prose represents both the vast network of marine ecology, from the shorelines to the deepest reaches of the sea floor, and the effects of seemingly mundane chemicals like DDT. In her writings about the ocean, ecological networks, and human-made toxins, Carson articulated and popularized a mode of speculative documentary suited to grappling with environmental problems, and especially with climate change, by making available a conception of the world in which ecological systems are estranged from and even unrecognizable to the humans who inhabit them. By undoing the familiarity of nature as a stable other to culture, Carson produces a documentary account capable of projecting the future from present-day actions and thus advocating for changes to behaviors that otherwise slowly, and perhaps invisibly, lead to catastrophe. This method has become central to environmentalist documentary. For example, Al Gore's award-winning account of climate change *An Inconvenient Truth* (2006) opens with a speculative invitation to readers: "Imagine with me now that . . . we have the chance to use our moral imaginations and to project ourselves across the expanse of time, 17 years into the future, and share a brief conversation with our children and grandchildren as they are living their lives in the year 2023."[5] This kind of speculative imagining is necessary to make climate change and other environmental problems visible. Carson's synthesis of nature writing, science writing, investigative journalism, and imaginations of the future initiated a mode within the documentary aesthetic capable of representing climate change, environmental harm, and the necessity of environmental activism in the late twentieth and early twenty-first centuries. Only through speculation about the future can environmentalist documentaries present climate change and other forms of environmental crisis as immediate problems.

Speculative Documentary

Silent Spring is about the proliferation of pesticide spraying programs after World War II. Documenting DDT and other pesticides' effects on water, soil, plants, fish, birds, and mammals (including humans), *Silent Spring* is written in a lyrical yet journalistic style, intertwining scientific data, industry history, and information about spraying programs with reflections about nature's importance, anecdotes about victims of pesticide toxicity, and apocalyptic imaginings of a world forever poisoned. As Gary Kroll has noted, *Silent Spring* is not a singular text but a "polysemous" one, appearing in multiple forms, from its initial magazine publication to its publication as a book and distribution through the Book of the Month Club.[6] Moreover, Carson's reportage on pesticides followed and relied upon earlier reports doubting DDT's safety. Employed by the U.S. Fish and Wildlife Service, Carson herself had written press releases warning fish-processing plants about DDT's toxicity in 1945 and 1946.[7] *Silent Spring*'s publication as a book, then, was part of a longer progression of reportage and dissemination, less a singular text than a process that could then be consolidated around a concrete object and through a cohering documentary style. Following the book's publication, Carson's account of pesticides would be disseminated even further through television and government documents, including, in 1963, an episode of the news program *CBS Reports* and a report on pesticides from President Kennedy's Science Advisory Committee.

Even before *Silent Spring* was published by Houghton Mifflin, Carson's writing was defining and propelling the environmentalist movement forward in the 1960s. As Rob Nixon, Rachel Carson Professor at the University of Wisconsin, Madison, noted in an editorial, *Silent Spring* and its reception had a sobering effect, a double-sided sense of both the possibilities for environmental change and its limits: "We can seldom expect outright environmental victories, just indispensable, heroic holding actions, in which writers of conscience—as interpreters and witnesses—have a vital role to play. Sure, Carson didn't live to see the Clean Water Act of 1972 and the Safe Drinking Water Act of 1974 that her writings helped inspire. But she also didn't live to see U.S. Vice President Dick Cheney, a former Halliburton chief executive, chair the energy task force that resulted in the 2005 bill exempting high-risk hydraulic fracturing (fracking) from the requirements of those same two acts."[8] As Nixon points out, celebrations of *Silent Spring*'s legislative impact can occlude the persistent and worsening problems of environmental pollution and escalating climate change, let alone legislative mandates that have undone or bypassed the regulations *Silent Spring* helped to put in place. Thinking of *Silent Spring* as speculative documentary, though, allows one to find in the book both an activist argument about government legislation and also a vision of the environment that foregrounds exploitation and its long-term effects, a recognition of the slow accumulation of damage and toxicity that cannot be fully repaired by regulatory triumphs. In this way, *Silent Spring* makes available both an activist orientation toward the state and corporations and a broader perspective that can reckon with a past and future that does not contain those entities. *Silent Spring*'s documentary aesthetic is both practical in its demands for legislative reform and speculative in its positing of a time before and after late capitalism.

Involvement in governmental reports was not new for Carson, who had worked for almost ten years for the U.S. Fish and Wildlife Service, where she "wrote pamphlets and press releases, and edited scientific papers generated by other Fish and Wildlife staff."[9] Owing to Carson's experience and the role her writings played in legislation, her work clearly partakes in and is an important late part of the tradition of government-sponsored documentary forms associated largely with the New Deal. These documentaries, like Pare Lorenz's film *The River* (1938), tend to celebrate technology, government, and humanity's ability to reshape the environment for the better. What makes Carson's work distinct from those government-sponsored, often sentimentally humanist forms, though, is her twinned focus on legislative action and the vast temporal sweep of ecology that displaces human society as central to the world. This ecological framework is evident in *Silent Spring,* but it was crafted and refined in Carson's earlier books about ocean ecology. These earlier ocean books—*Under the Sea-Wind* (1941), *The Sea Around Us* (1951), and *The Edge of the Sea* (1955)—engage in a hybrid documentary form much like *Silent Spring,* though they are descriptive rather than activist in their ultimate intent.[10] While rooted in federal patronage of oceanography and her own experiences working for the U.S. Fish and Wildlife Service, Carson's ocean writings importantly speculate as much as they report and disseminate scientific information.[11] As Philip Cafaro claims about Carson's first book, *Under the Sea-Wind,* she combines "an imaginative, phenomenological exploration of other consciousnesses with the latest researches in scientific natural history."[12] It is this imagining of other consciousnesses, such as *Under the Sea-Wind*'s character Scomber the Mackerel, coupled with her lyrical passages about deep time that produce a speculative documentary form, one that remains key to environmentalist documentary writing and film today.

Through her blend of science and nature writing with speculative imagining about the futures of an increasingly over-fished and toxic ocean, Carson's books often produce a sense of a doomed future. Indeed, in the 1952 documentary film adaptation of Carson's *The Sea Around Us,* written and directed by Irwin Allen, who would later make the successful disaster films *The Poseidon Adventure* (1972) and *The Towering Inferno* (1974), a series of Technicolor scenes of glaciers shedding ice into the ocean concludes the film on an ominous note about temperatures rising across the globe and the concomitant rise of ocean levels. The film concludes with the phrase "The End?," presaging both Allen's future career in disaster films and Carson's sublime approach to nature. Kroll notes that Carson was disappointed with Allen's adaptation of her book, and he cites a letter in which Carson wishes that the film version of *The Sea Around Us* had been made with the "beauty, the dignity, and the impressiveness of the Pare Lorenz script for *The River.*"[13] Pare Lorenz's New Deal documentary *The River* concludes with an account of how the Tennessee Valley Authority and the Farm Security Administration are improving farmland and restoring rivers, optimistically stating, "We had the power to take the valley apart—we have the power to put it together again." Though Carson was unhappy with it as a film adaptation, Allen's *The Sea Around Us* nonetheless captures, in its ominous conclusion's warning of environmental catastrophe, the way in which Carson presents a longer view than Lorenz's documentary, one that emphasizes not the rehabilitation of society but its ultimate and inevitable collapse. Rather than engaging in a sentimental humanist account of social flourishing and the renewed control of nature, as we see in *The River,* Carson offers, through speculation, a longer view of the environment over time that does not depend on human institutions.

Gesturing not to a hopeful future occasioned by liberalism but instead to a disastrous future facilitated by human interference with ecological systems, Carson's approach to the environment speculates about our apocalyptic future and in so doing challenges the public to imagine alternatives to their seemingly mundane activities. Indeed, Allen's 1961 science fiction film *Voyage to the Bottom of the Sea* would hinge on a giant fire in the sky that threatens to extinguish all life on Earth by raising the planet's temperature. Featuring crumbling glaciers and nuclear warheads, *Voyage to the Bottom of the Sea* dramatizes, in the guise of an adventure story, the kinds of apocalyptic visions lyrically and presciently documented in

Carson's writings about warming oceans and toxic environments.[14] Carson's prose trades in a kind of sensational imagining similar to Allen's, and it is only through that speculation that she is able to begin to describe the larger consequences of climate change.

As Michael Schudson states in his influential *Discovering the News,* literary journalism of the 1960s often took on a subjective, challenging tone in order to make visible what might otherwise be obscured by the "standard of objectivity" in print journalism.[15] Carson's contribution to this subversive, critical tradition in literary nonfiction is the synthesis of nature writing, lyrical reflection, and speculative representations of the future. Moving from ecosystems to pesticide production, Carson documents nature as a function of economic, oceanic, and biological processes rather than a static end in itself to be conserved and celebrated. *Silent Spring* takes part in both the traditions Schudson ascribes to critical journalism of the 1960s—"a literary tradition and a muckraking tradition."[16] At once investigative and speculative, Carson's prose blends a distinctively imaginative style with investigative strategies, including endnotes to support *Silent Spring*'s claims. This synthesis of the investigative and the speculative can be traced through Carson's own career, and it has led to a wide swath of speculative documentaries that seek to make visible environmental damage, the climate change crisis, and the need for largescale environmentalist reform.

In an influential essay that helped to define the shift from ecocriticism to what is commonly referred to now as the environmental humanities, Lawrence Buell claims that "contemporary toxic discourse effectively starts with *Silent Spring.*"[17] Moving beyond romantic notions of nature as separate from human activity, toxic discourse, in Buell's argument, "insists on the interdependence of ecocentric and anthropocentric values. It underscores the point that environmentalism must make concerns for human and social health more central and salient than it traditionally has if it is to thrive, perhaps even to survive."[18] However, in her *Sense of Place and Sense of Planet,* Ursula K. Heise notes that the discourse of toxicity often replicates what it purportedly disavows, "the fundamentally pastoral vision of ecology . . . a vision that understands ecological systems as harmonious and balanced networks and that sees nature as self-regenerating if left on its own."[19] Moving beyond this pastoral vision has proven difficult, and Heise argues in a later essay that science fiction is one site where ecology has been thought of as thoroughly enmeshed with human culture, as part of a global network that cannot be nostalgically bracketed off from late capitalism. As Heise asserts, modern environmentalism must imagine "a human society that will live its future life in Martian ecologies, no matter the planet."[20]

What Carson offers, even in her early writings on the ocean, is a blend of what Buell describes as toxic discourse and what Heise describes as imaginative representations of ecology as part of a global network. Carson is not nostalgic for pristine nature but instead imagines ecology as in a constant, yet slow, state of change and flow. In *The Sea Around Us,* Carson describes the sea as both one entity and not an entity at all but movement: "There is, then, no water that is wholly of the Pacific, or wholly of the Atlantic, or of the Indian or the Antarctic. The surf that we find exhilarating at Virginia Beach or at La Jolla today may have lapped at the base of antarctic icebergs or sparkled in the Mediterranean sun, years ago, before it moved through dark and unseen waterways to the place we find it now. It is by the deep, hidden currents that the oceans are made one."[21] Carson's network thinking—her emphasis on the fluidity of the ocean over our geographical boundaries—casts the ocean as fluid and porous, as something that undoes the names that describe it once one looks at water itself. That is, the ocean, and ecology more broadly, presents the nonfiction writer with a representational dilemma. Traditional nomenclature fails to capture the reality of the ocean, and Carson's speculative documentary prose aims to represent the "deep, hidden currents" otherwise obscured.

In *Under the Sea-Wind,* Carson describes writing about the ocean precisely as such:

> In planning this book I was confronted at the very outset with the problem of a central character. It soon became evident that there was no single animal—bird, fish, mammal, or any of the sea's lesser creatures—that could live in all the various parts of the sea I proposed to describe. That problem was instantly solved, however, when I realized that the sea itself must be the central character whether I wished it or not; for the sense of the sea, holding the power of life and death over every one of its creatures from the smallest to the largest, would inevitably pervade every page.[22]

Carson's central character, then, is a vast ecological network, one that makes human society seem temporary, yet also one that requires representation through a human framework, characterization. What Carson's prose stages and what allows her to engage in the various tropes and imaginings of *Silent Spring* is a dialectic representation of nature, as both other to human society and as the network on which human society is based. Toxicity and equilibrium, ultimately, are synthesized in Carson's view, as ecological systems were never stable entities in the first place but only in balance in a very short temporal view. This understanding of ecology engages in the documentary aesthetic by attempting to represent what cannot be directly observed or documented.

The Nature of *Silent Spring*

Like many of her earlier works about marine life and ocean ecology, Carson's *Silent Spring* was initially published in the *New Yorker,* a venue best known for its "smart" commentary on urban life. On the surface, Carson's writings seem at odds with the *New Yorker*'s editorial focus, yet as Jamin Creed Rowan has argued, Carson's ecological writings mirrored the magazine's understanding of the city as a network. Comparing Carson's prose to Jane Jacobs's writing about the city, Rowan demonstrates how "like the community of sea creatures Carson describes at sea's edge, the pedestrians on Hudson Street compose a deeply interconnected yet anonymous social web."[23] While her earlier works might, on first glance, fit within the tradition of nature writing continuous from nineteenth-century nonfiction such as Henry David Thoreau's *Walden* (1854), works which find in the natural world an escape and difference from culture, Carson's writing also makes clear how nature writing is, and always was, just as much about nature's intertwinement with culture as it is about drawing a stark dichotomy between the cultural and the natural. Carson's ecological networks mirror the urban flows of the postwar city, entailing, in the worst-case scenario, the naturalization of exploitative structures and, in the best-case scenario, the decentering of normalized hierarchies. In *Silent Spring,* especially, this enlarged vision of nature as culture is necessary, for only through that lens can one begin to understand the permanent, long-term, largescale effects of pesticide toxicity.

From *Silent Spring*'s title and its opening chapter, "A Fable for Tomorrow," Carson begins her record of increased organic pesticide use in the United States and its harmful effects on plants, animals, water supplies, and soil with a vision of future apocalypse. Like many works of environmentalist documentary to follow it, *Silent Spring* begins not with facts or experience but with speculation, a narrative about a before—"There was once a town in the heart of America where all life seemed to live in harmony with its surroundings"—and an after—"Then a strange blight crept over the area and everything began to change. . . . On the mornings that had once throbbed with the dawn chorus of robins, catbirds, doves, jays, wrens, and scores of other bird voices there was now no sound; only silence lay over the fields and woods and marsh."[24] Borrowing a familiar trope from *The Communist Manifesto,* Carson then concludes the first chapter of *Silent Spring* with a claim about what her documentary prose will make available as knowledge: "A grim specter has crept upon us almost unnoticed, and this imagined tragedy may easily become a stark reality we all shall know."[25]

Carson figures this possible "stark reality" in two temporal registers—the slow time of pollution, which results in small changes to the ecosystem that, compounded, become disastrous, and the immediate, catastrophic event. As she writes, "The full maturing of whatever seeds of malignancy have been sown by these chemicals is yet to come."[26] In this view toxicity is hidden until catastrophic—"an irreversible malignancy will slumber long and undetected until finally—its cause long forgotten and even unsuspected—it flares into the open as recognizable cancer"[27]; but Carson also documents more immediate, noticeable effects of toxicity. The central reference point for this is the death of songbirds, which is invoked in the book's fictionalized first chapter only to be returned to, as fact and not as fiction, in chapter eight: "Over increasingly large areas of the United States, spring now comes unheralded by the return of the birds, and the early mornings are strangely silent where once they were filled with the beauty of bird song. This sudden silencing of the song of birds, this obliteration of the color and beauty and interest they lend to our world have come about swiftly, insidiously, and unnoticed by those whose communities are as yet unaffected."[28] This alliterative "sudden silencing of the song of birds" echoes *Silent Spring*'s title, shushing through prose the silencing occasioned by DDT.

While Carson figures natural cycles and equilibrium as persistent and as inevitably returning after a disruption such as the use of DDT, *Silent Spring* also chronicles the irreversibility of some pollution and toxicity, the ways in which "the living world was shattered."[29] In the book's concluding chapter, "The Other Road," Carson argues that in forests, "with a minimum of help and a maximum of noninterference from man, Nature can have her way, setting up all that wonderful and intricate system of checks and balances that protects the forest from undue damage by insects."[30] In this contradiction—between nature as irreversibly damaged and nature as always striving to an equilibrium—lies Carson's conception of nature. At once beyond human interference and completely determined by human activity, nature in *Silent Spring* is a marker of an other to human culture and a figure for human culture's growing reliance on the manipulation and production of the natural world as a source of revenue.

Carson's images of apocalypse and deep time, of the inevitable washing away of human society, coupled with her representation of the irreversible changes human society has contributed to the environment, stages this dialectical approach to ecology, one in which humans are both temporary and permanent agents among other organic and inorganic entities in the environment, never certain about their place in a fluid system.

The permanent harm done by humans is rendered clear when Carson casts an everyday object as saturated with foreign toxins: "The common salad bowl may easily present a combination of organic phosphate insecticides. Residues well within the legally permissible limits may interact."[31] Carson then projects, through the toxic salad bowl, an apocalyptic vision of the environment:

> The world of systemic insecticides is a weird world, surpassing the imaginings of the brothers Grimm—perhaps most closely akin to the cartoon world of Charles Addams. It is a world where the enchanted forest of the fairy tales has become the poisonous forest in which an insect that chews a leaf or sucks the sap of a plant is doomed. It is a world where a flea bites a dog, and dies because the dog's blood has been made poisonous, where an insect may die from vapors emanating from a plant it has never touched, where a bee may carry poisonous nectar back to its hive and presently produce poisonous honey.[32]

Carson's representation of the "slow violence" of environmental degradation and displacement is punctuated by these moments of everyday toxicity, of sudden death and contamination.[33]

In his reading of the 1963 episode of *CBS Reports* titled "The Silent Spring of Rachel Carson," which gave Carson's warnings about pesticides an even broader audience, Finis Dunaway argues that the media spectacle produced around *Silent Spring*, similar to other media coverage of environmental problems such as nuclear testing, pollution, and climate change, "narrowed the scope of *Silent Spring* to single out DDT as the nation's sole pesticide danger. The repeated emphasis on DDT, while lending legitimacy to the ban, also worked to marginalize systemic critiques of industrial agriculture and the increasing reliance on pesticides."[34] The reduction of Carson's critique to DDT bypasses her larger ecological framework, in which DDT is merely one example of human society's slow violence, and in which human society is temporary, destined to be washed away. This perspective lends itself less to environmental policy than to science fiction, and this is perhaps why *Silent Spring*'s speculative vision of apocalypse is followed up with chapters and endnotes about the present, not the future. Carson's careful documentation and citation practices in *Silent Spring* are evidence of a pragmatic concern—that her documentary project will be received as merely speculative rather than founded on scientific evidence and principles. As Mark McGurl has noted, deep time lends itself to genre fiction, and especially science fiction and horror, for unlike literary realism, genre fiction is "willing to risk artistic ludicrousness in their representation of the inhumanly large and long."[35] This is, in part, evident in *Silent Spring,* and countered in the text by endnotes and citations. What makes *Silent Spring* unique, in this instance, is its dialectical staging of what McGurl refers to as a the "posthuman comedy" of deep time, in which human society is rendered absurd by the cosmos' grand history and the stasis and silence of postwar America. Carson's speculative documentary imagines an important shift from everyday life in the present to the future that our economic and social systems are making, thus grounding the time travel of speculative documentary in empirical data about everyday life in the present.

Silent Spring argues for a more mindful use of science in pest control, while also emphasizing how ecology is a vast system that exceeds human society. In *Silent Spring,* Carson traces how her ecosystem thinking, emergent alongside urban planning ideologies that would be appropriated into fantasies of organic synthesis between work and life, can produce not a sense of organic equilibrium but a recognition of dynamism, change, and political responsibility.[36] Prefiguring the ecological theories of thinkers such as Timothy Morton, *Silent Spring* denies nature's status as ontologically distinct from culture and politics.[37] Even more than this, though, Carson's mode of speculative documentary positions the speculative documentation of the future as central to environmental activism.

This imperative to document the future is taken up by later environmentalist documentaries, from the counterhistory in the film *Who Killed the Electric Car?* (2006) to the environmental damage described in Bill McKibben's *Eaarth: Making Life on a Tough New Planet* (2010). To focus briefly on another example: Werner Herzog's 1992 film *Lesson of Darkness* engages in the kind of estrangement from place and time that allows one to view our world as transient, as polluted and unsustainable, bound to give way. The film is composed of documentary footage shot in Kuwait after the first Gulf War. Centering on scenes of the Kuwaiti oil fires and the oil workers trying to contain them, the film is narrated by Herzog as an alien observer, introducing the footage in the film as being from "a planet in our solar system," and going on to say about an oil worker standing in front of a wall of flames, gesturing and stomping on the ground, "the first creature we encountered tried to communicate something to us." The communication is, of course, unintelligible. Perhaps the worker is showing us that the wall of flame is coming from below the ground, that the fire is crude oil aflame, but Herzog neither interviews the figure nor speculates about the meaning of his gestures. Instead, the viewer is left not with a sense of aestheticized violence (something that the film was initially accused of upon its first festival screenings) but with a sense of how environmental catastrophe estranges one from the environment, displaces the familiar and the everyday so completely as to render human communication and human agency moot. This rendering moot is also part of the documentary's temporal and spatial reach—one of the film's chapters is titled "A Dinosaur's Feast," featuring shots of large machinery moving around Kuwaiti oil fields. The chapter title's reference to the organic beings, the dinosaurs, who decomposed into petroleum, is ironic—it is not dinosaurs who feast on their crude remains but these large machines. The dinosaurs here are not reptiles but fossil-fuel burning engines, facing extinction on a burning planet. This kind of imaginary can capture the temporal span necessary for thinking of our everyday actions and structures of environmental exploitation as slowly leading to catastrophe.

Representing Capitalism and Climate Change

Central to *Silent Spring,* but not named as such, is the engine driving the exploitative use of pesticides: late capitalism. Indeed, *Silent Spring* spurred not only the environmentalism of the late twentieth century but also contemporary environmentalist politics that focus on capitalism and economics. As Nixon notes in his editorial on Carson, the ways in which legislation has been manipulated under neoliberalism to conform to corporate interests have actively impeded the legislative triumphs occasioned by *Silent Spring:* "Even the prescient Carson could not have imagined this: an America where corporations are now legally people, replete with human rights, thereby endangering the rights of us noncorporate humans—ordinary, mortal citizens whose right to an unpoisoned future Carson rose up to defend."[38] The problems facing us today require something more than the advocacy of legislation and regulation, and this was anticipated even in Carson's earlier books about the ocean. For Carson, ecological time necessitates a shift in perspective, a recognition of and sense of obligation toward the dark patches of unknown life that precede and will follow the human species.

In a chapter about eels in *Under the Sea-Wind*, for example, Carson imagines a distant future: "As the waiting of the eels off the mouth of the bay was only an interlude in a long life filled with constant change, so the relation of sea and coast and mountains ranges was that of a moment in geologic time. For once more the mountains would be worn away by the endless erosion of water and carried in silt to the sea, and once more all the coast would be water again, and the places of its cities and towns would belong to the sea."[39] This moment of speculative documentary poses a subtle counterpoint to the logic of conservation, as the environment is valuable not as a resource for human life but because it will exist after humans have vanished. With its focus on entrepreneurial individualism and free markets, the neoliberal imaginary is incapable of conceiving interests outside of the purview of human agents, and indeed it even figures nonhuman entities like corporations as human agents. Carson offers an early meditation on the necessity of radical alterity, as a foil to emergent neoliberalism's totalized field of human agents.

Silent Spring and the environmentalist documentary tradition that follows from it—in books such as Edward Abbey's *Desert Solitaire* (1968) and John McPhee's *Control of Nature* (1989), and more recently Elizabeth Kolbert's *The Sixth Extinction* (2014) and Naomi Klein's *This Changes Everything* (2014)—strive to represent the mutual imbrication of nature and culture through imaginings of the future available in the documentary aesthetic. Carson's sublime imagery often offsets capitalism as temporary, as in this passage from *The Sea Around Us* about humankind:

> In the artificial world of his cities and towns, he often forgets the true nature of his planet and the long vistas of its history, in which the existence of the race of men has occupied a mere moment of time. The sense of all these things comes to him most clearly in the course of a long ocean voyage, when he watches day after day the receding rim of the horizon, ridged and furrowed by waves; when at night he becomes aware of the earth's rotation as the stars pass overhead; or when, alone in this world of water and sky, he feels the loneliness of his earth in space. And then, as never on land, he knows the truth that his world is a water world, a planet dominated by its covering mantle of ocean, in which the continents are but transient intrusions of land above the surface of the all-encircling sea.[40]

Our place in this world is transient, Carson reminds us, even if our effects on this world will be permanent.

Contrary to Carson's faith in the decentering force of the sea, and as Allan Sekula documented in his work of photography and prose *Fish Story* (1995), late capitalism nonetheless transformed our relation to the sea at the time *Silent Spring* was being written, published, and read through the "containerization of cargo movement: an innovation pioneered initially by United States shipping companies in the latter half of the 1950s, evolving into the world standard for general cargo by the end of the 1960s. . . . Factories become mobile, ship-like, as ships become increasingly indistinguishable from trucks and trains, and seaways lose their difference with highways. . . . This historical change reverses the 'classical' relationship between the fixity of the land and the fluidity of the sea" (fig. 16).[41] Carson's ocean loses its difference from the land, yet this entails not the sea's taming by late capitalism but late capitalism's own instability, its own entrance into the speculative imaginaries that Carson associated with the sea. Sekula's *Fish Story* details how documentary representations of labor must always be provisional, and this provisionality is, in the work of Carson and other environmentalist documentarians, where speculation can chart possible pasts and futures.[42]

Like *Fish Story*, Richard Misrach and Kate Orff's *Petrochemical America* (2014) also documents in photographs and text the ways in which fossil fuels undergird our world, flush with goods that appear through petroculture's modes of circulation. In Misrach's photograph *Norco Cumulus Cloud*, for example, one can mistake the fluffy cloud for an idyllic landscape,

Figure 16. "Panorama. Mid-Atlantic" from *Fish Story*, Allan Sekula, 1989–95. (Courtesy of the Allan Sekula Studio)

until one reads the photo's caption: "Throughout the day, natural-looking clouds, nicknamed 'Norco cumulus,' hover over the site, created by the comingling of moisture and volatile hydrocarbons that originate in the process of refining gasoline" (fig. 17).[43] The natural is the petrochemical. The emissions cloud and its innocuous toxicity, though, is only part of the documentary effort in *Petrochemical America.* When read alongside the work's second half, a series of maps, charts, and glossaries, a longer vision than that of the momentary, uncanny Norco cloud becomes available. In Orff's map *From the Earth to the Sky,* carbon dioxide is mapped alongside the fossil record in Louisiana, bleeding off of the map to represent offshore pipelines and deepwater drilling sites, tracing the seep of petroculture into the future, toxicity above and below the surface. It is a vision of a system and timeline that makes the Norco cloud less a coincidence than a point on a continuum whose effects will outlast us all.[44]

Petrochemical America's collaborative mapping project differs substantially from another of Misrach's well-known works, *The Mysterious*

Figure 17. *Norco Cumulous Cloud, Oil Shell Refinery, Norco, Louisiana,* Richard Misrach, 1998. (© Richard Misrach, courtesy Fraenkel Gallery, San Francisco)

Opacity of Other Beings (2015). These photographs of individual humans floating in borderless water capture some of the sublimity of the ocean that so interested Rachel Carson (fig. 18). The water, in these photographs, offsets and renders ghostly the human body, making the body's materiality, and the materiality of the swimsuits each subject wears, a stark contrast against water without apparent end. Taken from an elevated vantage point so as to create the appearance of an infinite body of water, these photographs posit an unreal nature, an impossible relation between human and water, and a vision, perhaps, of the rising waters to come with rising global temperatures. In contrast, Misrach's photographs of Louisiana remain situated, rooted in context, history, extraction, and emission. Similar to the human/inhuman dialectic used by Carson to advocate for legislative reform and to posit a deep future where resources can no longer be thought of as resources, Misrach's photographic projects reveal both the resilience of the human and the economic forces that dwarf individual humans and render them immobile. The human is at once central and left behind, as in the photograph *Night Fishing, Near Bonnet Carré Spillway*

Figure 18. *Untitled (July 29, 2012 7:43PM),* Richard Misrach, 2012. (© Richard Misrach, courtesy Fraenkel Gallery, San Francisco)

(fig. 19). In this photograph, a blurry barge moves through the spillway and a refinery lights up the background. In contrast to this movement and light, a solitary figure stands immobile on the shore. His back to the camera, at the end of a grass-and-dirt patch leading up to the water, the fisherman is static, rendered as landscape against the barge in motion, even though he is in the foreground.

In A. Laurie Palmer's photobook *In the Aura of a Hole: Exploring Sites of Material Extraction* (2014), the stakes are less the interplay of humanity, mobility, and timeframes than the normalization of largescale extraction. In the work's chapter on sulfur, Palmer travels to and photographs a BP-owned Sulfur mine in California (fig. 20). While there, she learns of "extremophiles," bacteria found in hot springs and carbon deposits that seem to ingest sulfur and emit hydrogen. These organisms, Palmer notes, became part of a "science . . . [that] has been used to shore up a heretical and politically charged theory about oil and fossil fuel formation," namely,

Figure 19. *Night Fishing, Near Bonnet Carré Spillway, Norco, Louisiana,* Richard Misrach, 1998. (© Richard Misrach, courtesy Fraenkel Gallery, San Francisco)

Figure 20. *Sulfur Pile, Port of Long Beach, California,* A. Laurie Palmer, 2014. (Courtesy of the artist)

that fossil fuels are in fact renewable via these microorganisms.[45] Undercutting the technofuturist utopianism of this science, though, Palmer concludes her sulfur chapter with this postscript: "In 2012 BP sold its Carson refinery . . . to help pay for the cost of the explosion and spill at the Deepwater Horizon rig."[46] In Palmer's photograph *Sulfur Pile, Port of Long Beach, California,* a bright yellow pyramid amid trees and chain link fence positions extraction as the chief interest of energy corporations. Speculation about renewability is a mere smokescreen, a prop to alleviate anxiety about the limits of our economic system and a future possibility quickly monetized in the face of present-day crisis.

Since *Silent Spring,* environmentalist documentary has come to engage in both activism, often aimed at specific legislative action or consumer awareness, and speculation about what comes after our current economic and energy regime. Climate change has made this twofold mode of representation even more necessary, as it demands recognition of the role petroculture has played in reshaping the environment. This poses a representational problem, as Dipesh Chakrabarty has noted, because "one never experiences being a concept."[47] It is here that Carson's writings continue to be useful, for they do allow one to experience exactly this—the conceptual nature of deep time and the twin pulls of hopelessness and individual activism that can accompany a recognition of one's place within a system. Carson's engagement with the documentary aesthetic has informed even works of science fiction. James VanderMeer's Southern Reach trilogy is a series of novels about an othered environment not understood by the humans who live alongside it. VanderMeer once tweeted that his trilogy was "all based on the video game of Rachel Carson's Silent Spring." It is this kind of speculative imagining—a never-created video game of a work of documentary prose, leading to a science fiction trilogy about an environment unrecognizable by humans who formerly inhabited it—that *Silent Spring* has made possible. This kind of speculative yet also documentary thought may allow us to grapple with the reality of climate change, especially because addressing climate change requires collective action, a kind of action difficult to fathom within neoliberal culture.

Conclusion: The Meaning of Memoir

The documentary aesthetic is central to our age, and it is ubiquitous in a variety of artistic and cultural forms. Nowhere is this more evident than the widespread popularity of the memoir over the past three decades. While the speculative documentaries that have emerged to address climate change and the environment attempt to broaden our frames of reference, the memoir has solidified a framework for privileging individual determination, recovery, and uplift that informs not just literature but social media posts, reality television programs, advertisements for pharmaceuticals, and so much more. As I have argued throughout this book, documentary art from the 1960s to the present has articulated the ways in which neoliberal culture and finance capitalism have isolated and limited, while also championing and privileging, individual modes of being in the world. In this conclusion, I will document how the "memoir boom" and the aesthetic uses of the memoir genre that occured in the 1990s and 2000s reflect the cultural and ontological force of neoliberal reforms. By the 1990s, the entrepreneurial idealism of free market ideology was becoming visible as a solipsistic, isolated subject position. In response to this, contemporary artists and writers reimagined how relations work between subject and system, artist and reality. It is important that this younger generation of artists is a generation for whom neoliberalism was not a series of reforms that happened during their young adulthood (as it was for documentary artists of previous decades) but instead the reality of finance capitalism into which they were born. While the memoir is a genre we might assume to be solipsistic in its focus on one individual's story, memoirists and artists working in life narrative today move from self to structure, in modes that gesture to possibilities for subjectivity both beyond and within neoliberal culture's limits.

An example of this younger generation's mode of memoiristic thinking is Miranda July's art project the Somebody messaging service app, which was launched as a way to essentially "Uber" one's conversations. So, instead of saying something difficult to someone—such as, for example, breaking up with a boyfriend—users could post what they wished to say to the Somebody app, and then an agent in the vicinity of the person the user wished to communicate with said the message for them. One's most intimate interactions, then, become memoir, scripts that are written out, rather than said or merely felt, and then made virtually public. The intimate becomes a transaction, while also remaining personal at the same time. "Somebody," like all memoir today, is less a critique of the imbrication of finance capitalism into everyday life than an expression of that imbrication as a channel for feeling. What the memoir as genre does, then, under finance capitalism, is make the self visible as an object within a structure.

Indeed, as Ben Yagoda remarks in his history of the genre's contemporary prominence, "Memoir has become the central form of culture: not only the way stories are told, but the way arguments are put forth, products and properties marketed, ideas floated, acts justified, reputations constructed or salvaged."[1] As Yagoda notes, the "memoir boom" of the 1990s is exemplified by a handful of influential literary bestsellers, such as Tobias Wolff's *This Boy's Life* (1989), Mary Karr's *The Liar's Club* (1995), and Frank McCourt's *Angela's Ashes* (1996). The boom is also notable for other bestsellers such as Susanna Kaysen's *Girl, Interrupted* (1993), Dave Pelzer's *A Child Called "It": One Child's Courage to Survive* (1993), Elizabeth Wurtzel's *Prozac Nation: Young and Depressed in America* (1994), and Frances Mayes' *Under the Tuscan Sun: At Home in Italy* (1996). These works from the twentieth century were followed in the twenty-first century by bestsellers such as Augusten Burroughs's 2002 *Running with Scissors: A Memoir,* Elizabeth Gilbert's *Eat Pray Love: One Woman's Search for Everything across Italy, India, and Indonesia* (2006), and James Frey's *A Million Little Pieces* (2003), initially sold as a memoir but relabeled a work of fiction after a prominent scandal and public dressing-down by Oprah Winfrey.[2]

The popular memoir has been an easy target for literary critics and cultural studies scholars, who view its vision of self-realization, its dramatization of suffering, and its emphasis on individual self-fashioning as evidence of the genre's privileging of the entrepreneurial individual. Along with reality television and "chick lit"—two other popular media forms that resonate as similarly invested in authenticity, suffering, and redemption, and that are also often associated with female readers and viewers—the memoir is typically viewed as a mere symptom of neoliberalism. For example, Walter Benn Michaels brands the memoir an "entirely Thatcherite genre," and Pamela Thoma has posited that the "culinary memoir," such as *Eat Pray Love* or Julie Powell's *Julie and Julia: 365 Days, 524 Recipes, 1 Tiny Apartment Kitchen* (2005), "is connected to the seemingly limitless demands for women's flexible labor in the marketplace and at home."[3] In her study of the memoir boom, Julie Rak argues that the memoir is a unique genre precisely because memoirs are "produced, and not just written. Memoir is a creative product. . . . [It] can even be regarded as a brand produced by the publishing and book retailing industries."[4] Rak argues, too, that the memoir is an important site for the articulation of public values in our contemporary moment, and thus finds in the memoir a commodified and rigorously marketed iteration of the public discourse so central to Jürgen Habermas's or Michael Warner's accounts of the eighteenth century.[5] Despite their various approaches to the genre, all of the above critics seem to agree that the memoir matters not as literature but as a marker of something else: public ideals of citizenship in a fully commodified and branded literary marketplace, the privileging of moral character as a justification for economic inequality, or the promotion of neoliberal models of flexible labor and conventional gender roles. The memoir is a barometer of neoliberalism's idealization of entrepreneurial individualism, emphasis on constant production and consumption as markers of a good life, and erosion of the commons and public discourse. In short, the memoir is a neoliberal genre.

This account of the popular memoir is compelling, but the memoir's reach into contemporary aesthetics is more diverse and complicated than the ever-growing number of bestsellers adapted into Hollywood films and tell-all chronicles of B-list celebrities would suggest. In recent years, writers as diverse and varied in their forms, themes, and affiliations as Dave Eggers, Sheila Heti, Tao Lin, Maggie Nelson, Justin St. Germain, and Jesmyn Ward, to name but a celebrated few, have turned to nonfiction forms and a more material orientation toward reality that emphasize economic and political limits. By viewing the contemporary memoir as an extension of the New Journalism, I posit that the memoir genre is a literary mode for the representation of disappointments and disillusionments in the neoliberal age: the limits to economic growth, the narrowness of political engagement, the lack of upward mobility and individual wellness cast as widely available and desirable in venues like *The Oprah Winfrey*

Show. From the New Journalism to the memoir boom, we can trace a cultural history of the documentary aesthetic that occurs in tandem with, and in response to, the uneven economic and political implementations of neoliberal reforms and the establishment of finance capitalism.

After all, if one of neoliberalism's cultural accomplishments has been the idealization and isolation of the entrepreneurial individual as the benchmark of success, then the first-person voice in literature might rise to ubiquity as a genre convention because it is simply how our culture thinks of itself. Insofar as this mode is widespread, writers might just as well strive to articulate alternative models of subjectivity as reinforce hegemonic subjectivity through the first-person voice. The memoir and its attendant conventions need not signal one relation to the conditions that have occasioned their ubiquity. Charting the memoir's ties to the New Journalism of the 1960s and 1970s helps to make visible the political possibilities of the genre, the ways in which documentary can represent central tensions of finance capitalism rather than merely smooth out those tensions with an appeal to the palliative, authorial self.

Joan Didion, Dave Eggers, and Receding Lives

In his review of Joan Didion's critically and popularly successful 2005 memoir *The Year of Magical Thinking,* John Leonard links the book to Didion's entire body of work. He reads the book as a culmination of the style, affect, and relation to events that Didion had developed in her reportage and fiction. Regarding the book's somber subject, Leonard concludes his review with a single-sentence paragraph: "I can't imagine dying without this book."[6] Leonard's remarks would reflect the wider reception of Didion's memoir as a vital work that synthesized aesthetic and self-help values. *The Year of Magical Thinking* was awarded the National Book Award for Nonfiction, named a finalist for the National Book Critics Circle Award and the Pulitzer Prize for Autobiography/Biography, and adapted into a stage play of the same name, in which Didion was played by Vanessa Redgrave. The memoir documents the death of Didion's long-time husband John Gregory Dunne, the ultimately fatal illness of her daughter Quintana Roo Dunne Michael, and the author's process of grieving. In keeping with her earlier work's emphasis on narrative structures and their failures, Didion tries to make sense of her husband's death and her daughter's illness by reading books and analyzing life as one analyzes a work of literature, only to find no sense, no possible interpretation:

> I went to the UCLA Medical Center bookstore. I bought a book described on its cover as a "concise overview of neuroanatomy and of its function and clinical implications." . . . The book was by Stephen G. Waxman, M.D., chief of neurology at Yale-New Haven, and was called *Clinical Neuroanatomy.* I skimmed successfully through some of the appendices, for example "Appendix A: The Neurologic Examination," but when I began to read the text itself I could only think of a trip to Indonesia during which I had become disoriented by my inability to locate the grammar in Bahasa Indonesia, the official language used on street signs and storefronts and billboards. . . . *Clinical Neuroanatomy* seemed to be one more case in which I would be unable to locate the grammar.[7]

What the memoir makes clear is that no amount of reading, no amount of research will make sense of what happened. Instead, the memoir concludes with a memory and an embrace of that memory's ephemerality, its detachment from any grand narrative or control: "I think about swimming with him into the cave at Portuguese Bend, about the swell of clear water, the way it changed, the swiftness and power it gained as it narrowed through the rocks at the base of its point. The tide had to be just right. . . . Each time we did it I was afraid of missing the swell, hanging back, timing it wrong. John never was. You had to feel the swell change. You had to go with the change. He told me that."[8] *The Year of Magical Thinking* and Didion's follow-up memoir *Blue Nights* document fleeting moments that the author remembers, and Didion presents those moments as mattering only to her and as always at risk of being lost. As she writes at the end of *Blue Nights,* "The fear is for what is still to be lost."[9] Personal experience—the arbiter of truth in our neoliberal culture—turns out not to document anything of lasting significance, to have no bearing on the events that determine a life, and to be in constant danger of being further eroded, further hollowed out. For all of the memoir's personality, the personal has no larger bearing, no larger meaning. The aesthetic function of memory in Didion's memoirs of loss is also a dramatization of memory's unimportance, of the personal's negligible status under a regime for which personal initiative is purportedly all.

While Didion writes about the hollowness of the personal, Dave Eggers and his McSweeney's publishing ventures are dependent on valorizing the personal and the intimate, as the aesthetic category of the "new sincerity" often invoked to discuss McSweeney's denotes. A host of contemporary writers come to mind when one thinks of experimental riffs on the memoir—some of whom will be discussed in this chapter's final section—but Eggers has been centrally involved not just in the writing of but also the publication of and activism surrounding contemporary literature that blurs memoir, novel, and nonfiction. After making a celebrated debut with the self-ironizing memoir *A Heartbreaking Work of Staggering Genius,* Eggers has continued to use the tropes of the memoir even though he no longer writes about himself or his family. His two second-hand memoirs, *What Is the What* (2006) and *Zeitoun* (2009), the former labeled a novel, the latter labeled a work of nonfiction, share a formal design that privileges the personal voice as the sole arbiter of experience, a design that conforms to the hyperindividualism of neoliberal culture, while trying to renew ethical bonds between reader, writer, and character.

What Is the What and *Zeitoun* both foreground their own constructedness, but *What Is the What* begins with a preface authored by Valentino Achak Deng, the only piece of the novel purporting to be his autobiography that is penned by him. In the preface, Deng describes the process by which the novel was researched and written:

> This book was born out of the desire on the part of myself and the author to reach out to others to help them understand the atrocities many successive governments of Sudan committed before and during the civil war. To that end, over the course of many years, I told my story orally to the author. He then concocted this novel, approximating my own voice and using the basic events of my life as the foundation. Because many of the passages are fictional, the result is called a novel. . . . This is simply one man's story, subjectively told.[10]

Deng and Eggers's shared desire to "reach out to others" forms the basis for the text, a text that is classified as a novel because of its subjectivity, the very quality that also, of course, registers as a kind of aesthetic, if not factual, truth and authenticity. The novelized memoir, then, serves as an overtly activist form, an incitement by the author and subject to make sure that, in Deng's words, the readers of the novel do something "to prevent the same horrors from repeating themselves."[11] The expansiveness of Deng and Eggers's desire renders the text a kind of broad, sincere hope and faith in the potential of life narrative to produce recognition and change. As Deng narrates at the closing of the novel, "Whatever I will do, I will find a way to live, I will tell these stories. I have spoken to every person I have encountered these last difficult days, and every person who has entered this club [the gym where he works] during these awful morning hours, because to do anything else would be something less than human. I speak to these people, and I speak to you because I cannot help it. It gives me strength, almost unbelievable strength, to know that you are there."[12] This ethical, mutually empowering relation among text, subject, and author marks the formal aspiration of *What Is the What* and, arguably, Eggers's work more generally—the aspiration to produce a text that will function as an intimate, ethical interface, a connection that then transforms moral obligation into the pleasure of labor for the collective good.

If *What Is the What* is the utopian, expansive version of the memoir, then *Zeitoun* moves in a more cynical direction. A book that is described not as a novel but as a work of nonfiction, *Zeitoun* is written in the third person, and while it has the same expansiveness of possibility as *What Is the What,* the narrative also undercuts its own faith in the aesthetic and ethical bond generated by nonfiction narrative. Beginning with epigraphs from Cormac McCarthy's *The Road*—"in the history of the world it might even be that there was more punishment than crime"—and Mark Twain—"To a man with a hammer, everything looks like a nail"—*Zeitoun* foregrounds cynicism and violence.[13] The book is about Abdulrahman Zeitoun, a contractor who survived Hurricane Katrina in New Orleans. Zeitoun works to rebuild New Orleans in its aftermath, yet ultimately, and in keeping with the book's epigraphs, the narrator finds in Zeitoun's survival and commitment to work something tragic and sad. Strikingly, the text concludes much like *What Is the What,* with the articulation of a renewed ethical commitment:

> As he drives through the city by day and dreams of it at night, his mind vaults into glorious reveries—he envisions this city and this country not just as it was, but better, far better. It can be. . . . There is much work to do, and we all know what needs to be done. . . . So let us get up early and stay late, and, brick by brick and block by block, let us get that work done. If he can picture it, it can be. This has been the pattern of his life: ludicrous dreams followed by hours and days and years of work and then a reality surpassing his wildest hopes and expectations.[14]

Once again, the text seems to end with an aspirational commitment to a better world. But, then, *Zeitoun*'s final sentence is a question: "And so why should this be any different?" This closing question does not affirm Zeitoun's faith in hard work but makes clear that his optimism, however admirable, also entails an amnesia—that Katrina and its aftermath "diminished the humanity of them all."[15] Kathy, Zeitoun's wife, seems to cope with this through memory loss: "It's shredded, unreliable. The wiring in her mind has been snapped in vital places."[16] Eggers' narration of heroic, optimistic, ethical individuality falters in *Zeitoun,* as it becomes clear that the difference at the conclusion of the text is that Zeitoun's work ethic is misguided, clearly unsuited and insufficient to realize his dreams of upward mobility.

Like *What Is the What, Zeitoun* begins with a caveat: "This book does not attempt to be an all-encompassing book about New Orleans or Hurricane Katrina. It is only an account of one family's experiences before and after the storm."[17] Eggers's prefacing in both texts diffuses what Kenneth Goldsmith has described as the deeply uninteresting question of authenticity that plagues literature and, especially, the memoir today, mainly by making authenticity a function of form.[18] Eggers's memoirs call attention to their constructedness, thereby making clear that a text cannot conform to reality in an easy, mimetic relationship. Despite this careful prefacing, *Zeitoun,* like *A Heartbreaking Work of Staggering Genius* before it, became the subject of some controversy in 2012 when, contrary to Eggers's depiction of him as a loving husband, Abdulrahman Zeitoun was arrested for assaulting his wife (he was acquitted in 2013). Moreover, the formal caveats and explanations at the beginning of both texts serve to formalize the ethical commitment of the text. For that is, after all, what Eggers's texts hinge upon: the incitement of ethical action on the part of the reader. This is, arguably, the goal of much "historiographical metafiction," but Eggers' difference lies in his laying bare the neoliberal impetus of such a formal imperative. Rather than provoking some vague sense of victimhood, historical tragedy, or imperative that human rights violations happen "never again," *What Is the What* and *Zeitoun* force the reader to exit through the gift shop, as it were. The final pages of each text contain information about charities to support, making the ethical cast of the memoir and witnessing overtly economic rather than merely emotional.

Eggers's two second-hand memoirs are compelling for the way that they lay bare the instrumentality of literature in the service of ethics, and thus they implicitly brand a wide swath of contemporary literature a kind of literature of bad faith, insofar as it elicits a similar ethical response but without a proper channel for individual investment or expenditure. His novel *A Hologram for the King* (2012) is fiction, yet written in a way that is informed by corporate tell-alls such as Michael Lewis's memoir *Liar's Poker* (1989). The novel meditates on the question of what might be done to restore a sense of productivity, belonging, even dignity to white collar workers increasingly downtrodden and exploited during the economic "downturn" of 2008. Pico Iyer, in the *New York Times Book Review,* celebrated *Hologram* as a kind of "'Death of a Globalized Salesman,' alight with all of Arthur Miller's compassion and humanism," and one can see how this is an easy position to take on a novel that is preoccupied with its central character.[19] The generically yet symbolically named "Alan Clay" signifies both middle-manager whiteness and the malleability that is expected in today's economy from any worker. The novel does indeed dwell on Alan's failing prospects, as when he worries about having enough money to pay his daughter's college tuition: "Had he planned better, had he not been so incompetent, he would have whatever she needed. He had twenty years to save $200k. How hard was that? It was ten thousand a year. Much less assuming any interest on the money. . . . He thought he could make the $200k at will, in any given year. How could he have predicted the world losing interest in people like him?"[20] What this passage points to, though, is less the novel's fixation on eulogizing or even romanticizing the corporate employee than its insistence that the individual's voice, privileged by the literary form of the memoir and the regime of neoliberalism, no longer functions as a site of aspiration. The novel concludes with Alan in the empty King Abdullah Economic City in Saudi Arabia, a pet project of the Arab nation's ruler but one never fully realized. Alan is there, initially, to sell hologram technology to the king, but his U.S.-based company loses out to a Chinese firm. Alan decides to stay in the built but unpopulated city, and the novel's titular technology, the hologram, functions both as a plot point and as a figure for the forms of spectral presence that the memoir and Eggers's literary aesthetic attempt to generate. At the novel's conclusion, Alan gambles on his future usefulness to the king, the king who has never appeared. "He had to hope for amnesia," the narrator remarks, both his own amnesia and that of his potential audience. Amnesia would mean that Alan's own failure in the global economy would result not in disillusionment but in a renewed effort to become a properly entrepreneurial individual. Amnesia allows for the renewed production of personhood, a personhood that looks much more like a hologram than a flesh-and-blood agent. Alan's hologram serves as a figure for Eggers's own aesthetic project—the production of a spectral presence that promises a better world but one that, it turns out, cannot be articulated or even thought through the compromised, aspirational individual.

Memoir and Mediation

Perhaps in no other subgenre of the memoir is attention to mediation more visible than in the comics or graphic memoir.[21] Pioneered by comics artists like Justin Green and R. Crumb in the 1960s and 1970s, and made canonical by Art Spiegelman with the publication of *Maus* in the 1980s and 1990s, the comics memoir remained a prominent genre into the 2000s. For example, Alison Bechdel's 2006 *Fun Home: A Family Tragicomic* details through drawings of family snapshots, diary entries, recollections, and works of literature Bechdel's relationship with her closeted father. At the core of the text is Bechdel's belief that her father committed suicide, though she acknowledges that "there's no proof, actually, that my father killed himself."[22] Like Bechdel's supposition about her father's death, *Fun Home*'s drawn photographs, diary entries, literary references, and dramatic retellings make her mediation of events and family apparent on the page.

Similarly, Phoebe Gloeckner's 2002 work of prose and comics *The Diary of a Teenage Girl* consists, in part, of the diary that Gloeckner "kept as a teenager," though she has changed the diarist's name to Minnie Goetze and calls the work a novel: "Although I am the source of Minnie, she cannot be me—for the book to have real meaning, she must be all girls, anyone. This is not history or documentary or a confession, and memories will be altered or sacrificed, for factual truth has little significance in the pursuit of emotional truth."[23] The text itself also questions its own meaningfulness, as Minnie writes in a diary entry: "Would you or would you not consider this journal a creative endeavor? (Obviously, you must be reading what I write.) I ask this question because it seems to everyone else that I haven't been doing jack shit lately in the way of independent, self-broadening projects."[24] She goes on to ask, "Perhaps, you say, I'd be better off typing randomly at the keyboard, perhaps a jumble of letters resembling alphabet soup would be more interesting to behold?," followed by twelve lines of just that, random letters, symbols, and numbers strung together by hitting a keyboard. The opposition established between random letters and meaningful words serves as a commentary on the diary form itself and on *The Diary of a Teenage Girl*'s status as a crafted work of literature. A diary, for Gloeckner, has only particular, individualized meaning, while a work of literature or art has a general, perhaps even universal meaning. So, by transforming her diary into a "novel," she lays claim to meaning, makes what were otherwise meaningless marks into meaningful words. It is important, though, that the diary form is retained in this transition as the form through which Minnie's character is expressed, as the diary form connotes authenticity and intimacy even if it has been called fiction.

Like *The Diary of a Teenage Girl,* many texts that are written in the genre of the memoir are called works of fiction by their authors and publishers. In Gloeckner's case, calling the work a novel rather than autobiography gives it an artistic and literary meaning that transcends and moves beyond frequent "descriptions of [her] book as being about 'trauma' or 'the sexuality of the female adolescent.'"[25] Or laying claim to the category of fiction can be a strategy to avoid lawsuits and the kind of outrage that resulted in James Frey's "public stoning" (to use the phrase Frey himself used, and which artist Ed Ruscha used in a commission for Frey, after the *A Million Little Pieces* scandal).[26] Or it can just be a way to acknowledge that memory is always incomplete and that any memoir contains some degree of fabrication. Less practically, and perhaps more meaningfully, drawing attention to these limits may make visible a condition of subjecthood today.

Contemporary artists and writers employ the memoir to represent the often hidden reality of limits in our contemporary moment—limits to memory, limits to sympathy, for sure, but also limits to economic growth, limits to upward mobility, limits to individual desire and initiative. In many works of contemporary literature that either are explicitly memoirs or use the genre of the memoir while labeling themselves fiction, disconnection and irony become figures for literature's relationship to the reader and, more broadly, for individuals' connection to each other in the age of neoliberalism. Like Eggers in *What Is the What,* the great theorist of autobiography Philippe Lejenue and the great champion of literary identification Oprah Winfrey find in the memoir a marker of authenticity and the chance for the reader's self-realization through intimate contact with an other—that is, they offer an ethical account of the memoir. Contrary to this dominant understanding of the memoir, many contemporary writers seem to seize on the memoir to dramatize the inability to even formulate an ethical bond with others.[27] These works represent human relations—including relations between the reader and the writer—as impersonal and structural rather than as personal and ethical, and as limited by material realities often thought to be fluid by free market ideology.

These contemporary memoiristic works often stage human relations in repetitive, rule-bound, and ultimately irresolute scenes, dramatizing the lack of closure, the inability to realize something about the self, and the incapacity for subjects to identify with one another in our neoliberal era. Moreover, these scenes of disidentification and irresolution depend on descriptions of material limits, juxtaposing the fluidity and flexibility of the neoliberal subject with the structures of inequality that facilitate and constrict what counts as human action and thought. For example, in the concluding chapter of Sheila Heti's 2012 *How Should a Person Be?: A Novel from Life,* the narrator, named Sheila, watches two of her friends play squash. The two friends, Margaux and Sholem, are both painters, and they have decided to let a squash game decide which one of them won the "Ugly Painting Competition" that the friends had decided to hold. Sheila is "really eager to know who would win," so she comes along.[28] At the squash court, the game begins:

> The game went very slowly at first, then grew more and more focused. Soon Margaux and Sholem were running back and forth, breathing very heavily. They smacked the ball against the wall, dodged into each other's part of the court, and slammed against the back wall, groaning. They nodded briefly when the other made a good move. They rubbed sweat from their brows and hit the ball too high. They ran forward and bent low, and at one point Sholem threw himself to the ground. Margaux followed the rolling ball, walking very slowly, and tossed it to Sholem to serve. He smacked it high in the air and ran to the edge of the court and missed.[29]

After this goes on for "about half an hour," Sheila and her friends realize that they don't know the score. They focus their attention on the game,

> but none of us could hear anything from below except for explosions of laughter, moans, and cursing, and Sholem saying, "Fuck! I hate this fucking game!"
>
> We remained very still, and we watched. Then finally Jon said, in his sweetly caustic drawl, "I don't think they even know the rules. I think they're just slamming the ball around."
>
> And so they were.[30]

The semblance of a game that is merely the pained exertions of two artists is a fitting representation of the "new sincerity" aesthetic often associated with the McSweeney's school and our memoir culture more broadly. Artists are expected to suffer for us. Yet Heti's novel represents this game as a process, even though it doesn't make sense as a means of judging a painting contest. A game without rules that is nonetheless played as if it has rules comes to look more like art and less like competition. The circumscription of the scene—the court, the rackets, the ball, the walls, the players—frames the game, like a painting, photograph, or play, as an aesthetic pursuit. Concluding with this game still in progress, Heti's memoiristic novel arrives not at a unified self but instead at a recognition of how external forces determine the self.

A related sense of directionless action, of a structured activity that, in fact, has no meaning and no endpoint, occurs in the opening chapter of Tao Lin's 2013 novel *Taipei,* narrated by Paul, a New York–based, Taiwanese-American writer who, at one point in the novel, gives a public reading where he reads one of Tao Lin's own poems, making the connection between author and narrator explicit. On an airplane going to Taipei, Paul thinks about Taipei as an alternative to life in America:

> On the plane, after a cup of black coffee, Paul thought of Taipei as a fifth season, or "otherworld," outside, or in equal contrast with, his increasingly familiar and self-consciously repetitive life in America, where it seemed like the seasons, connecting in right angles, for some misguided reason, had formed a square, sarcastically framing nothing—or been melded, Paul vaguely imagined, about an hour later, facedown on his arms on his dining tray, into a door-knocker, which a child, after twenty to thirty knocks, no longer expecting an answer, has continued using, in a kind of daze, distracted by the pointlessness of his activity, looking absently elsewhere, unaware when he will abruptly, idly stop.[31]

As with the squash match that closes Heti's *How Should a Person Be?,* Lin's image of a child at the door knocker finds in the self only repetition within confining limitations, limits that are recognized by the participant and the narrator but unable to be transcended. Here, the memoiristic allows for the recognition of a narrow frame, the way in which the effusive self is circumscribed by the promise of unlimited play.

In Maggie Nelson's 2009 book *Bluets,* a collection of 240 prose pieces about the color blue written in the first person, the color blue and other colors become shorthand, a way of describing complex structures that pull us away from the world rather than attaching our language to it: "Fifteen days after we are born, we begin to discriminate between colors. For the rest of our lives, barring blunted or blinded sight, we find ourselves face-to-face with all these phenomena at once, and we call the whole shimmering mess 'color.' You might even say it is the business of the eye to make colored forms out of what is essentially shimmering. This is how we 'get around' in the world. Some might call it the source of our suffering."[32] *Bluets* dwells on how, as Nelson articulates it in an essay, "the most seemingly immaterial forces are, in fact, material."[33] This material basis for our perceptions, for our livelihoods, for our literary and aesthetic pleasures, when acknowledged, places the reader in a new awareness of her surroundings, a new space to contemplate the stubborn materiality of our world, often characterized as fluid, networked, immaterial.

This emphasis on material limits—a squash court, a door knock never to be answered, the shimmering relations that we reduce to the idea of "blue"—is the political accomplishment of nonfiction prose under neoliberalism. The juxtaposition of idealism and the self with material limits functions as an aesthetically inflected ideology critique, a bringing back from the flows of the free market into the stubborn material realities of finance capitalism and the limits neoliberal legislation and priorities place on individuals.

And, in the case of Jessamyn Lovell's photography project *Dear Erin Hart,* emphasizing the porous yet also rigid limits of the self is one way of thinking of subjecthood as an object within a structure. In *Dear Erin Hart,* Lovell explains that her identity was stolen—she found out about the identity theft when she received a court summons from San Francisco. A resident of New Mexico, Lovell had her wallet stolen from a photo gallery in San Francisco, and subsequently her driver's license and name had been used when a woman actually named Erin Hart had been arrested. After flying to San Francisco to clear her name, Lovell then gets angry and "decide[s] to track [Erin Hart] down and at least see who she was."[34] This proves harder than she imagines, as she gets three different mug shots of Hart. She eventually hires a private investigator to help her, and she returns to San Francisco and surreptitiously photographs Hart on the day she is released from prison, as Hart goes to a convenience store to buy cigarettes, shoplifts from a Goodwill clothing store, and then goes into a motel (fig. 21). Lovell returns a year later, only to find Hart's current address to be a strange, boarded-up mansion. Going through her photographs of the mansion, she finds a photo that she thinks might be of Hart, "after a year of 'living hard.'"[35] The project concludes with a sealed envelope, left at the San Francisco gallery where Lovell's photos and wall texts were installed, addressed to Hart (fig. 22). Hart was invited to the show yet did not appear. After the show closed, Lovell gave the letter to Hart's parole officer, who "confirmed giving Erin Hart a condensed version of what I had written." Lovell's project begins with anger. It is a kind of revenge, as she reclaims her identity by infringing on the privacy of another. Yet the project changes over time, as Lovell begins to identify with Hart (they are both from working-class backgrounds, they have both struggled with

Figure 21. "Extra Mile, 2013," from *Dear Erin Hart, 2011–2014,* Jessamyn Lovell. "With the help of Pete Siragusa and two other P.I.s I was able to find, follow, and photograph Erin Hart, the woman who stole my identity. I followed her from being released from county jail around San Francisco, including a gas station, on the bus, a Goodwill store, and a market." (Courtesy of the artist)

money). Lovell's identification with Hart can only go so far, though, as she never encounters or speaks to her. The sealed letter is never opened by Hart, the intimate connection is never established. Instead, Lovell can only view Hart from the distance of a private investigator—Hart is an object in motion, her feelings, thoughts, history, and future only a projection. What is felt as deeply personal to Lovell—her identity was stolen—also has nothing to do with the personal at all. And Lovell's photographs balance this tension, as in the mug shot of Hart fixed to an envelope. The photograph is at once vibrant and colorful yet also a photograph of a photograph, attached to a folder containing documents the viewer isn't allowed to read. The photograph discloses only the limits of Lovell's, and our own, ability to know who Hart is—a person who is only visible within structures that handle subjects as objects, but an object with whom Lovell can't help but imagine herself as being in an intimate relation.

Figure 22. "Letter to Erin Hart, 2014," from *Dear Erin Hart, 2011–2014,* Jessamyn Lovell. "I wrote this letter to Erin Hart, the woman who stole my identity. The sealed letter was installed in the exhibition *Dear Erin Hart,* at SF Camerawork in 2014. A wall tag gave instructions to the gallery staff to allow only Erin Hart to open and read the letter if she asked." (Courtesy of the artist)

Documentary's Promise

A striking example of how documentary can represent this pull between self and object, feeling and structure, is in a work of nonfiction reportage. Adrian Nicole LeBlanc's *Random Family* is painstakingly researched narrative journalism about a poor family in the Bronx. At the end of *Random Family,* a mother and her daughters visit the daughters' father, Cesar, who is going to be in jail for a long time still:

> Toward the end of the visit, Nautica begged Cesar to give her a pony ride, as he had when she was little, where he bounced her like a piece of popcorn on his knees. He did—for a good ten minutes. Then he held her lengthwise like a barbell and pushed her into the air. Mercedes watched, her awe and longing clear. When Cesar began to spin Nautica around, Mercedes couldn't contain her desire. "Can you do that to me?" she asked breathlessly.

> She caught herself as quickly, and her expression turned stony. The hope became a dare. Since she was a baby, no one had been able, or willing, to carry her. She weighed 130 pounds now.
>
> Cesar placed Nautica down and squatted before Mercedes. Drawing out the moment, he rubbed his chin. Then, very seriously, he examined his big hands. He measured the width of his grip below Mercedes's knees. Mercedes had braced herself for rejection; then, the next thing she knew, she was up in the air. She went rigid with excitement and terror. "No, *Daddy!*" she shrieked giddily.
>
> He adjusted her on his shoulders. She clutched his hair and dug her legs into his armpits. Then he paraded his daughter around the honor room and into the regular visiting area, where they took another lap past the inmates, who smiled and nodded as Cesar introduced his oldest girl. He pushed out the door to the enclosed cement courtyard. An April wind had whipped up, and everything was flying, so he quickly ducked back inside, exaggerating the drop as they went over the threshold.
>
> *"Daddyyy!"* Mercedes squealed, nearly losing her balance. She regained it as he steadied. He headed back to their table, where Nautica grinned and Coco gazed up at them, like a little girl in awe of a Christmas tree. Mercedes was trying not to smile but she couldn't help it. "I'm going to fall! Daddy! I'm too heavy!" she said urgently.
>
> "Relax, I ain't going to drop you, don't worry," Cesar assured her. He's been lifting weights almost daily for the last five years. To himself, he said, "Listen, you light as a feather to me."[36]

The lyricism of the passage and its use of dialogue, free indirect discourse, and explication all contribute to a heart-warming effect. It is hard for a book to make me cry, but this one does it every time. My response, though, has less to do with what is on the page than with the looming reality that the book sets up prior to this scene: Cesar is going to drop his daughter, figuratively. He is in prison, and even if he gets out, there is little for him in the world that awaits outside, a world of poverty, limited opportunities, and broken social services. The affective reach of this passage is not personal but structural. I cry not for Cesar but because of the limits that Cesar has no choice but to inhabit, that we all have no choice but to inhabit in one way or another.

In a 2013 interview marking the ten-year anniversary of *Random Family*'s publication, LeBlanc reflected on the book's reception: "I often felt disturbed that readers were surprised by the experiences of the people in the book. Many are shocked, I think, to discover that people in poverty have complicated, meaningful lives—in other words, that the people in the book are, in fact, human beings."[37] This humanity is a function not of identification and recognition but of the cruel distance between self and structure, made visible in documentary art today. In Justin St. Germain's 2013 memoir *Son of a Gun,* about the murder of his mother by his stepfather, he writes about watching his mother watch herself on television. A neighbor was murdered by her husband, and St. Germain's mother was interviewed by the local news. St. Germain remarks, "She'd never been on TV before, and she asked us if that was how she really looked, if that was her real voice. She didn't recognize herself."[38] This passage is a metatextual moment, a reference to St. Germain's own representation of his mother's murder and his awareness that his mother might not find herself recognizable in the pages of this book about her. Articulating a similar idea in her 2013 memoir *Men We Reaped,* a chronicle and memorial of the many young African American men the author knew who died young, Jesmyn Ward writes: "There is a great darkness bearing down on our lives, and no one acknowledges it."[39] At once a reference to institutionalized racism, crime, and drug abuse stemming from a lack of opportunities and to the erosion of public education and other services, Ward's sentence, like St. Germain's passage above, stages the major accomplishment of the documentary aesthetic—the representation of finance capitalism's structures and their reorganization of our everyday lives.

In her landmark 2008 essay "Men Explain Things to Me," Rebecca Solnit encapsulates the role that documentary art can have today. About the ways in which men assume mastery over women, Solnit's essay begins by recounting a party in Aspen, where a man described Solnit's own book to her as a book she "should have known." Solnit explains the man's error, but he "beg[ins] holding forth again" regardless. Solnit remarks that she "like[s] incidents of that sort, when forces that are usually so sneaky and hard to point out slither out of the grass and are as obvious as, say, an anaconda that's eaten a cow or an elephant turd on the carpet."[40] Making these subtle forces visible and recognizing their ubiquity in our lives, from structural racism and police violence to patriarchal privilege and sexual assault, have led to some of the most powerful social movements of today. These movements rely on documentary arts, from memoir and video to testimony and structural analysis, as they launch both critiques of finance capitalism's exploitation of subjects and visions of what renewed collective lives might be beyond exploitation. Documentary art at its best estranges us from ourselves and makes visible the structures that produce our subjectivities, the rules which bind us to a way of life that is in constant crisis and to which alternatives are emerging.

NOTES

Introduction

1. Glidden, *Rolling Blackouts,* 7.

2. Ibid.

3. Ibid., 6.

4. Shifts in print journalism and glossy magazines also contributed to the changing, more aesthetic role of photojournalism. As Julian Stallabrass has argued, the consolidation of media ownership under neoliberalism has pushed more conventional photojournalism into the art museum. "Even once serious publications" now focus on "food, fashion, cars, and the lives of TV personalities," and photographers such as Sebastião Salgado shift to "broad, synthetic work outside the daily pressures of conventional news coverage." Stallabrass, "Sebastião Sagado and Fine Art Photojournalism," 133–34.

5. Buffett, letter to the shareholders of Berkshire Hathaway Inc., 15.

6. Hayek, "Use of Knowledge," 526.

7. David Harvey characterizes contemporary financialization as an escalation of capitalism's drive to find profit through "fictitious capital" generated through complex financial instruments, the mechanisms of which "consisted of a labyrinth of countervailing claims that were almost impossible to value except by way of some mix of future expectations, beliefs and outright crazy short-term betting in unregulated markets." Harvey, *Seventeen Contradictions and the End of Capitalism,* 241.

8. See Jones, *Masters of the Universe,* as well as Mirowkski, "Postface." The longer intellectual history compliments and expands on the historical scope of neoliberalism that commonly finds neoliberalism's origins in 1970s reforms, as in Harvey, *Brief History of Neoliberalism.*

9. For an account of the Great Inflation period, see Bryan, "The Great Inflation."

10. See Jameson, "Postmodernism, or, the Cultural Logic of Late Capitalism."

11. There are many ways in which this historical and structural vertigo has been theorized. For prominent examples, see Crary, *24/7;* Fisher, *Capitalist Realism;* Jameson, *The Seeds of Time;* and Toscano and Kinkle, *Cartographies of the Absolute.*

12. See Nichols, *Speaking Truths with Film,* 13–33.

13. Grierson, "The Documentary Producer," 8.

14. Benjamin, "The Author as Producer," 771.

15. Agee, *Let Us Now Praise Famous Men,* 12.

16. Coles, *Doing Documentary Work,* 6.

17. Tagg, "Melancholy Realism," 38.

18. For an account of how documentary and journalistic forms have shifted due to digital, interactive interfaces, see Uricchio et al., *Mapping the Intersection of Two Cultures.*

19. On institutional critique's place in the art museum, see Fraser, "From the Critique of Institutions to an Institution of Critique."

20. White, *Figural Realism,* 24.

21. For an influential account of how documentary films by Claude Lanzmann and Errol Morris engage with history in relation to Jameson's definition of postmodernism, see Williams, "Mirrors without Memories."

22. For a historical account of the development of the "standard of objectivity" in American journalism, see Schudson, *Discovering the News,* and for a critique of classic documentary practice, see Rosler, "In, Around, and Afterthoughts."

23. Sontag, *On Photography,* 4.

24. Sontag, *Regarding the Pain of Others,* 81

25. Sontag's essay on the Abu Ghraib photographs was published shortly after *Regarding the Pain of Others.* See Sontag, "Regarding the Torture of Others."

26. The concept of art in the "expanded field" of postmodernism is in Krauss, "Sculpture in the Expanded Field."

27. *Powaqqatsi.*

28. Joselit, *After Art,* 92.

29. Stallabrass, "Sebatião Salgado and Fine Art Photojournalism," 145.

30. Michaels, *The Beauty of a Social Problem,* 36.

31. Campt, *Listening to Images,* 107.

32. *The 2015 Baltimore Uprisings,* n.p. For a reflection on the Baltimore uprising volume that has influenced my thinking here, see Clover, "Baltimore Riot. Baltimore Commune?"

33. Mailer, *The Presidential Papers,* 18.

34. Mailer, "The Armies of the Night, Handwritten Draft."

35. See Geyh, Leebron, and Levy, *Postmodern American Fiction.*

36. One of the key implications of this argument is that the way that we think about postmodern or postwar literature must be revised to more fully include and account for literary nonfiction, especially since critics and scholars of post-1945 literature have begun to seek alternate modes of periodizing late twentieth- and early twenty-first-century literature. The broader critical and literary historical context of this claim is laid out in Gladstone, "Introduction." While the overhauling of post-1945 literary studies has significantly changed the terms through which we view the period, nonfiction is still often absent from these considerations. In Mark McGurl's *The Program Era,* for example, literary nonfiction, though a part of the creative writing programs that he is analyzing, is not treated in any significant detail. Instead, McGurl notes that journalism and magazine writing are "importantly 'on the map' of the field of literary production to this day," though largely, as in his analysis of Kay Boyle's essay about the student strike at San Francisco State, as a kind of practical exercise on the way to producing literary fiction "in

quieter times" (30, 224). Michael Szalay's study of how postwar novelists such as Ralph Ellison, Norman Mailer, and William Styron were part of "a generation of novelists who helped a new technical elite . . . facilitate the transition of state-sponsored capitalism into a more properly neoliberal dispensation" has informed my thinking as well, especially insofar as cross-racial identification forms neoliberal styles (Szalay, *Hip Figures,* 28). But, again, Szalay's study focuses on novels, despite a writer like Mailer's major shift from novel writing to nonfiction prose in the 1960s and beyond.

1 / Money Trees

1. Jameson, *Postmodernism, or, the Cultural Logic of Late Capitalism,* 44.
2. Ibid., 44–45.
3. Ibid., 45.
4. Herr, *Dispatches,* 3.
5. Ibid., 43.
6. Ibid., 218.
7. Ibid., 188.
8. This is borne out by the fact that scholarship on Herr's *Dispatches* focuses on topics that we typically associate with reportage, such as ethics and accuracy, as well as its possible status as a work of "postmodern fiction." That the book can be read as both points to its documentary aesthetic, synthesizing journalistic modes with aesthetic practice. See Bartley, "The Hateful Self"; Lighter, "Michael Herr's Lurp Tale"; and Carpenter, "It Don't Mean Nothin.'"
9. For thorough critiques of documentary from this perspective, see Kael, "Current Cinema"; Rosler, "In, Around, and Afterthoughts"; and Sontag, *On Photography.*
10. Rosler, "In, Around, and Afterthoughts," 177.
11. Balsom and Peleg, "Introduction: The Documentary Attitude," 13.
12. The term "expanded field" is influentially used to describe postmodern aesthetics in Krauss, "Sculpture in the Expanded Field."
13. See Toscano and Kinkle, *Cartographies of the Absolute;* and Michaels, *The Beauty of a Social Problem.*
14. Michaels, "The Politics of a Good Picture," 183.
15. Crimp, "The Photographic Activity of Postmodernism," 100.
16. Beattie, *Dont Look Back,* 33.
17. Hall, "'Don't You Ever Just Watch?,'" 250.
18. Monteyne, "The Sound of the South Bronx," 101.
19. See Chang, *Can't Stop, Won't Stop;* Clover, *1989;* and Quinn, *Nothin' But a "G" Thang.*
20. Chang, *Can't Stop, Won't Stop,* 319.
21. Clover, *1989,* 36–37.
22. Quinn, *Nothin' but a "G" Thang,* 7.
23. Wallace and Costello, *Signifying Rappers,* 137.
24. Tate, "What Is Hip-Hop?," 240.
25. For accounts of rap and its connection to tropes of authenticity, see Keyes, *Rap and Street Consciousness,* 122–53; and the "authenticity debates" section of Forman, *That's the Joint!,* 69–224.
26. Bradley, *Book of Rhymes,* 168.
27. Chute, *Disaster Drawn,* 4.

28. See Nixon, *Slow Violence;* and Harvey, *The New Imperialism.*
29. Piskor, *Hip Hop Family Tree, Book 1,* 40.
30. Ibid., 109–11.
31. Ibid., 94.
32. Ibid., 60.
33. Ibid., 82.
34. Piskor, *Hip Hop Family Tree, Book 4,* 51, 81.
35. Piskor, *Hip Hop Family Tree, Book 1,* 90.
36. Ibid.
37. See Piskor, *Hip Hop Family Tree: Hip Hop/Comics Connection Pt. 2.*
38. Piskor, *Hip Hop Family Tree, Book 1,* 85–88.
39. "Kahlil Joseph."
40. Brown, "Side B (Dope Song)."
41. Pusha T, "M.F.T.R."
42. Leovy, Ghettoside, 241.
43. California Legislative Black Caucus, *The State of Black California,* 18.
44. Ibid., 33.
45. See Knafo and Kirkham, "For-Profit Prisons Are Big Winners of California's Overcrowding Crisis."
46. Leovy, *Ghettoside,* 317.
47. Williams, "Intertextuality and Lineage," 304.
48. Rose, *Hip Hop Wars,* 236.
49. Ascher, *Portfolio Society,* 123.
50. Ibid., 124.
51. Quinn, "Occupy," 94–95.

2 / Emergence in Retrospect

1. Didion, *The White Album,* 11.
2. Ibid.
3. For accounts of the New Journalism's problematization of the divide between fact and fiction, as well as its connections to more conventional forms of journalism, see Hartsock, *A History of American Literary Journalism;* Hellman, *Fables of Fact;* Hollowell, *Fact and Fiction;* Lehman, *Matters of Fact;* and Sims, *Literary Journalism.* The collection that gives "New Journalism" its force as a term for describing narrative or immersive journalism, the nonfiction novel, and literary reportage, is Wolfe and Johnson, *The New Journalism.*
4. Nelson, *Tough Enough,* 147.
5. Ibid., 149.
6. Codinha, "Céline Unveils Its Latest Poster Girl."
7. Jacobs, "Joan Didion on the Céline Ad."
8. See Harvey, *Brief History of Neoliberalism;* and Jones, *Masters of the Universe.*
9. Mirowski, "Postface: Defining Neoliberalism," 431.
10. Joan Didion, *Slouching Towards Bethlehem,* 85.
11. Ibid., 128.
12. Ibid., 123.
13. Sontag, "One Culture and the New Sensibility," 303.
14. See Hutcheon, *A Poetics of Postmodernism;* and Jameson, "Third-World Literature."

15. Almeida, *Waves of Protest,* 178.
16. Pratt, *Imperial Eyes,* 221.
17. Ibid., 205.
18. See Jameson, "Postmodernism."
19. Didion, *Salvador,* 13.
20. Didion, *Political Fictions,* 54.
21. Stuelke, "Reparative Politics," 767.
22. Didion, *Salvador,* 14.
23. Ibid.
24. Ibid., 26.
25. Ibid., 31.
26. Ibid., 34–35.
27. Ibid., 108.
28. See Almeida, *Waves of Protest.*
29. Didion, *The White Album,* 206.
30. Ibid., 208.
31. Haacke, *Shapolsky et al.,* 92.
32. Ibid., 93.
33. Ibid., 96.
34. Messer qtd. in Deutsche, "Property Values," 153.
35. Buchloh, "Hans Haacke," 49.
36. Deutsche, "Property Values," 155.
37. Schwabsky, "Inside Out."
38. Ibid.
39. Deutsche, "Property Values," 157.
40. Mirowski, *Never Let a Serious Crisis Go to Waste,* 15.
41. Friedman and Friedman, *Two Lucky People,* 400.
42. Long, "Chile Recognises 9,800 More Victims of Pinochet's Rule."
43. Friedman and Friedman, *Two Lucky People,* 408.
44. Ibid., 399.

3 / Neoliberal Style

1. West with Jay-Z, "Diamonds from Sierra Leone."

2. The subject position of the "entrepreneurial individual," or, more broadly, "homo economicus," is central to Foucault's early analysis of neoliberalism in *The Birth of Biopolitics.* See also Lemke, "The Birth of Bio-politics"; and Read, "A Genealogy of Homo Economicus."

3. As Adam Bradley remarks, Jay-Z's sense of rap as a kind of competition is central to the form: "Far from disqualifying rap as a poetic form, rap's combative nature actually binds it more securely to the spirit of competition at the heart of the some of the earliest poetic expressions" (Bradley, *Book of Rhymes,* 177). What Bradley sees as predominantly aesthetic—Jay-Z's emphasis on competitive (or entrepreneurial) individualism—I see as also an element of neoliberal ideology. My approach to rap music here has been influenced by the reading of rap in relation to free market economics in Clune, *American Literature and the Free Market,* 127–46.

4. In *Decoded,* Jay-Z notes that there are "two kinds of rhythm": the beat and the flow. While the beat is "like time itself, ticking off relentlessly in a rhythm that never varies

and never stops," the flow is "like life. . . . Flow is what we do with that time, how we live through it." This form/content schema is unified through the hustle, which "is the ultimate metaphor for the basic human struggles." Jay-Z, *Decoded,* 10–11, 18.

5. Rose, *Hip Hop Wars,* 202.

6. Jay-Z, *Decoded,* 309.

7. Norris qtd. in Jay-Z, *Decoded,* 311.

8. The book's layout and use of images also reinforces its aesthetic and political purposes. For an analysis of *Decoded* in relation to other hip-hop memoirs, see Balestrini, "Strategic Visuals."

9. Jay-Z, *Decoded,* 311.

10. For an extended reading of Jay-Z's performance at Pace Gallery and its relation to both celebrity and the art world, see Gabrillo, "The Rapper Is Present."

11. Jay-Z, *Decoded,* 311.

12. For other histories of neoliberalism's emergence, see Duggan, *The Twilight of Equality;* Harvey, *Brief History of Neoliberalism;* Peck, *Constructions of Neoliberal Reason;* and Steger and Roy, *Neoliberalism.*

13. Brown, "The End of Educated Democracy," 23.

14. "Structure of feeling" is a reference to Raymond Williams' influential concept, one which accompanies and even anticipates economic change. Neoliberal style functions this way, as it emerges in nonfiction narrative before neoliberal reforms become hegemonic under, for example, the Reagan presidency or the Thatcher premiership. See Williams, *Marxism and Literature,* 128–35.

15. Harvey, *Brief History of Neoliberalism,* 4.

16. De Saussure, *Course in General Linguistics,* 68. Neoliberalism has become a key term, as evidenced by the following, just a sampling of some recent works on the subject: Dávila, *Culture Works;* Elliot and Harkins, *Genres of Neoliberalism;* Gilbert, *Neoliberal Critique;* Harkins, *Everybody's Family Romance;* Huehls, *After Critique;* Jones, *Masters of the Universe;* Ouellette, *Better Living through Reality TV;* Peck, *Constructions of Neoliberal Reason;* and Smith, *Affect and American Literature.*

17. Harvey, *Brief History of Neoliberalism,* 12.

18. Ibid., 13.

19. On the decline of per capita GDP growth in Europe and the United States from 1950 to 2012, see Piketty, *Capital in the Twenty-First Century,* 96–99.

20. Miller, *Jane Austen,* 48.

21. Foucault, *Birth of Biopolitics,* 279.

22. The neoliberal style that I am charting in Haley and Thompson extends to contemporary literature as well, as can be seen in Caren Irr's reading of William T. Vollmann's "intensely monadic anti-political aesthetic, his monster of self-consciousness absorbing and obsessively scrutinizing its relation to all that crosses its path" (Irr, "Anti-Capitalism and Anti-Realism," 189). This first-person obsession is indicative of neoliberal style's persistence into contemporary prose.

23. Jay-Z, *Decoded,* 30.

24. Thompson, *Fear and Loathing at Rolling Stone,* 512.

25. Haley does not appear in the *Norton Anthology*'s table of contents, though an excerpt from *The Autobiography of Malcolm X,* attributed only to Malcolm X, is included. In the biographical and contextual sketch before the excerpt, it is noted that the *Autobiography* was "written in conjunction with Alex Haley," that it "became a best-seller in 1964,

the year that it was published," and that it "remains a classic of American autobiography" (Gates, *Norton Anthology of African American Literature,* 1816). The unproblematized use of "autobiography" to describe the text, along with the misidentification of the book's publication date as 1964, when it was actually published after Malcolm X's assassination in 1965, elides Haley's pivotal role in shaping the text.

26. Ferguson, *Reorder of Things,* 192.

27. Haley, *Alex Haley: The Playboy Interviews,* 4.

28. Ibid., 5.

29. Fraterrigo, *Playboy and the Making of the Good Life,* 149.

30. Haley, *Alex Haley: The Playboy Interviews,* 10.

31. Ibid., 14.

32. Ibid., 18.

33. Marable, *Malcolm X,* 220.

34. Balk, "Black Merchants of Hate," 72–73.

35. Ibid., 73.

36. Ibid., 74.

37. For an account of this article's differences from the *Autobiography,* see Abernethy, *The Iconography of Malcolm X,* 76–80. As Marable has argued, the *Autobiography* ultimately casts Malcolm X as "a pragmatic liberal, not a revolutionary," and it "does not read like a manifesto for black insurrection, but much more in the tradition of Benjamin Franklin's autobiography" (Marable, *Malcolm X,* 466).

38. Glass, *Counterculture Colophon,* 155.

39. Graeme Abernethy describes the *Autobiography* as "leav[ing] one with an impression of a series of selves cultivated under constant (if mutating) apprehension of death," which he links to the iconographic tradition in Christianity (Abernethy, *Iconography of Malcolm X,* 74). Abernethy's reading of the mutability of Malcolm X as an icon meshes well with my reading of Haley here, as Malcom X's ideological and iconographic functions point to the ways in which neoliberal economics penetrate and transform radical politics.

40. Berlant, *Cruel Optimism,* 23–50.

41. Malcolm X and Haley, *Autobiography of Malcolm X,* 358–59.

42. Ibid., 416.

43. Ibid., 418.

44. Ibid., 4.

45. Ibid., 523.

46. In a letter to *Playboy,* Acosta would claim that he and Thompson were equally responsible for the creation of "gonzo journalism": "In point of fact, Doctor Duke [Thompson] and I—the world famous Doctor Gonzo—together we both, hand in hand sought out . . . the term and methodology of reporting crucial events under fire and drugs, which are of course essential to any good writing in this age of confusion" (Acosta, *Oscar Zeta Acosta,* 109). For a reading of Acosta's conflicted relationship with the white counterculture and Thompson, see Martinez, *Countering the Counterculture,* 149–80.

47. Thompson, *Fear and Loathing at Rolling Stone,* 25.

48. Thompson, *Fear and Loathing in Las Vegas,* 4.

49. Ibid.

50. Thompson, *Fear and Loathing at Rolling Stone,* 29.

51. Ibid., 46–47.

52. Ibid., 65–66.
53. Thompson, *Fear and Loathing in Las Vegas,* 44.
54. DeKoven, *Utopia Limited,* 89.
55. Thompson, *Fear and Loathing in Las Vegas,* 68.
56. Ibid.
57. Venturi, Brown, and Izenour, *Learning from Las Vegas,* 52.
58. See Panitch and Gindin, *The Making of Global Capitalism,* 133–59.
59. Thompson, *Hey Rube,* 222.

4 / True Crime

1. Didion, *Slouching Towards Bethlehem,* 13.
2. Ibid.
3. Ibid., 21.
4. Ibid., 22.
5. Wakefield, "Slouching Towards Bethlehem."
6. Didion, *Slouching Towards Bethlehem,* 29.
7. Bugliosi with Gentry, *Helter Skelter,* 629.
8. Ibid., 359.
9. Rule, *The Stranger Beside Me,* 219.
10. Ibid., 78.
11. Wilson, *Learning to Live with Crime,* 16.
12. Cooper, *Family Values,* 313.
13. Malcolm, *The Journalist and the Murderer,* 3, 71, 72.
14. Ibid., 5.
15. McGinniss, *Fatal Vision,* 848.
16. Morris, *A Wilderness of Error,* 382.
17. Ibid., 490.
18. Segal qtd. in ibid., 246.
19. "A Wilderness of Error."
20. Chapter 7 transcript, *S Town,* http://stownpodcast.org.
21. Kael, "Current Cinema," 112.
22. "Chapter 6: What the Hell Did I Do?," *The Jinx.*
23. See Seltzer, "Serial Killers (II)," 124–25.
24. Simon, *The Innocents,* 70.
25. Nelson, *The Red Parts,* 2.
26. Ibid., 11.
27. Ibid., 113.
28. Ibid., 174.
29. Ibid.
30. Ibid., 174–75.
31. Ibid., 27.
32. Ibid., 194.
33. Ibid., 195.
34. Ibid., 180.
35. Ibid., 109.
36. For an account of the complexities of women's testimony in particular, see Gilmore, *Tainted Witness.*

37. Michaels, *The Beauty of a Social Problem,* 22.

38. Khan-Cullors and bandele, *When They Call You a Terrorist,* 11.

39. Ibid., 204.

5 / Speculative Ecology

1. Haacke, "On Social Grease," 143.

2. See Clover, *Riot Strike Riot.*

3. For an account of modes of imagining a post-oil future and their limits, see Szeman, "Crude Aesthetics."

4. The concept of "slow violence" comes from Nixon, *Slow Violence.*

5. Gore, *An Inconvenient Truth,* 11.

6. Kroll, "The 'Silent Springs' of Rachel Carson," 404.

7. See Souder, *On a Farther Shore,* 113–14.

8. Nixon, "Rachel Carson's Prescience."

9. Souder, *On a Farther Shore,* 23.

10. As Gary Kroll has noted about *The Sea Around Us,* the bestseller that allowed Carson to leave the U.S. Fish and Wildlife Service to work as a full-time writer, the book is "part nature writing" and "an equal participant in the literature of science writing. As an established form of journalism, science writing emerged in the 1920s as an effort to inform the lay public of the many scientific advances of the day." Kroll, "Rachel Carson's *The Sea Around Us,*" 120.

11. As Kroll argues, Carson's ocean books participated in and documented the scientific discoveries gained from the "federal patronage lavished [on] the oceanographic sciences in return for important data on a large range of ocean statistics that were crucial for the military's execution of the war effort—a new partnership that lasted well into the Cold War." Kroll, "Rachel Carson's *The Sea Around Us,*" 120.

12. Cafaro, "Rachel Carson's Environmental Ethics," 68.

13. Carson qtd. in Kroll, "Rachel Carson's *The Sea Around Us,*" 128.

14. For more on science fiction and environmentalism, see Canavan, *Green Planets.*

15. Schudson, *Discovering the News,* 160–94.

16. Ibid., 187.

17. Buell, "Toxic Discourse," 645.

18. Ibid., 639–40.

19. Heise, *Sense of Place and Sense of Planet,* 140.

20. Heise, "Martian Ecologies and the Future of Nature," 469.

21. Carson, *The Sea Around Us,* 147.

22. Carson, *Under the Sea-Wind,* 3.

23. Rowan, "The New York School of Urban Ecology," 603.

24. Carson, *Silent Spring,* 1–2.

25. Ibid., 3.

26. Ibid., 226.

27. Ibid., 233.

28. Ibid, 105.

29. Carson, *Silent Spring,* 68.

30. Ibid., 293.

31. Ibid., 32.

32. Ibid., 32–33.

33. See Nixon, *Slow Violence.*

34. Dunaway, *Seeing Green,* 31.

35. McGurl, "The Posthuman Comedy," 538.

36. For a reading of how Carson's ecology mirrors Jane Jacobs's urban planning vision, and how both reinforce social hierarchies within late capitalism, see Kinkela, "The Ecological Landscapes of Jane Jacobs and Rachel Carson."

37. See Morton, *Ecology without Nature.*

38. Nixon, "Rachel Carson's Prescience."

39. Carson, *Under the Sea-Wind,* 162.

40. Carson, *The Sea Around Us,* 15.

41. Sekula, *Fish Story,* 49.

42. For an account of *Fish Story* and labor, see Entin, "Working Photography."

43. Misrach, *Petrochemical America,* 6.

44. Ibid., 120–21.

45. Palmer, *In the Aura of a Hole,* 51.

46. Ibid.

47. Chakrabarty, "The Climate of History," 220.

Conclusion

1. Yagoda, *Memoir,* 28.

2. For a reading of the James Frey controversy, see Rak, *Boom!,* 179–205.

3. Michaels, "Going Boom"; Thoma, "What Julia Knew," 130. See also Gilmore, "American Neoconfessional"; Williams, "Eat, Pray, Love"; and, for a related take on reality television, McCarthy, "Reality Television."

4. Rak, *Boom!,* 44.

5. See Habermas, *The Structural Transformation of the Public Sphere;* and Warner, *The Letters of the Republic.*

6. Leonard, "The Black Album."

7. Didion, *The Year of Magical Thinking,* 104.

8. Ibid., 227.

9. Didion, *Blue Nights,* 188.

10. Eggers, *What Is the What,* 5.

11. Ibid.

12. Ibid., 474–75.

13. Eggers, *Zeitoun,* 7.

14. Ibid., 335.

15. Ibid., 246.

16. Ibid., 303.

17. Ibid., 9.

18. See Goldsmith, *Uncreative Writing,* 6–8.

19. Iyer, "Desert Pitch"

20. Eggers, *A Hologram for the King,* 135.

21. For scholarly accounts of comics memoir, see Chute, *Graphic Women;* and Chaney, *Graphic Subjects.*

22. Bechdel, *Fun Home,* 27.

23. Gloeckner, *The Diary of a Teenage Girl,* xv. The podcast *Mortified* features adults who share embarrassing materials from their adolescence, in a way that is both

reminiscent of Gloeckner's use of the diary form and yet another example of the force that memoir has in our contemporary culture. See http://getmortified.com/podcast/.

24. Gloeckner, *The Diary of a Teenage Girl,* 65.

25. Ibid., xvi.

26. See Powers, "Ed Ruscha."

27. See Lejeune, *On Autobiography,* 3–30; and on Oprah Winfrey, see Peck, *The Age of Oprah,* 175–210.

28. Heti, *How Should a Person Be?,* 305.

29. Ibid., 305–6.

30. Ibid., 306.

31. Lin, *Taipei,* 16.

32. Nelson, *Bluets,* 20.

33. Nelson, "All That Is the Case," 156.

34. Lovell, *Dear Erin Hart.*

35. Ibid.

36. LeBlanc, *Random Family,* 403–4.

37. Altman, "'Random Family' Ten Years On."

38. St. Germain, *Son of a Gun,* 95.

39. Ward, *Men We Reaped,* 250.

40. Solnit, "Men Explain Things to Me," 3.

BIBLIOGRAPHY

Abernethy, Graeme. *The Iconography of Malcolm X*. Lawrence: UP of Kansas, 2013.

Acosta, Oscar Zeta. *Oscar Zeta Acosta: The Uncollected Writings*. Ed. Ilan Stavans. Houston: Arte Público P, 1996.

Agee, James, and Walker Evans. *Let Us Now Praise Famous Men*. Boston: Mariner, 2001.

Almeida, Paul. *Waves of Protest: Popular Struggle in El Salvador, 1925–2005*. Minneapolis: U of Minnesota P, 2008.

Altman, Anna, and Katia Bachko. "'Random Family' Ten Years On: An Interview with Adrian Nicole LeBlanc." *New Yorker* (26 July 2013).

Ascher, Ivan. *Portfolio Society: On the Capitalist Mode of Prediction*. Brooklyn: Zone, 2016.

Balestrini, Nassim. "Strategic Visuals in Hip-Hop Life Writing." *Popular Music and Society* 38.2 (2015): 224–42.

Balk, Alfred, and Alex Haley. "Black Merchants of Hate." *Saturday Evening Post* (26 Jan. 1963).

Balsom, Erika, and Hila Peleg. "Introduction: The Documentary Attitude." *Documentary Across Disciplines*. Ed. Erika Balsom and Hila Peleg. Cambridge: MIT P, 2016. 10–19.

Bartley, Aryn. "The Hateful Self: Substitution and the Ethics of Representing War." *Modern Fiction Studies* 54.1 (Spring 2008): 50–71.

Beattie, Keith. *Dont Look Back*. New York: BFI/Palgrave, 2016.

Bechdel, Alison. *Fun Home: A Family Tragicomic*. New York: Mariner, 2007.

Benjamin, Walter. "The Author as Producer." Trans. Edmund Jephcott. *Selected Writings, Vol. 2: 1927–1934*. Ed. Michael W. Jennings, Howard Eiland, and Gary Smith. Cambridge: Harvard UP, 1999. 768–82.

Berlant, Lauren. *Cruel Optimism.* Durham: Duke UP, 2011.

Bradley, Adam. *Book of Rhymes: The Poetics of Hip Hop.* New York: Basic, 2009.

Brouillette, Sarah. *Literature and the Creative Economy.* Stanford: Stanford UP, 2014.

Brown, Danny. "Side B (Dope Song)." *Old.* Fool's Gold Records, 2013.

Brown, Wendy. "The End of Educated Democracy." *Representations* 116.1 (2011): 19–41.

Bryan, Michael. "The Great Inflation: 1965–1982." *Federal Reserve History* (22 Nov. 2013).

Buchloh, Benjamin. "Hans Haacke: From Factographic Sculpture to Counter-Monument." *Hans Haacke: For Real, Works 1959–2006.* Ed. Matthias Flügge and Robert Fleck. Düsseldorf: Richter, 2006. 42–59.

Buell, Lawrence. "Toxic Discourse." *Critical Inquiry* 24.3 (Spring 1998): 639–65.

Buffett, Warren E. Letter to the shareholders of Berkshire Hathaway Inc. (21 Feb. 2003). http://www.berkshirehathaway.com/letters/2002pdf.pdf.

Bugliosi, Vincent, with Curt Gentry. *Helter Skelter: The True Story of the Manson Murders.* New York: Norton, 1994.

Cafaro, Philip. "Rachel Carson's Environmental Ethics." *Rachel Carson: Legacy and Challenge.* Ed. Lisa H. Sideris and Kathleen Dean Moore. Albany: SUNY P, 2008.

California Legislative Black Caucus. *The State of Black California.* 2007.

Campt, Tina M. *Listening to Images.* Durham: Duke UP, 2017.

Canavan, Gerry, and Kim Stanley Robinson, eds. *Green Planets: Ecology and Science Fiction.* Middletown: Wesleyan UP, 2014.

Capote, Truman. *In Cold Blood: A True Account of a Multiple Murder and Its Consequences.* New York: Random House, 1966.

Carpenter, Lucas. "'It Don't Mean Nothin'': Vietnam War Fiction and Postmodernism." *College Literature* 30.2 (Spring 2003): 30–50.

Carson, Rachel. *The Sea Around Us.* New York: Oxford UP, 1991.

———. *Silent Spring.* New York: Houghton Mifflin, 2002.

———. *Under the Sea-Wind.* New York: Penguin, 2007.

Chakrabarty, Dipesh. "The Climate of History: Four Theses." *Critical Inquiry* 35 (Winter 2009): 197–222.

Chaney, Michael, ed. *Graphic Subjects: Critical Essays on Autobiography and Graphic Novels.* Madison: U of Wisconsin P, 2011.

Chang, Jeff. *Can't Stop, Won't Stop: A History of the Hip-Hop Generation.* New York: Picador, 2005.

Chile, Obstinate Memory. Dir. Patricio Guzmán. In *The Battle of Chile.* Icarus Films, 1998.

Chute, Hillary. *Disaster Drawn: Visual Witness, Comics, and Documentary Form.* Cambridge: Harvard UP, 2016.

———. *Graphic Women: Life Narrative and Contemporary Comics.* New York: Columbia UP, 2010.

Clover, Joshua. "Baltimore Riot. Baltimore Commune?" Verso Books blog (25 April 2016). https://www.versobooks.com/blogs/2614-baltimore-riot-baltimore-commune.

———. *1989: Bob Dylan Didn't Have This to Sing About.* Berkeley: U of California P, 2009.

———. *Riot Strike Riot: The New Era of Uprisings.* New York: Verso, 2016.

Clune, Michael W. *American Literature and the Free Market, 1945–2000.* New York: Cambridge UP, 2009.

Codinha, Alessandra. "Céline Unveils Its Latest Poster Girl: Joan Didion." *Vogue* (6 Jan. 2015).

Coles, Robert. *Doing Documentary Work.* New York: Oxford UP, 1997.

Cooper, Melinda. *Family Values: Between Neoliberalism and the New Social Conservatism.* Brooklyn: Zone, 2017.

Crary, Jonathan. *24/7: Late Capitalism and the Ends of Sleep.* New York: Verso, 2013.

Crimp, Douglas. "The Photographic Activity of Postmodernism." *October* 15 (Winter 1980): 91–101.

Dávila, Arlene. *Culture Works: Space, Value, and Mobility across the Neoliberal Americas.* New York: New York UP, 2012.

Dekoven, Marianne. *Utopia Limited: The Sixties and the Emergence of the Postmodern.* Durham: Duke UP, 2004.

de Saussure, Ferdinand. *Course in General Linguistics.* Trans. Wade Baskin. Ed. Perry Meisel and Haun Saussy. New York: Columbia UP, 2011.

Deutsche, Rosalind. "Property Values: Hans Haacke, Real Estate, and the Museum." *Hans Haacke.* Ed. Rachel Churner. Cambridge: MIT P, 2015. 137–62.

Didion, Joan. *Blue Nights.* New York: Knopf, 2011.

———. *Political Fictions.* New York: Knopf, 2001.

———. *Salvador.* New York: Vintage, 1994.

———. *Slouching Towards Bethlehem.* New York: Farrar, Straus and Giroux, 2008.

———. *The White Album.* New York: Farrar, Straus and Giroux, 1990.

———. *The Year of Magical Thinking.* New York: Knopf, 2005.

Dont Look Back. Dir. D. A. Pennebaker. Criterion Collection, 2015.

Duggan, Lisa. *The Twilight of Equality?: Neoliberalism, Cultural Politics, and the Attack on Democracy.* Boston: Beacon, 2003.

Dunaway, Finis. *Seeing Green: The Use and Abuse of American Environmental Images.* Chicago: U of Chicago P, 2015.

Eggers, Dave. *A Hologram for the King.* San Francisco: McSweeney's, 2012.

———. *What Is the What.* San Francisco: McSweeney's, 2006.

———. *Zeitoun.* San Francisco: McSweeney's, 2009.

Elliot, Jane, and Gillian Harkins, eds. "Genres of Neoliberalism." Special issue of *Social Text* 31.2 (2013).

Entin, Joseph B. "Working Photography: Labor Documentary and Documenting Labor in the Neoliberal Age." *Remaking Reality: U.S. Documentary Culture after 1945*. Ed. Sara Blair, Joseph B. Entin, and Franny Nudelman. Chapel Hill: U of North Carolina P, 2018.

Ferguson, Roderick. *The Reorder of Things: The University and Its Pedagogies of Minority Difference*. Minneapolis: U of Minnesota P, 2012.

Fisher, Mark. *Capitalist Realism: Is There No Alternative?* Winchester, UK: Zero, 2009.

The Fog of War transcript. http://www.errolmorris.com/film/fow_transcript.html.

Forman, Murray, and Mark Anthony Neal, eds. *That's the Joint!: The Hip-Hop Studies Reader*. 2nd ed. New York: Routledge, 2011.

Foucault, Michel. *The Birth of Biopolitics: Lectures at the Collège de France, 1978–1979*. Trans. Graham Burchell. Ed. Michel Senellart. New York: Palgrave Macmillan, 2008.

Fraser, Andrea. "From the Critique of Institutions to an Institution of Critique." *Artforum* 44.1 (Sept. 2005): 278–83.

Fraterrigo, Elizabeth. *Playboy and the Making of the Good Life in Modern America*. New York: Oxford UP, 2011.

Fried, Michael. *Why Photography Matters as Art as Never Before*. New Haven: Yale UP, 2008.

Friedman, Milton, and Rose D. Friedman. *Two Lucky People: Memoirs*. Chicago: U of Chicago P, 1998.

Gabrillo, James. "The Rapper Is Present: Sound Art, Liveness, and the Negotiation of Identity in Jay Z's 'Picasso Baby.'" *Journal of Popular Music Studies* 29 (2017): 1–10.

Gates, Henry Louis, Jr., and Nellie Y. McKay, eds. *The Norton Anthology of African American Literature*. New York: Norton, 1997.

Geyh, Paula, Fred G. Leebron, and Andrew Levy, eds. *Postmodern American Fiction: A Norton Anthology*. New York: Norton, 1997.

Gilbert, Jeremy, ed. "Neoliberal Culture." Special issue of *New Formations* 80–81 (2013).

Gilmore, Leigh. "American Neoconfessional: Memoir, Self-Help, and Redemption on Oprah's Couch." *Biography* 33.4 (Fall 2010): 657–79.

———. *Tainted Witness: Why We Doubt What Women Say about Their Lives*. New York: Columbia UP, 2017.

Gimme Shelter. Dir. David Maysles, Albert Maysles, and Charlotte Zwerin. Criterion Collection, 2000.

Gladstone, Jason, and Daniel Worden. "Introduction: Postmodernism, Then." *Twentieth-Century Literature* 57.3–4 (Fall/Winter 2011): 291–308.

Glass, Loren. *Counterculture Colophon: Grove Press, the Evergreen Review, and the Incorporation of the Avant Garde*. Stanford: Stanford UP, 2013.

Glidden, Sarah. *Rolling Blackouts: Dispatches from Turkey, Syria, and Iraq*. Montreal: Drawn & Quarterly, 2016.

Gloeckner, Phoebe. *The Diary of a Teenage Girl: An Account in Words and Pictures*. Revised ed. Berkeley: North Atlantic, 2015.

Goldsmith, Kenneth. *Uncreative Writing: Managing Language in the Digital Age.* New York: Columbia UP, 2011.

Gore, Al. *An Inconvenient Truth: The Planetary Emergency of Global Warming and What We Can Do about It.* New York: Rodale, 2006.

Grierson, John. "The Documentary Producer." *Cinema Quarterly* 2.1 (Autumn 1933): 7–9.

Haacke, Hans. "On Social Grease." *Art Journal* 42.2 (Summer 1982): 137–43.

———. *Shapolsky et al. Manhattan Real Estate Holdings, a Real-Time Social System, as of May 1, 1971.* In *Hans Haacke: Unfinished Business.* New York and Cambridge: New Museum of Contemporary Art/MIT P, 1986. 92–97.

Habermas, Jürgen. *The Structural Transformation of the Public Sphere: An Inquiry into a Category of Bourgeois Society.* Trans. Thomas Burger. Cambridge: MIT Press, 1991.

Haley, Alex. *Alex Haley: The Man Who Traced America's Roots.* New York: Reader's Digest, 2007.

———. *Alex Haley: The Playboy Interviews.* Ed. Murray Fisher. New York: Ballantine, 1993.

Hall, Jeanne. "'Don't You Ever Just Watch?': American Cinema Verité and *Dont Look Back.*" *Documenting the Documentary: Close Readings of Documentary Film.* Ed. Barry Keith Grant and Jeannette Sloniowski. Detroit: Wayne State UP, 2013. 237–53.

Harkins, Gillian. *Everybody's Family Romance: Reading Incest in Neoliberal America.* Minneapolis: U of Minnesota P, 2009.

Hartsock, John C. *A History of American Literary Journalism: The Emergence of a Modern Narrative Form.* Amherst: U of Massachusetts P, 2000.

Harvey, David. *A Brief History of Neoliberalism.* New York: Oxford UP, 2005.

———. *The New Imperialism.* New York: Oxford UP, 2003.

———. *Seven Contradictions and the End of Capitalism.* New York: Oxford UP, 2014.

Hayek, Friedrich A. "The Use of Knowledge in Society." *American Economic Review* 35.4 (Sept. 1945): 519–30.

Heise, Ursula K. "Martian Ecologies and the Future of Nature." *Twentieth-Century Literature* 57.3–4 (Fall/Winter 2011): 447–71.

———. *Sense of Place and Sense of Planet: The Environmental Imagination and the Global.* New York: Oxford UP, 2008.

Hellman, John. *Fables of Fact: The New Journalism as New Fiction.* Urbana: U of Illinois P, 1981.

Herr, Michael. *Dispatches.* New York: Vintage, 1991.

Heti, Sheila. *How Should a Person Be?: A Novel from Life.* New York: Henry Holt, 2012.

Hollowell, John. *Fact and Fiction: The New Journalism and the Nonfiction Novel.* Chapel Hill: U of North Carolina P, 1977.

Huehls, Mitchum. *After Critique: Twenty-First Century Fiction in a Neoliberal Age.* New York: Oxford UP, 2016.

Hungerford, Amy. *Making Literature Now.* Stanford: Stanford UP, 2016.
Hutcheon, Linda. *A Poetics of Postmodernism: History, Theory, Fiction.* New York: Routledge, 1988.
Irr, Caren. "Anti-Capitalism and Anti-Realism in William T. Vollmann's *Poor People.*" *Reading Capitalist Realism.* Ed. Alison Shonkwiler and Leigh Clare Le Barge. Iowa City: U of Iowa P, 2014. 177–94.
Iyer, Pico. "Desert Pitch: 'A Hologram for the King' by Dave Eggers." *New York Times* (19 July 2012).
Jacobs, Alexandra. "Joan Didion on the Céline Ad." *New York Times* (7 Jan. 2015).
Jameson, Fredric. "Postmodernism, or, the Cultural Logic of Late Capitalism." *New Left Review* 146 (July/August 1984): 53–92.
———. *Postmodernism, or, the Cultural Logic of Late Capitalism.* Durham: Duke UP, 1991.
———. *The Seeds of Time.* New York: Columbia UP, 1994.
———. "Third-World Literature in the Era of Multinational Capitalism." *Social Text* 15 (Autumn 1986): 65–88.
Jay-Z. *Decoded.* New York: Spiegel & Grau, 2011.
———. *Picasso Baby: A Performance Art Film.* Dir. Mark Romanek. 2013. http://lifeandtimes.com/jay-z-picasso-baby-a-performance-art-film.
The Jinx: The Life and Deaths of Robert Durst. Dir. Andrew Jarecki. HBO, 2015.
Jones, David Steadman. *Masters of the Universe: Hayek, Friedman, and the Birth of Neoliberal Politics.* Princeton: Princeton UP, 2012.
Joselit, David. *After Art.* Princeton: Princeton UP, 2013.
Kael, Pauline. "Current Cinema." *New Yorker* (19 Dec. 1970).
"Kahlil Joseph: *Double Conscience.*" Museum of Contemporary Art Los Angeles. http://www.moca.org/exhibition/kahlil-joseph-double-conscience.
Keyes, Cheryl L. *Rap Music and Street Consciousness.* Urbana-Champaign: U of Illinois P, 2002.
Khan-Cullors, Patrisse, and asha bandele. *When They Call You a Terrorist: A Black Lives Matter Memoir.* New York: St. Martin's P, 2017.
Kinkela, David. "The Ecological Landscapes of Jane Jacobs and Rachel Carson." *American Quarterly* 61.4 (Dec. 2009): 905–29.
Knafo, Safi, and Chris Kirkham. "For-Profit Prisons Are Big Winners of California's Overcrowding Crisis." *Huffington Post* (25 Oct. 2013). http://www.huffingtonpost.com/2013/10/25/california-private-prison_n_4157641.html.
Krauss, Rosalind. "Sculpture in the Expanded Field." *October* 8 (Spring 1979): 30–44.
Kroll, Gary. "Rachel Carson's *The Sea Around Us,* Ocean-Centrism, and a Nascent Ocean Ethic." *Rachel Carson: Legacy and Challenge.* Ed. Lisa H. Sideris and Kathleen Dean Moore. Albany: SUNY P, 2008.
———. "The 'Silent Springs' of Rachel Carson: Mass Media and the Origins of Modern Environmentalism." *Public Understanding of Science* 10 (2001): 403–20.

La Berge, Leigh Clare. *Scandals and Abstraction: Financial Fiction of the Long 1980s.* New York: Oxford UP, 2015.

Lamar, Kendrick. *Good Kid, M.A.A.D. City.* Top Dawg/Aftermath, 2012.

LeBlanc, Adrian Nicole. *Random Family: Love, Drugs, Trouble, and Coming of Age in the Bronx.* New York: Scribner, 2003.

Lehman, Daniel. *Matters of Fact: Reading Nonfiction over the Edge.* Columbus: Ohio State UP, 1997.

Lejeune, Philippe. *On Autobiography.* Trans. Katherine Leary. Ed. Paul John Eakin. Minneapolis: U of Minnesota P, 1989.

Lemke, Thomas. "'The Birth of Bio-politics': Michel Foucault's Lecture at the Collège de France on Neo-liberal Governmentality." *Economy & Society* 30.2 (2001): 190–207.

Leonard, John. "The Black Album." *New York Review of Books* (20 Oct. 2005).

Leovy, Jill. *Ghettoside: A True Story of Murder in America.* New York: Spiegel & Grau, 2015.

Lessons of Darkness. Dir. Werner Herzog. Anchor Bay, 2004.

Lighter, Jonathan. "Michael Herr's Lurp Tale." *War, Literature, and the Arts* 28 (2016): 1–12.

Lin, Tao. *Taipei.* New York: Vintage, 2013.

Littler, Francis W. "Agricultural Spray Emulsion Concentrates and Their Method of Manufacture." U.S. Patent 3,098,789. 23 July 1963.

Long, Gideon. "Chile Recognizes 9,800 More Victims of Pinochet's Rule." *BBC News* (18 Aug. 2011).

Lovell, Jessamyn. *Dear Erin Hart.* San Francisco: Cameraworks, 2015.

Mailer, Norman. *Advertisements for Myself.* Cambridge: Harvard UP, 1992.

———. "The Armies of the Night, Handwritten Draft." 1967–68. Folder 2, Box 77, Norman Mailer Papers, Harry Ransom Center, University of Texas at Austin.

———. *The Fight.* New York: Random House, 2013.

———. "Modes and Mutations: Quick Comments on the American Novel." *Commentary* (1 March 1966).

———. *The Naked and the Dead.* New York: Picador, 2000.

———. *The Presidential Papers.* New York: Putnam, 1963.

Malcolm, Janet. *The Journalist and the Murderer.* New York: Vintage, 1990.

Malcolm X and Alex Haley. *The Autobiography of Malcolm X.* New York: Ballantine, 1992.

———. "I'm Talking to You, White Man." *Saturday Evening Post* (12 Sept. 1964).

Marable, Manning. *Malcolm X: A Life of Reinvention.* New York: Penguin, 2012.

Martin, Theodore. *Contemporary Drift: Genre, Historicism, and the Problem of the Present.* New York: Columbia UP, 2017.

Martinez, Manuel Luis. *Countering the Counterculture: Rereading Postwar American Dissent from Jack Kerouac to Tomas Rivera.* Madison: U of Wisconsin P, 2003.

McCarthy, Anna. "Reality Television: A Neoliberal Theater of Suffering." *Social Text* 25.4 (Winter 2007): 17–41.

McGinnis, Joe. *Fatal Vision*. New York: Signet, 2012.

McGurl, Mark. "The Posthuman Comedy." *Critical Inquiry* 38 (Spring 2012): 533–53.

———. *The Program Era: Postwar Fiction and the Rise of Creative Writing*. Cambridge: Harvard UP, 2009.

McLanahan, Annie. *Dead Pledges: Debt, Crisis, and Twenty-First-Century Culture*. Stanford: Stanford UP, 2016.

Michaels, Walter Benn. *The Beauty of a Social Problem: Photography, Autonomy, Economy*. Chicago: U of Chicago P, 2015.

———. "Going Boom." *Bookforum* (February/March 2009).

———. "The Politics of a Good Picture: Race, Class, and Form in Jeff Wall's *Mimic*." *PMLA* 125.1 (January 2010): 177–84.

Miller, D. A. *Jane Austen, or, the Secret of Style*. New York: Columbia UP, 2003.

Mirowski, Philip. *Never Let a Serious Crisis Go to Waste: How Neoliberalism Survived the Financial Meltdown*. New York: Verso, 2013.

———. "Postface: Defining Neoliberalism." *The Road from Mont Pèlerin: The Making of the Neoliberal Thought Collective*. Ed. Philip Mirowski and Dieter Plehwe. Cambridge: Harvard UP, 2015.

Misrach, Richard, and Kate Orff. *Petrochemical America*. New York: Aperture, 2014.

Monteyne, Kimberley Bercov. "The Sound of the South Bronx: Youth Culture, Genre, and Performance in Charlie Ahearn's *Wild Style*." *Youth Culture in Global Cinema*. Ed. Timothy Shary and Alexandra Seibel. Austin: U of Texas P, 2007. 87–105.

Moraru, Christian. *Cosmodernism: Narrative, Late Globalization, and the New Cultural Imaginary*. Ann Arbor: U of Michigan P, 2011.

Morris, Errol. *A Wilderness of Error: The Trials of Jeffrey MacDonald*. New York: Penguin 2012.

Morton, Timothy. *Ecology without Nature: Rethinking Environmental Aesthetics*. Cambridge: Harvard UP, 2007.

Nealon, Jeffrey T. *Post-Postmodernism: or, The Cultural Logic of Just-in-Time Capitalism*. Stanford: Stanford UP, 2012.

Nelson, Deborah. *Tough Enough: Arbus, Arendt, Didion, McCarthy, Sontag, Weil*. Chicago: U of Chicago P, 2017.

Nelson, Maggie. "All That Is the Case: Some Thoughts on Fact in Nonfiction and Documentary Poetry." *Lit from Within: Contemporary Masters on the Art and Craft of Writing*. Ed. Kevin Haworth and Dinty W. Moore. Athens: Ohio UP, 2011.

———. *Bluets*. Seattle: Wave, 2009.

———. *The Red Parts: A Memoir*. New York: Free P, 2007.

Nichols, Bill. *Speaking Truths with Film: Evidence, Ethics, Politics in Documentary*. Berkeley: U of California P, 2016.

Nixon, Rob. "Rachel Carson's Prescience." *Chronicle of Higher Education* (3 Sept. 2012).
———. *Slow Violence and the Environmentalism of the Poor.* Cambridge: Harvard UP, 2011.
Ouellette, Laurie. *Better Living through Reality TV: Television and Post-Welfare Citizenship.* Malden: Blackwell, 2008.
Palmer, A. Laurie. *In the Aura of a Hole: Exploring Sites of Material Extraction.* London: Black Dog, 2014.
Panitch, Leo, and Sam Gindin. *The Making of Global Capitalism: The Political Economy of American Empire.* New York: Verso, 2012.
Peck, Jamie. *Constructions of Neoliberal Reason.* New York: Oxford UP, 2010.
Peck, Janice. *The Age of Oprah: Cultural Icon for a Neoliberal Era.* Boulder: Paradigm, 2008.
Piketty, Thomas. *Capital in the Twenty-First Century.* Trans. Arthur Goldhammer. Cambridge: Harvard UP, 2014.
Piskor, Ed. *Hip Hop Family Tree, Book 1: 1970s–1981.* Seattle: Fantagraphics, 2013.
———. *Hip Hop Family Tree, Book 4: 1984–1985.* Seattle: Fantagraphics, 2016.
———. *Hip Hop Family Tree: Hip Hop/Comics Connection Pt. 2.* Seattle: Fantagraphics, 2014.
Powaqqatsi. qatsi.org, 2014. http://www.koyaanisqatsi.org/films/powaqqatsi.php.
Powers, Bill. "Ed Ruscha." *W Magazine* (Nov. 2007).
Pratt, Mary Louise. *Imperial Eyes: Travel Writing and Transculturation.* 2nd ed. New York: Routledge, 2008.
Pusha T. "M.F.T.R." *King Push: Darkest Before the Dawn, The Prelude.* Def Jam/GOOD Music, 2015.
Quinn, Eithne. *Nothin' But a "G" Thang: The Culture and Commerce of Gangsta Rap.* New York: Columbia UP, 2004.
———. "Occupy Wall Street, Racial Neoliberalism, and New York's Hip-Hop Moguls." *American Quarterly* 68.1 (March 2016): 75–99.
Rak, Julie. *Boom!: Manufacturing Memoir for the Popular Market.* Waterloo: Wilfred Laurier UP, 2013.
Read, Jason. "A Genealogy of Homo Economicus: Neoliberalism and the Production of Subjectivity." *Foucault Studies* 6 (2009): 25–36.
The River. Dir. Pare Lorentz. 1938. http://xroads.virginia.edu/~1930s/film/lorentz/river.html.
Rose, Tricia. *The Hip Hop Wars: What We Talk about When We Talk about Hip Hop—and Why It Matters.* New York: Basic, 2008.
Rosler, Martha. "In, Around, and Afterthoughts (On Documentary Photography)." *Decoys and Disruptions: Selected Writings, 1975–2001.* Cambridge: MIT P, 2004. 151–206.
Rowan, Jamin Creed. "The New York School of Urban Ecology: The *New Yorker,* Rachel Carson, and Jane Jacobs." *American Literature* 82.3 (Sept. 2010): 583–610.
Rule, Ann. *The Stranger Beside Me.* New York: Pocket, 2009.

Sacco, Joe. *Safe Area Goražde: The War in Eastern Bosnia.* Seattle: Fantagraphics, 2001.

Schudson, Michael. *Discovering the News: A Social History of American Newspapers.* New York: Basic, 1978.

Schwabsky, Barry. "Inside Out." *Nation* (6 May 2015).

The Sea Around Us. Dir. Irwin Allen. Warner Brothers, 2010.

Sekula, Allan. *Fish Story.* Düsseldorf: Richter Verlag, 1995.

Seltzer, Mark. "Serial Killers (II): The Pathological Public Sphere." *Critical Inquiry* 22.1 (Autumn 1995): 122–49.

Simon, Taryn. *The Innocents.* New York: Umbrage, 2003.

Sims, Norman, ed. *Literary Journalism in the Twentieth Century.* New York: Oxford UP, 1990.

Smith, Rachel Greenwald. *Affect and American Literature in the Age of Neoliberalism.* New York: Cambridge UP, 2015.

Smith, Terry. *What is Contemporary Art?* Chicago: U of Chicago P, 2009.

Solnit, Rebecca. "Men Explain Things to Me." *Men Explain Things to Me.* Chicago: Haymarket, 2014. 1–15.

Sontag, Susan. "One Culture and the New Sensibility." *Against Interpretation and Other Essays.* New York: Farrar, Straus and Giroux, 1966. 293–304.

———. *On Photography.* New York: Noonday P, 1989.

———. *Regarding the Pain of Others.* New York: Picador, 2003.

———. "Regarding the Torture of Others." *New York Times* (23 May 2004).

Souder, William. *On a Farther Shore: The Life and Legacy of Rachel Carson.* New York: Broadway, 2012.

St. Germain, Justin. *Son of a Gun: A Memoir.* New York: Random House, 2013.

Stallabrass, Julian. "Sebastião Sagado and Fine Art Photojournalism." *New Left Review* 223 (May–June 1997): 131–60.

Steger, Manfred B., and Ravi K. Roy. *Neoliberalism: A Very Short Introduction.* New York: Oxford UP, 2010.

Stuelke, Patricia. "The Reparative Politics of the Central America Solidarity Movement Culture." *American Quarterly* 66.3 (Sept. 2014): 767–90.

Szalay, Michael. *Hip Figures: A Literary History of the Democratic Party.* Stanford: Stanford UP, 2012.

Szeman, Imre. "Crude Aesthetics: The Politics of Oil Documentaries." *Oil Culture.* Ed. Ross Barrett and Daniel Worden. Minneapolis: U of Minnesota P, 2014. 350–65.

Tagg, John. "Melancholy Realism: Walker Evans's Resistance to Meaning." *Narrative* 11.1 (Jan. 2003): 3–77.

Tate, Greg. "What is Hip-Hop?" *Flyboy 2: The Greg Tate Reader.* Durham: Duke UP, 2016. 239–42.

Thin Blue Line transcript. http://www.errolmorris.com/film/tbl_transcript.html.

Thoma, Pamela. "What Julia Knew: Domestic Labor in the Recession-Era Chick Flick." *Gendering the Recession: Media and Culture in an Age of Austerity.* Ed. Diane Negra and Yvonne Tasker. Durham: Duke UP, 2014.

Thompson, Hunter S. *Fear and Loathing at Rolling Stone: The Essential Writings of Hunter S. Thompson.* Ed. Jann S. Wenner. New York: Simon and Schuster, 2011.

———. *Fear and Loathing in Las Vegas: A Strange Journey to the Heart of the American Dream.* New York: Vintage, 1998.

———. *Hey Rube: Blood Sport, the Bush Doctrine, and the Downward Spiral of Dumbness.* New York: Simon and Schuster, 2004.

Toscano, Alberto, and Jeff Kinkle. *Cartographies of the Absolute.* Winchester, UK: Zero, 2015.

The 2015 Baltimore Uprising: A Teen Epistolary. New York: Research and Destroy, 2015.

Uricchio, William et al. *Mapping the Intersection of Two Cultures: Interactive Documentary and Digital Journalism.* MIT Open Documentary Lab/MacArthur Foundation, 2015. http://opendoclab.mit.edu/interactivejournalism/.

VanderMeer, Jeff. Twitter post. 23 Oct. 2014, 11:46 a.m. https://twitter.com/jeffvandermeer/status/525357671839326208.

Venturi, Robert, Denise Scott Brown, and Steven Izenour. *Learning from Las Vegas.* Revised ed. Cambridge: MIT P, 1977.

Wakefield, Dan. "Slouching Towards Bethlehem." *New York Times* (21 July 1968).

Wallace, David Foster. "Consider the Lobster." *Consider the Lobster and Other Essays.* New York: Back Bay, 2005. 235–54.

———. "E Unibus Pluram: Television and U.S. Fiction." *Review of Contemporary Fiction* 13.2 (Summer 1993): 151–94.

Wallace, David Foster, and Mark Costello. *Signifying Rappers.* New York: Back Bay, 2013.

Ward, Jesmyn. *Men We Reaped: A Memoir.* New York: Bloomsbury, 2013.

Warner, Michael. *The Letters of the Republic: Publication and the Public Sphere in Eighteenth-Century America.* Cambridge: Harvard UP, 1990.

West, Kanye, with Jay-Z. "Diamonds from Sierra Leone (Remix)." *Late Registration.* Def Jam, 2005.

White, Hayden. *Figural Realism: Studies in the Mimesis Effect.* Baltimore: Johns Hopkins UP, 1999.

Wild Style. Dir. Charlie Ahearn. Music Box Films, 2013.

"A Wilderness of Error: The Trials of Jeffrey MacDonald." Pentagram. https://www.pentagram.com/work/.

Williams, Justin A. "Intertextuality and Lineage in The Game's 'We Ain't' and Kendrick Lamar's 'M.A.A.D. City.'" *The Pop Palimpsest: Intertextuality in Recorded Popular Music.* Ed. Lori Burns and Serge Lacasse. Ann Arbor: U of Michigan P, 2018. 291–312.

Williams, Linda. "Mirrors without Memories: Truth, History, and the New Documentary." *Film Quarterly* 46.3 (Spring 1993): 9–21.

Williams, Raymond. *Marxism and Literature.* New York: Oxford UP, 1977.

Williams, Ruth. "*Eat, Pray, Love:* Producing the Female Neoliberal Spiritual Subject." *Journal of Popular Culture* 47.3 (June 2014): 613–33.

Wilson, Christopher P. *Learning to Live with Crime: American Crime Narrative in the Neoconservative Turn.* Columbus: Ohio State UP, 2010.

Wolfe, Tom, and E. W. Johnson, eds. *The New Journalism.* New York: Harper and Row, 1973.

Yagoda, Ben. *Memoir: A History.* New York: Riverhead, 2009.

INDEX

Page numbers in italics refer to illustrations.

Abbey, Edward, 119
Abernethy, Graeme, *The Iconography of Malcolm X,* 152n39
Abramovič, Marina, 70, 85
Abu Ghraib, 13
Acosta, Oscar Zeta, 80, 82, 83, 85, 152n46
Adams, Randall, 95
Agee, James, *Let Us Now Praise Famous Men,* 10–11
Ahearn, Charlie, *Wild Style,* 18, 26, 28–29, 32, 34, 46
Allen, Irwin, 111–12
Allende, Salvador, 65
Almeida, Paul, 56, 59
Apocalypse Now (Coppola), 58
Armies of the Night, The (Mailer), 16, 17, 52
Ascher, Ivan, *Portfolio Society,* 44–45
audio, 5, 7, 16, 37, 95–96
Augustine, 6
autobiography, 9, 47, 137, 152n25. *See also* memoir
Autobiography of Malcolm X, The (Malcolm X and Haley), 19, 69, 70, 72–80, 84, 85, 152n25, 152n37, 152n39
autonomy, 23, 25

Balk, Alfred, 77
Balsom, Erika, 23
Bambaataa, Afrika, in *Hip Hop Family Tree,* *33*
bandele, asha, *When They Call You a Terrorist,* 104
"Battle of Aspen, The" (Thompson), 80–82
Battle of Chile, The (Guzmán), 65–66
Beastie Boys, 35
Beatles, the, 83
Beattie, Keith, *Dont Look Back,* 27
Beauty of a Social Problem, The (Michaels), 103–4
Bechdel, Alison, 20, 32; *Fun Home,* 136
Beckett, Samuel, 55
Benjamin, Walter, "The Author as Producer," 10
Berlant, Lauren, *Cruel Optimism,* 78
Big Short, The (McKay), 5–6
Black Lives Matter, 10, 104
"Black Merchants of Hate" (Balk and Haley), 77
Blade Runner (Scott), 16
Blaze, Jess, 44
Blondie, 36
Blue Nights (Didion), 131
Bluets (Nelson), 139–40
Boetticher, Budd, 55
Bonaventure Hotel, 21, 57
Bourdain, Anthony, 6

Bourke-White, Margaret, 11
Bowery in Two Inadequate Descriptive Systems, The (Rosler), 22–23
Boyle, Kay, 148n36
Bradley, Adam, *Book of Rhymes*, 31–32, 151n3
Bronx, 29, 31
Brouillette, Sarah, *Literature and the Creative Economy*, 18
Brown, Danny, "Side B (Dope Song)," 39
Brown, Wendy, "The End of Educated Democracy," 70–71
Brown Power, 82
Buchloh, Benjamin, "Hans Haacke," 61, 63
Buell, Lawrence, "Toxic Discourse," 112–13
Buffett, Warren, letter to shareholders of Berkshire Hathaway Inc., 7
Bugliosi, Vincent, *Helter Skelter*, 88–89
Bundy, Ted, 19, 89
Buñuel, Luis, 10
Burroughs, Augusten, 128
Burroughs, William S., 55
Burtynsky, Edward, 17
Busy Bee Starski, in *Hip Hop Family Tree*, 28, 36–37, *37*

Cafaro, Philip, "Rachel Carson's Environmental Ethics," 110
Campt, Tina M., *Listening to Images*, 14
Capote, Truman, *In Cold Blood*, 17, 87
Carson, Rachel, 19, 107–20, 122, 124–25, 155n11; *The Sea Around Us*, 110, 111, 113, 119, 155n10; *Silent Spring*, 19, 107–19, 124–25; *Under the Sea-Wind*, 110, 113, 119
Céline, 49–50
Chakrabarty, Dipesh, "The Climate of History," 124
Chang, Jeff, *Can't Stop, Won't Stop*, 30
Chile, 65–67
Chile, Obstinate Memory (Guzmán), 65–66, 67
Chute, Hillary, *Disaster Drawn*, 32
cinéma verité, 7, 8, 15, 26–27
Clay, Cassius, 73
climate change, 20, 107–10, 112, 124–25, 127
Clover, Joshua, "Baltimore Riot. Baltimore Commune?," 148n32; *1989*, 30; *Riot Strike Riot*, 106–7
Codinha, Alessandra, 49–50
Cold War, 4–5, 58
Coles, Robert, *Doing Documentary Work*, 11
comics, 1–4, 5, 6, 7, 9, 11, 25–26, 32–38, 46, 136–37
Communist Manifesto, The (Marx), 115
conceptual art, 7, 11, 13, 15, 25–26, 47–48, 61–65, 105–6
Conrad, Joseph, *Heart of Darkness*, 58
Cooper, Melinda, *Family Values*, 89
Coppola, Francis Ford, 58; *Apocalypse Now*, 58
Corporation, The, 88
counterculture, 47, 48–49, 53–56, 70–71, 80–85
creative writing, 13
crime, 19, 42–43, 86–104, 140–41, 144
Crimp, Douglas, "The Photographic Activity of Postmodernism," 25
Crumb, R., 34, 136

Davis, Miles, 73–76, 77
Dear Erin Hart (Lovell), 140–41, *141*, *142*
debt, 44–45, 60
Decoded (Jay-Z), 19, 68–70, 151n4
DeKoven, Marianne, *Utopia Limited*, 83
Deng, Valentino Achak, 132
de Saussure, Ferdinand, *Course in General Linguistics*, 71
Deutsche, Rosalyn, "Property Values," 63, 65
Deutsche Bank, 6
"Diamonds from Sierra Leone (Remix)" (West and Jay-Z), 68
Diary of a Teenage Girl, The (Gloeckner), 136–37
Dickinson, Emily, 69
Didion, Joan, 9, 17, 19, 20, 48–61, 67; *Blue Nights*, 131; "Insider Baseball," 58; "On the Morning after the Sixties," 60; *Salvador*, 56–60; *Slouching Towards Bethlehem*, 53–55, 86–88; "Some Dreamers of the Golden Dream," 86–88; "The White Album," 48–49, 50; *The Year of Magical Thinking*, 130–31
Dirty John (podcast), 87
Dispatches (Herr), 21–22, 25, 26, 149n8
documentary: as aesthetic, 3–4, 5, 6–10, 11–13, 15, 18, 20, 21–24, 25, 46, 47–48, 50–51, 85, 96–97, 103, 105–7, 114, 127–30, 144–45; across media, 5, 6–7, 8, 10, 11–13, 15, 23–24, 25–26, 36–39, 46, 47–48, 90, 144–45, 148n18; and music, 26–46; as speculative, 107–25, 127
Dont Look Back (Pennebaker), 18, 26–28, 29, 46
Doors, the, 48

Do the Right Thing (Lee), 29
Double Indemnity, 86–87
Dr. Dre, 30, 40, 44
Dunaway, Finis, *Seeing Green*, 115
Dunne, John Gregory, 48, 130
Dunne Michael, Quintana Roo, 50, 130
Durst, Robert, 96
Dylan, Bob, 19, 26–27, 46, 68

E-40, 42
Eat Pray Love (Gilbert), 128, 129
Eazy-E, 36
ecocriticism, 112
ecology, 105–25
Eggers, Dave, 20, 129, 131–35, 137; *A Heartbreaking Work of Staggering Genius*, 132, 134; *A Hologram for the King*, 134–35; *What Is the What*, 132–33, 137; *Zeitoun*, 132, 133–34
Eliot, T. S., 69
El Salvador, 56–60
environmentalism, 19–20, 105–25, 127
Environmental Protection Agency, 107
Esquire, 22
Evans, Walker, 10–11
Evers, Medger, 27
exploitation, 41, 104

Fab Five Freddy, 28
Fatal Vision (McGinniss), 90, 91–92
Fear and Loathing in Las Vegas (Thompson), 52, 80, 81, 83 84
Ferguson, Charles, 5
Ferguson, Roderick, 73–74
film, 4–5, 6, 7, 9, 10, 11, 12, 13, 17, 22–23, 26–29, 38–39, 46, 47–48, 65–66, 90, 94–96, 111, 117–18
finance capitalism, 7–10, 15, 18, 26, 31, 44–46, 51–52, 63, 71, 127, 128, 130, 144–45, 147n7
financial crisis of 2008, 5–6, 7, 135
Fish Story (Sekula), 19, 29, 120, *120*
Flaherty, Robert, 10, 12
Fog of War, The (Morris), 4–5
Foucault, Michel, *The Birth of Biopolitics*, 72, 151n2
Fraga, Dan, 36
Fraterrigo, Elizabeth, *Playboy and the Making of the Good Life in Modern America*, 74
Freak Power, 80–82, 84
free market, 7–8, 20, 51–52, 66–67, 68, 74, 76, 77, 82, 84, 88, 119, 127, 137, 140
Frey, James, *A Million Little Pieces*, 38, 128, 137
Frey, John, 48
Friedman, Milton, 48, 51; *Two Lucky People*, 66–67
Friedman, Rose, 48; *Two Lucky People*, 66–67
Fun Home: A Family Tragicomic (Bechdel), 136

Galindo, Guillermo, 23
Gates, Henry Louis, Jr., *Norton Anthology of African American Literature*, 73
Gentry, Curt, *Helter Skelter*, 88–89
Gilbert, Elizabeth, *Eat Pray Love*, 128
Gillot, Marie-Agnes, 50
Gimme Shelter (Maysles brothers), 94–95
Glass, Loren, *Counterculture Colophon*, 78
Glass, Philip, *qatsi* trilogy scores, 13
Glidden, Sarah, 32; *Rolling Blackouts*, 1–4, *2*, *3*, *5*, *6*, *9*
Gloeckner, Phoebe, 20, 156n23; *The Diary of a Teenage Girl*, 136–37
Godard, Jean-Luc, 55
Goldsmith, Kenneth, *Uncreative Writing*, 134
Gomez, Selena, 6
Good Kid, M.A.A.D. City (Lamar), 18, 26, 38–46, *39*
Gore, Al, *An Inconvenient Truth*, 108
Gosling, Ryan, 6
graffiti, 28–29, 31, 34
Grandmaster Flash and the Furious Five, in *Hip Hop Family Tree*, 33, *33*, *34*
Gray, Freddie, 14
Green, Justin, 136
Grierson, John, "The Documentary Producer," 10
Grove Press, 78
Guggenheim Museum, 61, 65
Gulf War, 117–18
Guzmán, Patricio, 19, 48; *The Battle of Chile*, 65–66; *Chile, Obstinate Memory*, 65–66, 67

Haacke, Hans, 19, 67; *Shapolsky et al. Manhattan Real Estate Holdings*, 47–48, 61–65, *62*; *On Social Grease*, 105–6, *106*; *Solomon R. Guggenheim Museum Board of Trustees*, 65

Habermas, Jürgen, *The Structural Transformations of the Public Sphere,* 129
Haley, Alex, 70–80; *The Autobiography of Malcolm X,* 19, 69, 70, 72–80, 84, 85, 152n25, 152n37, 152n39; "Black Merchants of Hate," 77; *Roots,* 72, 73
Hall, Jeanne, "Don't You Ever Just Watch?," 27
Hamilton, Ann, 23
Harris, David Ray, 95
Harry, Debbie, 36
Hart, Erin (subject of *Dear Erin Hart*), 140–41, *141, 142*
Harvey, David, 32; *A Brief History of Neoliberalism,* 71; *Seven Contradictions and the End of Capitalism,* 147n7
Hayek, Friedrich A., 51, 72; "The Use of Knowledge in Society," 7–8
Heartbreaking Work of Staggering Genius, A (Eggers), 132, 134
Heart of Darkness (Conrad), 58
Heise, Ursula K., "Martian Ecologies and the Future of Nature," 112–13
Helios Design Labs, 23
Hell's Angels, 94–95
Hell's Angels (Thompson), 58
Helter Skelter (Bugliosi and Gentry), 88–89, 90
Herr, Michael, *Dispatches,* 21–22, 25, 26, 149n8
Herzog, Werner, *Lessons of Darkness,* 19–20, 117–18
Heti, Sheila, 20, 129; *How Should a Person Be?,* 138–39
hip hop, 9, 17, 28–46, 68–70. *See also* rap
Hip Hop Family Tree (Piskor), 18, 26, 32–38, *33, 34, 37, 38,* 46
Hogan's Alley (Outcault), and *Hip Hop Family Tree,* 33, *34*
Hologram for the King, A (Eggers), 134–35
How Should a Person Be? (Heti), 138–39
Huehls, Mitchum, *After Critique,* 18
Hungerford, Amy, *Making Literature Now,* 18
Hunter, Meredith, 94–95
Hurricane Katrina, 133–34
hustler, 19, 45, 68–70, 72–73, 77, 78–79, 85. *See also* individualism
Hutcheon, Linda, *A Poetics of Postmodernism,* 56

Image Comics, 36
In Cold Blood (Capote), 17, 87, 90
Inconvenient Truth, An (Gore), 108
individualism, 15, 52, 56, 60, 67, 76, 81–82, 84–85, 88, 92, 94, 95, 127–30, 132, 140; as entrepreneurial, 20, 29, 31, 45, 51, 68–70, 85, 88, 89, 105, 119, 127–30, 131, 135, 151nn2–3. *See also* hustler
Innocents, The (Simon), 90, 97–99, *98, 99*
"Insider Baseball" (Didion), 58
installation art, 7, 8, 11, 23, 38, 61–65
Interrotron, 4–5, 6, 85
In the Aura of a Hole (Palmer), 20, 123–24, *124*
Iraq, 1, 3, 9
Irr, Caren, "Anti-Capitalism and Anti-Realism in William T. Vollmann's *Poor People,*" 152n22
Iyer, Pico, "Desert Pitch," 135

Jacobs, Jane, 114, 156n36
Jagger, Mick, in *Gimme Shelter,* 94–95
Jameson, Fredric, 9, 56, 57; *Postmodernism, or, the Cultural Logic of Late Capitalism,* 21–22
Jane: A Murder (Nelson), 100, 103
Jarecki, Andrew, *The Jinx,* 96
Jay Rock, 41
Jay-Z, 72–73, 80, 85, 151n3; *Decoded,* 19, 68–70, 151n4; "Diamonds from Sierra Leone (Remix)," 68; *Picasso Baby,* 70
jazz, 74–76
Jinx, The (Jarecki), 96
Jones, David Steadman, *Masters of the Universe,* 8
Joselit, David, *After Art,* 14
Joseph, Kahli, 38, 43
journalism, 1–4, 5, 6, 11, 12, 16–17, 22, 25–26, 32, 50, 61, 70, 74–78, 80–83, 87, 90–91, 112, 142–43, 147n4, 148n18, 148n22, 148n36, 149n8, 155n10
Journalist and the Murderer, The (Malcolm), 90–91
Jujubee (game studio), 23
July, Miranda, 20; Somebody app, 128

Kael, Pauline, "Current Cinema," 94–95
Karr, Mary, 128
Kaysen, Susanna, 128
Kennedy, John F., 94, 109
Khan-Collors, Patrisse, *When They Call You a Terrorist,* 104
King, Martin Luther, Jr., 73, 76

Kinkle, Jeff, 23
Kissinger, Henry, 73
Klein, Naomi, 119
Kolbert, Elizabeth, 119
Kool Moe Dee, in *Hip Hop Family Tree*, 37, *38*
Kroll, Gary, 109, 111, 155nn10–11
Kuwait, 117–18

La Berge, Leigh Clare, *Scandals and Abstractions*, 18
Lady Pink, 28
Lamar, Kendrick, 17, 18–19; *Good Kid, M.A.A.D. City*, 26, 38–46, *39*
Las Vegas, 83–84
Lawrence, Freya, 50
Learning from Las Vegas (Venturi, Brown, and Izenour), 84
LeBlanc, Adrian Nicole, 20; *Random Family*, 142–44
Lee, Spike, 36; *Do the Right Thing*, 29
Leibovitz, Annie, 50
Leiterman, Gary, 103
Lejeune, Philippe, 137
Leonard, John, 130
Leovy, Jill, 42, 43
Lerner, Ben, *10:04*, 23
Lessons of Darkness (Herzog), 19–20, 117–18
Let Us Now Praise Famous Men (Agee and Evans), 10–11
Lewis, Michael, 5, 134
liberalism, 8–9, 47, 58, 111
Lichtenstein, Roy, 35
Liefeld, Rob, 36
Lin, Tao, 20, 129; *Taipei*, 139
literature, 9, 47–60, 68–85, 99–104, 107–20, 127–40, 142–44, 148n36, 152n22
Lorenz, Pare, 110, 111
Los Angeles, 40–44, 82
Louisiana, 120–23. *See also* New Orleans
Lovell, Jessamyn, 20; *Dear Erin Hart*, 140–41, *141*, *142*

m.A.A.d. (Joseph), 38, 43, 44
MacDonald, Jeffrey, 19, 91–92
Mademoiselle, 55
Magaña, Álvaro, 59
Mailer, Norman, 90, 148n36; *The Armies of the Night*, 16–17, 47, 52
Malcolm, Janet, *The Journalist and the Murderer*, 90–91
Malcolm X, 38, 72–73, 76–80; *The Autobiography of Malcolm X*, 19, 69, 70, 72–80, 84, 85, 152n25, 152n37, 152n39
Manson, Charles, 19, 48, 88–89
Marable, Manning, *Malcolm X*, 77, 152n37
Martin, Theodore, *Contemporary Drift*, 18
Mayes, Frances, 128
Mayes, Larry, 97–98, *99*
Maysles, Albert and David, *Gimme Shelter*, 94–95
McCarthy, Cormac, 133
McCourt, Frank, 128
McGinniss, Joe, *Fatal Vision*, 90, 91–92, 94
McGurl, Mark, "The Posthumous Comedy," 18, 117, 148n36
McKay, Adam, *The Big Short*, 5–6
McKibben, Bill, 117
McLanahan, Annie, *Dead Pledges*, 18
McLemore, John, 92–94
McNamara, Robert, 4–5, 6
McPhee, John, 119
McSweeney's, 131, 138
memoir, 3, 9–10, 20, 25–26, 32, 38, 39, 47, 66–67, 68–70, 85, 99–104, 127–39, 144, 156n23. *See also* autobiography
"Men Explain Things to Me" (Solnit), 144
Men We Reaped (Ward), 144
Michaels, Walter Benn, 14, 23, 24–25, 103–4, 129; *The Beauty of a Social Problem*, 103–4
Miller, D. A., *Jane Austen*, 72
Miller, Lucille, 86–87
Million Little Pieces, A (Frey), 38, 128, 137
Mimic (Wall), *24*, 24–25, 26
Mirowski, Philip, 52, 65
Misrach, Richard, 23; *The Mysterious Opacity of Other Beings*, 121–22, *122*; *Petrochemical America*, 20, 120–23, *121*, *122*, *123*
Mixer, Jane (subject of *Jane: A Murder*), 100–104
modernism, 10–12, 23
Monteyne, Kimberley Bercov, "The Sound of the South Bronx," 28
Moraru, Christian, *Cosmodernism*, 18
Morris, Errol, 6, 85, 95; *The Fog of War*, 4–5; *The Thin Blue Line*, 29, 95–96; *A Wilderness of Error*, 91–92, *93*
Morrison, Norman, 4
Morton, Timothy, *Ecology without Nature*, 117
music, 9, 12, 16, 17, 18–19, 25–46, 68–70, 74–76, 85

Mysterious Opacity of Other Beings, The (Misrach), 121–22, *122*

N.W.A., 29–30
Nanook of the North, 12
Nation of Islam, 73, 76–80, 84
nature writing, 107–20, 155n10
Nealon, Jeffrey, *Post-Postmodernism,* 18
Nelson, Deborah, *Tough Enough,* 49
Nelson, Maggie, 19, 23, 129; *Bluets,* 139–40; *Jane: A Murder,* 99–100, 103; *The Red Parts,* 90, 99–104
neoliberalism, 6, 8–10, 15, 17–18, 20, 26, 35, 44–46, 47–48, 51–52, 73–74, 84–85, 88, 89, 95, 97, 106–7, 118–119, 125, 127–30, 131, 132, 134, 135, 137, 140, 151nn2–3; emergence of, 47–67, 76, 107, 147n8; and foreign policy, 48, 51–52, 56–60, 65–67; as style, 49–51, 67, 68–85, 148n36, 152n14, 152n22
New Deal, 12–13, 23, 107–8, 110, 111
New Journalism, 7, 8, 15, 17, 25–26, 47–60, 70–85, 129–30, 150n3
New Orleans, 133–34
new sincerity, 85, 131, 138
Newton, Huey P., 48
New Yorker, 94–95, 114
New York Review of Books, 56
New York Times, 50, 87, 135
Nichols, Bill, *Speaking Truths with Film,* 10
Nixon, Richard, 107
Nixon, Rob, 109, 118; "slow violence," 32
Nixon shock, 8, 84
Norris, Kathleen, 68–70

objectivity: in documentary, 12, 15; in journalism, 2–3, 12, 22, 112, 148n22
Occupy Wall Street, 45
oil, 9, 105–7, 117–18, 120–24
On Social Grease (Haacke), 105–6, *106*
"On the Morning after the Sixties" (Didion), 60
Orff, Kate, *Petrochemical America,* 20, 120–21

Paglen, Trevor, 23
Palmer, A. Laurie, *In the Aura of a Hole,* 20, 123–24, *124*
Passaro, Alan, 94
Peleg, Hila, 23
Pelzer, Dave, 128
Pennebaker, D. A., *Dont Look Back,* 18, 26–28, 29
Pentagon, march on, 4
Pentagram (design firm), 91–92, *93*
performance art, 7, 13, 29, 70, 85
Petrochemical America (Misrach and Orff), 20, 120–23, *121, 123*
photography, 3, 5, 7, 8, 9, 10, 11, 13, 17, 22–23, 24–25, 38, 39, 47–48, 49–50, 53–55, 61–65, 87, 97–99, 102, 104, 120–25, 136, 140–41. *See also* photojournalism
photojournalism, 3, 6, 13, 29, 53–55, 147n4
Picasso Baby (Jay-Z), 70
Pinochet regime, 66–67
Piper, Adrian, 29
Piskor, Ed, *Hip Hop Family Tree,* 18, 26, 32–38, *33, 34, 37, 38,* 46
Playboy, 72, 73–76, *75,* 152n46
podcasts, 87, 90, 92–94, 156n23
poetry, 6, 7
postmodernism, 9, 15–18, 21–22, 25, 30–31, 56, 84, 148n36, 149n8
Postmodernism, or, the Cultural Logic of Late Capitalism (Jameson), 21–22
Powaqqatsi (Reggio), 13–14
Powell, Julie, 129
Pratt, Mary Louise, *Imperial Eyes,* 56–57
prison, 42–43
privatization, 20, 32, 42–43, 51–52, 58, 59, 70–71, 84, 89
Public Enemy, 29–30, 31
Pusha T, 39

Quinn, Eithne, *Nothin' But a "G" Thang,* 29, 45
Quiñones, Lee (star of *Wild Style*), 28

Rak, Julie, *Boom!,* 129
Random Family (LeBlanc), 142–44
Rankine, Claudia, *Citizen,* 23
rap, 12, 17, 28–46, 68–70, 85, 149n25, 151n3. *See also* hip hop
Rauschenberg, Robert, 55
Reader's Digest, 72, 73, 76
Reagan administration, 8, 30, 57–60, 89
real estate, 42, 61–65
Redgrave, Vanessa, 130
Red Parts, The (Nelson), 90, 99–104
Reggio, Godfrey, *Powaqqatsi,* 13–14
Renger-Patzsch, Albert, 10
Reynolds, Debbie, 83
River, The (Lorentz), 110, 111
Robbie, Margot, in *The Big Short,* 6

Robinson, Sylvia, 35, 36
Rockwell, Norman, 53
Rolling Blackouts (Glidden), 1–4, *2*, *3*, 5, 9
Rolling Stone, 72, 80–84
Rolling Stones, the, and *Gimme Shelter*, 94–95
Romero, Óscar, 57
Roots (Haley), 72, 73
Rose, Tricia, *The Hip Hop Wars*, 44, 68
Rosler, Martha, *The Bowery in Two Inadequate Descriptive Systems*, 22–23
Rowan, Jamin Creed, "The New York School of Urban Ecology," 114
Rubin, Rick, in *Hip Hop Family Tree*, 35
Rule, Ann, *The Stranger Besie Me*, 89
Run-DMC, in *Hip Hop Family Tree*, 35
Ruscha, Ed, 137

Sacco, Joe, *Safe Area Goražde*, 26, 32
Salazar, Ruben, 82
Salvador (Didion), 56–60
Salvadoran Civil War, 56–60
San Bernardino, 86–88
San Francisco, 48, 53–55, 83–84, 140
Satrapi, Marjane, 32
Saturday Evening Post: and Didion, 48, 53–55, *54*, 87; and Haley, 72, 76–77
Saudi Arabia, 135
Schneemann, Carolee, 85
Schudson, Michael, *Discovering the News*, 112
Schwabsky, Barry, "Inside Out," 63–64
science fiction, 111, 112, 116–17, 125
science writing, 107–20, 155n10
Sea Around Us, The (Carson), 110, 111, 113, 119, 155n10
Segal, Bernard, 91
Sekula, Allan, *Fish Story*, 19, 29, 120, *120*
Seltzer, Mark, "Serial Killers (II)," 96
Serrano, Andres, 70
Shapolsky et al. Manhattan Real Estate Holdings (Haacke), 47–48, 61–65, *62*
Signifying Rappers (Wallace and Costello), 30–31
Silent Spring (Carson), 19, 107–19, 124–25
Simmons, Russell, in *Hip Hop Family Tree*, 35
Simon, Taryn, 17, 19, 23, 104; *The Innocents*, 90, 97–99, *98*, *99*
Slouching Towards Bethlehem (Didion), 53–55, 86–88
"Slouching Towards Bethlehem" (Didion), 53–55, *54*
Smith, Rachel Greenwald, *Affect and American Literature in the Age of Neoliberalism*, 18
Smith, Terry, *What Is Contemporary Art?*, 18
social media, 3, 10, 14–15, 125, 127–28
Solnit, Rebecca, "Men Explain Things to Me," 144
Solomon R. Guggenheim Museum Board of Trustees (Haacke), 65
"Some Dreamers of the Golden Dream" (Didion), 86–88
Son of a Gun (St. Germain), 144
Sontag, Susan, 13, 55
Spiegelman, Art, 26, 29, 32, 136
Stallabrass, Julian, 14, 147n4
Stevens, Earl, 42
St. Germain, Justin, 20, 129; *Son of a Gun*, 144
S Town (podcast), 92–94
Stranger Beside Me, The (Rule), 89, 90
"Strange Rumblings in Aztlan" (Thompson), 82
Streshinsky, Ted, 53, *54*
Stuelke, Patricia, 58
Stuteville, Sarah, 1, *3*
Sudan, 132
Sugarhill Gang, 33
Sugarhill Records, 36
sulfur, 123–24
Supremes, the, 55
Szalay, Michael, *Hip Figures*, 148n36

Tagg, John, "Melancholy Realism," 11
Taipei (Lin), 139
Tate, Greg, "What Is Hip Hop?," 31
television, 5, 17, 87, 90, 96, 101, 116, 127, 128
testimony, 3–5, 6, 95–96, 144
Thin Blue Line, The (Morris), 29, 95–96
Thoma, Pamela, "What Julia Knew," 129
Thompson, Hunter S., 17, 47, 70–73, 80–85, 152n46; "The Battle of Aspen," 80–82; *Fear and Loathing in Las Vegas*, 52, 80, 81, 83–84; *Hell's Angels*, 58; "Strange Rumblings in Aztlan," 82
Thoreau, Henry David, 114
Tone Loc, 31
Top Dawg Records, 40
Toscano, Alberto, *Cartographies of the Absolute*, 23

totality, 23
T-Pain, 16
true crime, 19, 86–104
Twain, Mark, 133
2015 Baltimore Uprising, The, 14–15
Two Lucky People (Friedman and Friedman), 66–67

Under the Sea-Wind (Carson), 110, 113, 119
University of Chicago, 51, 59, 66
U.S. Fish and Wildlife Service, 109, 110, 155n10

Valech Commission, 66
VanderMeer, Jeff, 125
Vennett, Jared, 6
Vertov, Dziga, 10
video games, 23, 125
Vietnam War, 4–5, 7, 13, 21–22, 25, 58
Village Voice, 31
Vogue, 49
Vollmann, William T., 152n22
Voyage to the Bottom of the Sea (Allen), 111

Wakefield, Dan, 87
Wall, Jeff, 18; *Mimic,* 24, *24–25,* 26
Wallace, David Foster, *Signifying Rappers,* 30–31
Ward, Jesmyn, 20, 129; *Men We Reaped,* 144
Warner, Michael, *The Letters of the Republic,* 129
Webb, Troy, 97, *98*
West, Kanye, "Diamonds from Sierra Leone (Remix)," 38
"What Is Hip-Hop?" (Tate), 31
What Is the What (Eggers), 132–33, 137
White, Hayden, *Figural Realism,* 12
"White Album, The" (Didion), 48–49, 50
Widener, Jeff, 29
Wilderness of Error, A (Morris), 91–92, *93*
Wild Style (Ahearn), 18, 26, 28–29, 32, 34, 46
Williams, Justin A., 44
Williams, Raymond, *Marxism and Literature,* 152n14
Wilson, Christopher P., *Learning to Live with Crime,* 89
Wilson, Fred, 23
Winfrey, Oprah, 128, 129–30, 137
Winnicott, D. W., 100, 101
Wolfe, Tom, 17
Wolff, Tobias, 128
World War II, 4
Wurtzel, Elizabeth, *Prozac Nation,* 128

Yagoda, Ben, 128
Year of Magical Thinking, The (Didion), 130–31
Yellow Kid, in *Hip Hop Family Tree,* 33, *34*

Zapruder film, 94
Zeitoun (Eggers), 132, 133–34
Zeitoun, Abdulrahman, 133–34

Recent books in the series
Cultural Frames, Framing Culture

Daniel Worden
Neoliberal Nonfictions: The Documentary Aesthetic from Joan Didion to Jay-Z

Len Gutkin
Dandyism: Forming Fiction from Modernism to the Present

Marian Eide
Terrible Beauty: The Violent Aesthetic and Twentieth-Century Literature

Mary Paniccia Carden
Women Writers of the Beat Era: Autobiography and Intertextuality

Josh Toth
Stranger America: A Narrative Ethics of Exclusion

Lauren S. Cardon
Fashion and Fiction: Self-Transformation in Twentieth-Century American Literature

Ann Brigham
American Road Narratives: Reimagining Mobility in Literature and Film

Jinny Huh
The Arresting Eye: Race and the Anxiety of Detection

James J. Donahue
Failed Frontiersmen: White Men and Myth in the Post-Sixties American Historical Romance

Eric Aronoff
Composing Cultures: Modernism, American Literary Studies, and the Problem of Culture

Samuel Chase Coale
Quirks of the Quantum: Postmodernism and Contemporary American Fiction

Stephanie Harzewski
Chick Lit and Postfeminism

Stephanie L. Hawkins
American Iconographic: "National Geographic," Global Culture, and the Visual Imagination

Rachel Hall
Wanted: The Outlaw in American Visual Culture